Dear Mike & Lindy

May this be your legal Right hand

Love always
Mom & Dad

Sandy Bh Shore Clearwater Fl. 12/77. * 9.93

SUPER THREATS

Books by John M. Striker and Andrew O. Shapiro
Mastering the Draft
Super Tenant: New York City Tenant Handbook

Books by Andrew O. Shapiro
Media Access: Your Rights to Express Your Views on Radio and Television

SUPER THREATS
How to Sound Like a Lawyer and Get Your Rights on Your Own

John M. Striker
and
Andrew O. Shapiro

Rawson Associates Publishers, Inc.
NEW YORK

Louis Shapiro
Betty Shapiro

For
Michael S. Striker (1905–1975)
Hilda Striker

Library of Congress Cataloging in Publication Data
Striker, John M.
　Super threats.
　Includes index.
　1. Consumers—United States.　2. Consumer education.　3. Letter-writing, English.
4. Threat (Psychology)　I. Shapiro, Andrew O., joint author.　II. Title.
HC79.C63S77　　1977　　381'.3　　76–53879
ISBN 0-89256-015-0

Copyright © 1977 by John M. Striker and
Andrew O. Shapiro
All rights reserved
Published simultaneously in Canada by
McClelland and Stewart, Ltd.
Manufactured in the United States of America
by The Book Press, Brattleboro, Vermont
Designed by Gene Siegel
Second Printing August 1977

Acknowledgments

We find ourselves in the curious position of not being able to thank dozens of people who provided us with much valuable information. In the course of our research, we interviewed people who worked for department stores, insurance companies, mail-order outfits, credit bureaus, travel agencies, utilities, repair shops—in short, "the other side." Those interviewees whose confidence we gained and who believed in the need for this book revealed much to us about how their companies would react to a super threat. In return, we assured our sources complete anonymity. So to them we can say no more than thank you for all the insights you gave us.

To our literary agent, Don Congdon, we wish to express our gratitude for his candor, good humor, and, at all times, his loyalty to us and our book.

Ken Rawson took an immediate and sincere interest in this book from the moment it was first proposed. Together with our able editor, Sandi Gelles-Cole, Ken helped us greatly to develop the most suitable literary approach to our subject.

Beside drawing on interviews and personal experience with clients, we did extensive legal research in order to substantiate this book. For facilitating our wide-ranging search, we are indebted, as we were on our previous three books, to Julius Marke, Ed Bander, Jerry Leone, and the rest of the staff of the law library at the New York University School of Law.

Preface

People have been indirectly asking us to write this book for years. Hardly a week goes by without some friend of ours—or a friend of a friend—calling our office and, after a little obligatory chitchat, saying, "I wonder if you could write a letter for me. You see, I've been having this hassle with . . ." What always follows is a genuine tale of woe, involving perhaps a defective $29.00 coffee maker or a $55.98 billing error or a $45.00 overcharge at a repair shop.

These are real problems. Almost without exception, the caller's legal rights have been violated. Yet, few lawyers, if any, will handle such problems. There's simply no way to earn a living handling small-money cases—unless, of course, the aggrieved party is willing to pay fifty dollars an hour (or more) for a lawyer's time. Legal services are so expensive that, for many violations of the law, poor and middle-class Americans cannot afford to get their rights.

Which explains why we get phone calls. The callers don't want to retain counsel. They simply want to ask a favor: Could we write a letter to some ripoff artist, which will resolve the caller's problem without further worry, time, and expense?

Our reply surprises most callers. You can write this letter yourself, we explain. "But how?" comes the invariable refrain. "How will I know what to say—and what *not* to say? How can I show the other side I mean business? And *how can I sound like a lawyer?*"

We've answered these questions many times in the ten years since we graduated from law school. We've explained to people what their rights were in a wide array of legal problems. And we've helped people to write informed, legally valid complaints, which in the vast majority of instances resolved problems quickly, easily, and satisfactorily.

Why do we do this? Because we happen to believe that politicians pass laws and judges make rulings for *all* Americans—not just those with money enough to hire legal guns. To the extent that any American forgoes his or her rights because of insufficient funds, then the law, which we took an oath to uphold, is demeaned. Idealistic? Of course. Realistic? Not in the current state of private legal practice for profit. Nevertheless, holding these beliefs and trying to live up to them makes us feel better and stronger about being lawyers.

We could, of course, maintain our ideals by writing letters for the people who call us. But that would conflict with another goal of ours: namely *the demystification of the law*. Too often, the law is regarded as an inaccessible set of rules and exceptions, which only lawyers can decipher. This common misconception deprives people of the confidence and satisfaction that come with discovery and self-help. You can learn about your legal rights, and you can even learn to enforce them on your own.

Convinced after years of experience that people like yourself could solve their own problems by writing strong, legally valid letters, we decided to disclose our entire system, so that as many people as possible might take advantage of it. Understand that this book is not intended as a substitute for the services of an attorney. For the best advice that money can buy, you must retain an attorney whom you trust. But before you do that, you owe it to yourself to take a crack at solving the problem on your own. Our super-threat system will help you to do just that.

J.M.S.
A.O.S.

New York City
February, 1977

Contents

	Preface	ix
Chapter 1	The Strategy behind the Super Threat	3
	"Are You Threatening Me?"	3
	From Crank Letter to Super Threat	6
	The Crank Letter	7
	The Polite Complaint Letter	12
	The SOS Letter	15
	The Super Threat	19
Chapter 2	How to Write a Super Threat	30
	Will a Super Threat Work?	30
	Where Is the Soft Spot?	32
	When Should You Send a Super Threat?	34
	What Do You Say in a Super Threat?	40
Chapter 3	Troublesome Neighbors	47
	Bad Business Neighbors	47
	Malicious Neighbors	51
Chapter 4	Troublesome Animals	55
	Noisy Animals	55
	Dangerous Animals	59

x CONTENTS

Chapter 5	Neighborhood Hazards	65
Chapter 6	Utility Companies	69
Chapter 7	Tenant Problems	75
	Common Tenant Gripes	75
	Repair-and-Deduct	77
	Landlord's Liability for Negligence	86
	Warranty of Habitability	92
	Landlord's Liability for Crime	101
Chapter 8	Product Warranties	111
Chapter 9	Deceptive Trade Practices	127
Chapter 10	Fraud	141
Chapter 11	Buying by Mail	154
	Mail-order Merchandise	154
	Negative-option Plans	159
	Mail Fraud	165
Chapter 12	Credit Problems	173
	Upholding Your Credit Rating	174
	Truth in Lending	185
	Correcting Billing Errors	193
	Fighting Bill Collectors	201
Chapter 13	Up Against the Internal Revenue Service	211
Chapter 14	Collecting on an Insurance Policy	220
Chapter 15	Travel and Moving	234
	Travel Agents	234
	Charter Flights	241
	Moving Companies	245

Appendix A	Sample Super Threats	254
Appendix B	Repair-and-Deduct Statutes and Cases	265
Appendix C	Warranty-of-Habitability Statutes and Cases	273
Appendix D	Uniform Commercial Code State Citations	277
Appendix E	Deceptive-Trade-Practices Statutes	279
Appendix F	Federal Trade Commission Regional Offices	291
Appendix G	Trial Locations for Small-Tax Cases	293
Appendix H	State Insurance Commissioners	295
Appendix I	Interstate Commerce Commission Field Offices	306
	Index	317

SUPER THREATS

1

The Strategy behind the Super Threat

"Are You Threatening Me?"

You have probably been asked this question on occasion—that is, unless you're the kind of person who takes things lying down. No doubt, you had reached the end of your rope with some scoundrel: for example, that "old pal" who borrowed fifty dollars from you and then gave you excuses for months; or the dog lover down the street who let his pet Doberman, "Fang," romp on *your* lawn every day, terrorizing your children; or those college kids who rented the cottage next to yours last summer and danced all night to the blaring rhythm of Tito Puente albums.

When all your polite reminders, your stern requests, and your desperate pleas fell on deaf ears, you finally blew up: "If you don't pay me back [chain that dog/turn off that racket], I'll call your boss [the dog pound/the cops]!" Just at that moment of fury, when you were all puffed up with righteous indignation, the target of your wrath skillfully applied the time-tested needle of the scoundrel: "Are you threatening me?"

"No, I'm not threatening you," you responded defensively, "I'm just giving you fair warning." Like most people, you retreated as soon as you were confronted with your own menacing behavior. Why? Why let a scoundrel off the hook? You're the one who's been getting the short end of the stick. You've been polite, reasonable, cooperative, and probably overly patient. The scoundrel hasn't made the slightest attempt to meet you halfway. So where does he get the gall to make you feel guilty with that "Are-you-threatening-me?" routine?

Chances are, it's not so much a matter of gall, as it is shrewdness. The scoundrel senses instinctively that you're uncomfortable in the threatening posture you've assumed. Making threats is not generally regarded as a *nice* thing to do. You know that; the scoundrel knows it; and he knows that you know it. So he plays upon your guilty knowledge. When he asks, "Are you threatening me?" he's really making an accusation: You're no better than a bully who *threatens* to beat up a weak playmate—a skyjacker who *threatens* to blow up an airplane—a kidnapper who *threatens* to kill a hostage—a major employer who *threatens* to pull out of a small town—a cloudy sky that *threatens* to rain out a ball game. You're clearly a bad person bent on doing harm. (After all, who ever heard of the Red Cross making threats? or Santa Claus? Would Bambi threaten a chipmunk? Would Kate Smith threaten not to sing the National Anthem? Never!)

Even if you check the word "threat" in Webster's Dictionary, you find this nasty definition: "1a: an expression of an intention to inflict evil, injury, or damage on another usu. as retribution or punishment for something done or left undone ... 1b: expression of an intention to inflict loss or harm on another by illegal means and esp. by means involving coercion or duress of the person threatened." There's no doubt about it, making threats has a bad press.

Well, no more! If this book does nothing else, it will dramatize the positive, healthy, productive aspects of making threats. Follow this book, and within a matter of weeks you will not only shake that negative "No-I'm-not-threatening-you" frame of mind, but will also clear your mental decks for the planning and launching of a battery of *super* threats.

Does this mean we are going to teach you how to join the underground and use plastic explosives? No. *Super Threats* is not a cookbook for anarchists. Quite the contrary is true: *Super Threats* is going to teach you about a wide array of hard-core, well-established legal rights—the sort of civilized cement that any respectable anarchist would blast to smithereens. We are not, however, going to leave you stranded with a fistful of empty principles—or "paper rights," as they're sometimes sneeringly called. Instead, we aim to put those rights to work for you. We will teach you a method, a *modus operandi,* for taking a firm grip on your rights and wielding them as a club over the heads of scoundrels.

One thing you can be sure of: After you launch a super threat, you're not going to hear that pseudoindignant whine, "Are you threatening me?" Your target will *know* that you're threatening him—indeed, super-threatening him. More important, he'll know that you're well within your rights in doing so. And unless he's a total crook or a fool (or both), he'll accommodate you—not because he's seen the light and suddenly realizes you're in the right, but simply because *resisting your threat is not in his self-interest.* And appealing to a scoundrel's self-interest is what getting your rights is all about.

From Crank Letter to Super Threat

What is a super threat?

Physically, it's just a piece of paper with words on it.

Psychologically, it's an edge that you gain over your adversary.

Spiritually, it's the satisfaction you get in knowing you've done the best you could in the least amount of time you could spare from your busy life.

Perhaps the most instructive way to introduce the concept and technique behind the super threat is to start off with an example of a super threat in action. For this purpose, let's invent a beleaguered hero and future super-threatener, Saul David, and cast him in the role of a worried big-city tenant. Now let's typecast as Saul's big-city landlord the mean, smug, cigar-chewing Rocky Goliath.

The scene is the dimly lit vestibule of the apartment building where Saul lives. Enter Saul. He stands stock-still in the front doorway, appalled to discover that the door lock—his first line of defense between the cold cruel world and home sweet home—is broken and completely inoperative. Anyone from the cold cruel world can easily intrude. Saul hurries through the dimly lit hallway and up the stairs to his apartment. He assumes—unwisely—that Rocky Goliath will repair the door lock in short order.

No such luck. A week passes without Goliath lifting a finger. In the meantime, two purses are lifted in the vestibule by muggers who walked right into the building and preyed on unsuspecting tenants. Then an apartment is burglarized.

Fed up with living in fear, David decides to confront Goliath—easier said than done. Goliath is much too smart to waste time listening to complaining tenants. So whenever

Saul David calls Goliath's office, the elusive landlord is, alas, "not in." Regardless of how many urgent messages Saul leaves, no attempt is made to repair the front door.

Exasperated, Saul decides that he will write to Goliath. Roughly speaking, there are four kinds of messages Saul can send:
1. a crank letter
2. a polite complaint letter
3. an SOS letter
4. a super threat.

Let's examine each one critically with an eye to assessing Saul's chances of compelling Goliath to fix the front-door lock.

First comes the crank letter.

The Crank Letter

A word of caution: We are about to have a few laughs at Saul David's expense, because crank letters like the one that follows are amusing—sadly so. Regrettably, crank letters are by no means uncommon. They are not literary aberrations churned out by little old ladies in tennis sneakers. They are written every day by well-dressed men and women who go to work each morning, make important decisions, earn good salaries, and then go blotto when it comes to composing a complaint letter.

January 25, 1977

Dear Goliath:

You're Just about the hardest guy in the world to get a hold of!!! What's the matter, are you afraid to talk to your tenants? I called that so-called office of yours all last week.

Whoever it was who answered claimed that you weren't "in" (are you ever??), and of course you never once had the decency to call me back. The only halfway considerate person I ever got through to was your so-called handyman, who answered your phone last Monday but said he was too busy to talk right then, because the boiler had broken down (again???) and he had to be "on call" (oh sure!) whenever the emergency mobile unit arrived from the furnace company (Janson's? Jensen's? Johnson's?).

BY THE WAY, WHEN IS THAT DAMN FURNACE GOING TO BE FIXED ONCE AND FOR ALL??? Every morning I get up, I never know if I'm going to have enough hot water to shave with. The next time that boiler goes on the blink, I'M REPORTING YOU TO THE PROPER AUTHORITIES!!!

There are laws in this city, Goliath, and you'd better start paying attention to them. You can't just rent apartments to people and then forget about them. The law prescribes steps you must take, and IGNORANCE OF THE LAW IS NO EXCUSE. You think you can get away with anything: up the rents, freeze the pipes, let bulbs burn out. How are people supposed to survive this inflation-recession-depression when they have to call somebody like you all week and never get an answer. We have a government of laws—not landlords—Goliath. So whenever it's convenient, why don't you defrost this freezer we live in; thaw things out to about 40 degrees for a change.

What I was actually calling about was to complain about the front door to this firetrap we live in; it's a disgrace the way things are let go here year after year, while you go on rent-gouging. The lock on the front door has been broken for almost two weeks now. That's what I wanted to tell you but couldn't since it's impossible to telephone a ghost.

This whole neighborhood's on the skids. Muggers snatched two purses in our vestibule last week, and an apart-

ment was ripped off. Better fix that lock or there's going to be hell to pay.
HOW WOULD YOU LIKE TO LIVE IN THIS BUILDING? Think about it, and try answering your phone when tenants call. Please act soon.

/s/ Saul David

This letter manages to commit every one of the deadly sins generally found in authentic American crank letters:

1. *Appearance.* Saul's crank letter is an eyesore. It assaults the reader with a formidable blob of type. Probably half of all crank letters are written without any paragraphing at all—just a monolithic block of words stretching from one edge of the paper to the other, as though the writer were obsessed with blotting out all white space. Face facts: If you write a sloppy, crowded letter, it stands an excellent chance of not even being read, let alone considered.

2. *Opening.* Crank letters generally get off on the wrong foot. That's because the crank tends to dash off the first thing that pops into his or her head. Saul David's letter is no exception. It opens with a petty and peripheral matter: Goliath's inaccessibility. Obviously, Goliath's elusiveness preoccupied Saul and prevented him from getting right to the point: the broken lock.

3. *Organization.* A universal weakness in crank letters is their lack of organization. The writer cannot resist the temptation to digress—to recount all the woes of his or her life, however tenuous their relationship to the problem at hand may be. For instance, a shopper complaining about a defective toaster may feel compelled to mention the surliness of the salesperson, the inconvenience created by the store's limited shopping hours, or the poor parking facilities. All of

these grievances may be legitimate and should be raised with the store's management—but not in a complaint about a nonworking toaster!

Saul David exhibits this same penchant for gab. He flies off in all directions, railing against the handyman's incompetence, boiler breakdowns, rent-gouging, and the deterioration of the neighborhood. Lost in this farrago of charges is Saul's complaint about the broken door lock. The regrettable impression that such disorganization creates is one of aimless griping. Since an aimless griper is likely to be an aimless person in general, his or her complaint can be safely ignored, without much fear of the consequences.

4. *Tone.* Saul commits the cardinal sin of the crank-letter-writer: *He gets personal.* Time and again, Saul indulges in taunts, cheap shots, and gratuitous insults. Like many cranks, Saul apparently thinks that he can wear his adversary down with scornful abuse. Such tactics are invariably self-defeating, because they portray the writer as a bellyacher, who is more concerned with name-calling than resolution of a problem. Besides, the recipient of a crank letter—even if he's as thick-skinned as Rocky Goliath—is only human. If your insults irk him enough, he may just exact silent retribution by ignoring your letter entirely.

5. *Length.* Most crank letters are gargantuan. They run four, five, six pages. (Frequently clients have come to our law office after their ten-page handwritten complaint letters failed to stir the recipient—out of a deep slumber, no doubt.) Regardless of how poignant or earthshaking you may think your situation is, the rest of the world does not agree. The rest of the world is slightly hung over, slouched at a cluttered desk, waiting for its morning coffee, listening to three phones ringing, when in comes your six-page lament. On the basis of weight alone, your letter will sink to the bottom of the correspondence pile, if not to the bottom of the wastepaper can.

6. *Authority.* The lack of authoritativeness is a problem not just with crank letters but with all complaint letters. (It is precisely this shortcoming that makes the super threat so essential, as we shall soon see.) Does Saul David really think he's impressing Goliath with: "The next time that boiler goes on the blink, I'M REPORTING YOU TO THE PROPER AUTHORITIES!!!"? In resorting to capitalization (underlining is another overused gimmick in crank letters) Saul betrays his own impotence. Does he really believe that Goliath will be prodded into action by "Better fix that lock or there's going to be hell to pay"? Chances are, Goliath knows that prices are lower in hell than at the locksmith's. The point is: If you don't know what you're talking about, *shut up.* After getting personal, the second-most-grievous sin of the crank letter is making idle threats; they simply expose you for the creampuff that you are.

Well, having lambasted Saul David's letter, there is no need to speculate at length upon its probable reception. It will arrive in the morning mail and depart in the evening trash. Moral: Don't *ever* write *anything* that exhibits *any* of the characteristics of a crank letter.

Perhaps we have overemphasized this point, but in our law practice we are constantly amazed not only at the proliferation of crank-type letters, but also at the caliber of people who write them. Sober, intelligent adults consult us with problems that seem insurmountable to them. Ironically, the obstacle that is preventing a satisfactory resolution is often a crank-type letter, which has hopelessly clouded the issue, alienated the other side, and made any meeting of the minds virtually impossible.

If you will permit us some amateur psychoanalytical guesswork, we are convinced that many of the people who write crank-type letters *don't want their problems to be solved.* They tend to regard the cold cruel world as a place where you inevitably get ripped off, no matter how circumspect you are about entering into transactions. Since everything's essentially hopeless, and everyone's against you, why bother to go about helping yourself in a logical, well-thought-out manner? How much easier—albeit self-defeating—to indulge yourself in a futile *cri de coeur:* a crank letter.

Lest we lose all faith in our would-be hero, Saul David, let's move right on to the letter he should have written in the first place: a polite complaint letter. Whenever you, like Saul, have the urge to indulge in a crank letter, get hold of yourself ("Stifle yourself," as Archie Bunker says) and buckle down to a polite complaint letter instead.

The Polite Complaint Letter

The second possible message that Saul could send to Rocky Goliath is a polite complaint letter. Such letters can be instrumental in resolving almost any problem—whether it's a tenant problem like Saul's, a consumer hassle, or a billing error. Often enough, the recipient will respond favorably to a polite complaint letter, especially if the recipient places a premium on maintaining reliability and good public relations. And if the polite complaint doesn't work, it serves as an ideal launch pad for a super threat.

We can learn the necessary ingredients of the polite complaint letter by examining what Saul David should write to Rocky Goliath:

Certified Letter No. 12345678

January 25, 1977

          Saul David
          Mailing address
          City, state, zip code

Rocky Goliath
Mailing address
City, state, zip code

         Re: Broken front-door lock

Dear Mr. Goliath:
  The lock on the front door of your apartment building at [street address here] is broken. Since the door can no longer be locked, any stranger can enter the building.
  I called your office on Monday, January 17, 1977, when I first discovered the broken lock. Since you were not there I left a message about the lock, which I have repeated in three subsequent calls.
  Within the past week, there have been two purse snatchings in the building's vestibule, as well as one apartment burglary. So you can see how urgent it is that security be restored by fixing the lock.
  Please repair the front door lock immediately.

             Sincerely,
             /s/ Saul David

  Saul's letter is simple, clear, and direct, as every polite complaint letter should be. Contrast Saul's second letter with his first one:

1. *Appearance.* Unlike his previous eyesore, Saul's polite complaint is neat and businesslike. Rocky Goliath will not groan the moment he looks at the letter.

2. *Opening.* Saul gets right to the point: The front-door lock is broken. From the outset, Rocky is not being led astray by any bellyaching about his inaccessibility.

3. *Organization.* Whereas the crank letter was all over the lot, here Saul sticks to the key grounds for his complaint: The lock is broken. Saul has telephoned several times. Criminals are getting into the building. It is urgent that the lock be repaired immediately. End of complaint. Forget about the furnace, and rent-gouging, and the deteriorating neighborhood—at least, in this letter.

4. *Tone.* Saul maintains a calm, rational tone throughout; he never gets personal with Goliath.

5. *Length.* While crank letters often simulate the end product of a paper drive, polite complaint letters are invariably one single sheet in length—no more!

6. *Authority.* There is a difference in authoritativeness between Saul's crank letter and the polite complaint. This difference derives less from what went into the second letter than what stayed out of it. By eliminating all idle threats, personal insults, and digressions, Saul has streamlined his letter down to the point where it is obviously the product of a logical mind. And logical thinkers cannot be safely ignored, because if they do not succeed at first, they'll just keep at you with renewed determination. Consequently, the impression that the polite letter creates is one that commands a certain basic respect, if not obedience. Maybe this respect, combined with Goliath's sense of responsibility, will lead him to repair the lock. If so, fine; case closed. If not, however, Saul will have to resort to some authority more compelling than a polite complaint letter. He will have to hit Rocky Goliath with a super threat.

The SOS Letter

Before we show you Saul's super threat, there is one other form of complaint that we feel compelled to discuss—not because we recommend its use (we don't!), but because so many other consumer advisers do. We dub this type of complaint the "SOS letter," because it resembles, at least in principle, the radio distress signal which a sinking ship might send out to any and all ships in the neighborhood.

When might an SOS letter be appropriate? After a polite complaint letter has already been sent and has failed to produce results. For example, Saul David mailed his polite complaint letter on January 25, 1977. If Goliath takes no productive steps in the week that follows, Saul could send off this SOS letter:

Certified Letter No. 12345678

February 3, 1977

Saul David
Mailing address
City, state, zip code

Rocky Goliath
Mailing address
City, state, zip code

Re: Broken front-door lock

Dear Mr. Goliath:
The lock on the front door of your apartment building at [street address here] has been broken and has been in nonworking condition since at least January 17, 1977.

On that day, I called your office and reported the broken lock. During the following week, I repeated that message in three subsequent calls. On January 25, 1977, I sent you a letter, again complaining about the lock and requesting its repair. In my letter, I alerted you to three thefts that had been committed in the building, presumably by strangers who walked right through the unlocked front door.

To date you have made no effort to repair the lock. While I remain hopeful that you will still do so, I believe the matter is urgent enough to warrant outside intervention. I am, therefore, sending copies of this letter to the agencies and officials listed below.

Sincerely yours,

/s/ Saul David

cc: Local Department of Buildings
    Local Police Department
    Office of the Mayor
    Office of the local State Legislator
    Office of the local Representative to Congress
    Local Building Owners' Trade Association
    Local Tenants' Organization
    Consumer-help Reporter on local TV station

Just by reading Saul's letter, especially the list at the end ("cc" means "carbon copies" [to]), you can understand why we've dubbed this sort of complaint the SOS letter. Saul is appealing for assistance to a wide array of outside sources —eight, to be exact. He will make eight copies of his SOS letter, plus one for himself, and send them to the agencies and officials listed.

What is the purpose behind this SOS letter? First, Saul is renewing his complaint and his request for repairs. The mere fact of this repeated correspondence shows Rocky Goliath that Saul is keeping after him. Second, Saul hopes that Goliath will feel pressured into acting because of the outside sources which are now being informed about the broken door lock. Third, help may come from one of the outside sources with the authority and the will to intervene on Saul's behalf.

Will the SOS letter work? Maybe. Maybe the local department of buildings will send out an inspector to check the front door. Maybe a cop will put the heat on Rocky about the crime wave inside his building. Maybe one of Saul's local elected officials will try to help out a beleaguered constituent. Maybe Rocky's fellow landlords in the building owners' trade association will warn him to shape up and not give them all a bad name. Maybe the local tenants' organization will picket in front of Rocky's building. Maybe the local station's consumer-help reporter will broadcast a story on Rocky's dereliction.

Maybe, maybe, maybe—and, then again, maybe not! The chief drawback of the SOS letter is that it's so iffy. Saul doesn't really know whether the department of buildings has any regulations about front-door locks and even if they do exist, are they enforced? What are the police supposed to do —arrest Goliath for not fixing a door? As for Saul's elected officials, they're also Goliath's elected officials; in fact, Goliath may well have "elected" them with his campaign contributions. Which brings us to Goliath's pals down at the building owners' trade association ... Which brings us to the local tenants' organization. This group may turn out to be Saul's best bet—that is, if they're big enough and militant enough. Similarly, a dedicated consumer-help reporter may just take a fancy to Saul's plight and swoop down on Goliath's building with all the heat and light that only TV can muster. (But remember, there are eight million stories in the Naked City!)

A second drawback to the SOS letter is that it may actually thwart outside intervention, rather than invite it. Put yourself in the shoes of someone who receives one of the eight copies of Saul David's letter. Your natural reaction might well be: Why get mixed up in this mess when one of these other groups will probably take care of it? No sense in a lot of duplication of effort.

A third drawback to the SOS letter lies in the hint of desperation that it suggests, at least to a canny adversary. No matter how firmly worded an SOS letter may be, it still tends to convey an underlying admission: I'm just about at the end of my rope; no more aces in the hole; no more tricks up my sleeve; have to hope that somebody else cares enough to help.

Finally, the SOS letter is a pain in the neck to prepare. You have to figure out all the places that you're going to send copies to; you have to make all the necessary copies, address all the extra envelopes, stuff them, stamp them, and mail them. Then, if you're really diligent, you'll have to follow up on your SOS letter by telephoning all the places where you sent it, until, God willing, somebody does something.

Perhaps you are stalwart enough to carry out an SOS-letter crusade without being carried out yourself, frothing at the mouth and chattering "cc...cc...cc...cc...." Apparently a lot of consumer advisers have unbounded faith in your fortitude, because there's hardly a how-to-complain article or book written nowadays that doesn't recommend some variation on the SOS letter.

We do not recommend use of the SOS letter, because it has too many drawbacks. We are not saying that it's worthless to contact outside agencies and individuals. On the contrary, precisely that course of action, with sample letters, will be advised at various times in this book. However, we advise that you communicate with one outside source at a time, choosing that source deliberately on the basis of what it can actually do for you. Most important, your communication with that outside source will *not* be in the form of an SOS letter. Such a letter makes too indirect an appeal for intervention; all the outside source receives from you is a copy of your correspondence to someone else, and exactly what you expect the outside source to do may not be at all clear. Therefore, you will have to address the outside source directly and request specific action if you really expect to get results. The best way to do this is in a standard polite complaint letter written and sent to the outside source.

The Super Threat

Let's assume that Saul David does not waste time sending an SOS letter to Rocky Goliath. As important as repair of the door lock is to Saul, he decides that he doesn't want to make it his life's work. And embarking upon an SOS-letter campaign seems a bit much. Above all else, Saul wants to settle the matter quickly—one way or another.

Saul assesses his situation. He has telephoned the landlord's office several times, to no avail. He has written a polite complaint letter, which provoked no response. What Saul wants is a lightning stroke, some unexpected gesture that will catch Goliath off guard and overcome him before he can regain his balance. So Saul sends Goliath the following super threat.

NOTICE

IN THE MATTER OF personal tort
liability for the commission
of third-party crimes

Rocky Goliath
Mailing address
City, state, zip code

Date of mailing:
February 3, 1977

NOTICE OF NEGLIGENT BREACH OF SECURITY

PLEASE TAKE NOTICE: Pursuant to *Kline* v. *1500 Massachusetts Avenue Apartment Corporation*, 439 F.2d 477 (D.C. Cir. 1970), you are in open breach of the implied warranty of security and are negligently enhancing the risk of criminal intrusions in this residential premises.

STATEMENT OF COMPLAINT

The lock on the front door of the aforementioned premises has been broken and in nonworking condition since at least January 17, 1977. This serious breach in building security was more fully described to you in my letter of January 25, 1977, a copy of which is enclosed.

DEMAND FOR ACTION

In order that you may cease and desist from negligently enhancing the risk of criminal intrusions in the aforementioned premises, it is incumbent upon you to forthwith repair the aforementioned broken front-door lock.

ULTIMATUM

If you negligently fail to satisfy the above demand and, as is reasonably foreseeable to any ordinarily prudent man, your negligence is the proximate cause of any unauthorized person or persons gaining access to the aforementioned premises and therein committing any crimes against person or property, including but not limited to burglaries, robberies, assaults, rapes, or homicides, then you shall be held personally liable in money damages to the full extent of any jury verdict based upon the personal injuries or property losses sustained by tenants or their lawful invitees.

[Your signature]
Saul David

Mailing address
City, state, zip code

Certified Mail No. 12345678

This "Notice" to Rocky Goliath demonstrates well the basic formula for writing all super threats. The formula is not new. In fact, it's been time-tested for generations, but only among a limited circle of professionals—namely, attorneys. Over the decades, attorneys have wielded great power, simply because they have known how to "scare action" out of people by writing them intimidating letters. These letters have rightfully earned a reputation; they are known and feared as *lawyers' letters*.

The lawyer's letter will be our constant model in the construction and launching of super threats. While our super threats may vary somewhat, they will all follow six guidelines, which are generally applied in any good lawyer's letter:

1. *Go for the soft spot.* Always isolate the recipient's weakest point, his *soft spot,* and then put pressure on it. Rocky Goliath's soft spot happens to be his apprehension of a severe financial loss—a common soft spot indeed. Saul's super threat put pressure on this soft spot by raising the prospect of an expensive lawsuit if some tenant, victimized by a criminal intruder, were to sue Rocky for negligence. Notice, Saul did not say that there would definitely be a lawsuit and that it would seek X dollars in damages. Saul had no way of knowing either of these things for certain; nor did he have to. The mere possibility of such a lawsuit seemed plausible enough to give Goliath cause for thought. Personal liability for negligence was something Goliath had not even considered when Saul first complained about the lock. Now along came this super threat, introducing a disturbing new element into Rocky's train of thought: What if I am sued? Rocky was forced to speculate. What if it's up to a jury (probably all tenants!) to decide how much I have to pay...?

What if? what if? Therein lies the real thrust of Saul's super threat: *the creation of sufficient uncertainty in the recipient's mind to make him reconsider.* So long as the doubts cannot be brushed aside, one question will keep nagging at the recipient: Is sticking to my current course of action worth the risk it entails? In Rocky's case, that question translates into: Is saving fifty or sixty bucks on a new lock worth the risk, however remote, of a fifty- or sixty-thousand-dollar jury verdict?

While worry about a potential financial loss is the most common soft spot for individuals and businesses alike, there are others, as we shall see. The soft spot of a slipshod mail-order business, for example, is the fear that daily mail delivery might be cut off. If the United States Post Office slaps a "mail stop-order" on the business, no more mail will be delivered to that business. Good-bye business; and good riddance, too, if it's a firm that bilked you.

2. *Invoke some legal authority.* Obviously, a lawyer is well equipped to do this in his or her letters. Citing statutes, court cases, and impressive-sounding Latin doctrines is a lawyer's stock in trade. No doubt, if some lawyer threatened facetiously to swear out a "writ of hocus-pocus," some benighted soul would leap to attention.

With a little coaching, you can invoke genuine legal authorities in your super threats. Saul David did. The first paragraph of his super threat cited the court case of *Kline v. 1500 Massachussetts Avenue Apartment Corporation* and went on to charge that Goliath had breached the "implied warranty of security." *Kline* happens to be a landmark federal case which established the legal doctrine that goes by the fancy name of "implied warranty of security." (Both the doctrine and the case are fully explained in Chapter 7.) Under it the landlord has a responsibility to protect tenants from crime.

While this book will teach you about many basic rights and the laws that support them, your aim in citing laws will not be merely to convince the other side of the legal justification for your position. An equally important function of legal citations is to intimidate. The unstated message of any citation in a super threat is that *you know something which the recipient doesn't know.* Superior knowledge suggests superior resources; it implies that you've got more tricks up your sleeve, and you'll pull them out if necessary.

Imagine Rocky Goliath's reaction when he stumbled across *Kline v. 1500 Massachussetts Avenue Apartment Corporation* and the implied warranty of security: The implied warranty of *what?* Kline versus *who?* Goliath probably began to experience stomach contractions. Any tenant who can cite some court case or toss off a rule or law must have the state —and maybe even God—on his side. Better not tangle with this hombre.

3. *Set a deadline.* The trouble with too many complaint letters is that they leave the recipient far too much leeway for evasion and delay. There comes a point at which an ultimatum must be given: If you fail to do x within y days, then z will happen. Otherwise, the long-drawn-out process of complaining begins to take more out of you than the solution to your problem is worth.

A specific deadline will almost always be stated in a super threat. Even in Saul David's super threat, which named no particular date, a deadline was clearly implied. Putting a person like Rocky Goliath on notice of his negligence is like planting a time bomb. So long as the negligence continues unabated, the bomb keeps ticking; it may go off at any moment, given the right convergence of people and events. So the implicit deadline for Rocky was one that continued from moment to moment; so long as he left the lock unrepaired, he shouldered the constant risk of disaster. In short, Rocky *failed* to act, at his peril.

4. *Provide an escape hatch.* Never use a super threat to back someone against a wall. Pushing for more than you deserve is both rash and counterproductive. It may indicate that you are twisting the law for some improper purpose. Furthermore, unreasonable demands will tend to stiffen, rather than overcome, resistance. Instead of building up any more resistance, you want to grease the tracks for swift compliance.

Therefore, when applying pressure in a super threat, you must always leave an escape hatch. Ideally, this outlet will afford the recipient an opportunity to comply without sustaining unreasonable expense or inconvenience. If the pressure applied is great enough, and the escape hatch is easy enough, the recipient is likely to give in. He will be persuaded that continued resistance is no longer in his self-interest; it's just not worth running the risk posed by your super threat. Giving in will seem easier, faster, cheaper, and, above all, wiser, than resisting.

Saul David's super threat repeated the same demand that he had been making all along: Fix the lock. Saul did not use the dire consequences raised in his "Ultimatum"—namely, a potential crime and a large jury verdict—as an occasion for leaning too hard on Goliath. Saul did not demand, for example, that Goliath institute twenty-four-hour uniformed-doorman service or install a closed-circuit electronic surveillance system with a TV monitor in every apartment. Such excessive demands might well have backfired, because Goliath would have rejected the super threat as simply a highhanded scheme to get something for nothing.

Considering the fair demand that Saul did make, Goliath will be hard pressed to deny it, especially in light of the unattractive alternative. Even if Rocky Goliath is a penny-pincher, and uncaring to boot, is he really so imprudent as to risk the possibility of a huge lawsuit over a cheesy little lock? No, in all likelihood Rocky will take the escape hatch offered; he'll fix the lock.

5. *Sound like a lawyer.* You will almost inevitably begin to sound like a lawyer if you follow the preceding four guidelines; they are, after all, the hallmarks of a typical lawyer's letter. What we are focusing on now is largely a matter of tone.

You want to sound detached, calculating, and inexorable. There is no better way to do this than to write your super threat in *legalese*. Legalese is that rigid, redundant, tooth-busting terminology lawyers have developed over the centuries as a substitute for plain English. You will no doubt recall the legalese that studded Saul David's super threat, like so much exposed plumbing: "You are ... negligently enhancing the risk of criminal intrusions"; "In order that you may cease and desist"; "as is reasonably foreseeable to any ordinarily prudent man"; "including but not limited to"; "personally liable in money damages." The beauty of such turgid phrases is their numbing impact; they just hammer away at the senses, like the terms of an insurance contract that aces you out of everything you're entitled to.

6. *Gain the edge over your adversary.* The ultimate goal of a super threat is *to be the one letter in ten that gets action.* Successful complaining is a highly competitive sport. You not only have to be good to win, you have to be distinctive.

Picture your adversary seated at a desk, reading through ten complaints. Four are crank-type letters, which go immediately to the bottom of the pile. Four are polite complaint letters; they deserve higher priority, but any response can probably be stalled off for several weeks. Then there's one of those ornery SOS letters. Well, since copies of the darn thing have already been scattered around, there's not much incentive to get on the stick. After all, the damage—if any—has already been done. Might as well wait awhile and see if anyone responds to the SOS.

Finally, there's one distinctive letter. It doesn't look or sound like any of the others. In fact, it's not really a letter at all, but a "Notice." Most disturbing of all, it is impossible to forget. It lingers through lunch—even a three-martini lunch—and follows you home after work. It's the kind of correspondence that you respond to first thing, just so it won't keep haunting you. A super threat rises to the top of any pile of complaints, not because it is devastating, but because it gains enough of a foothold in the reader's imagination to compel attention. The aim here is only to get an edge, not a preemptive nuclear first strike.

Consider how unsettling Saul David's super-threat notice must have been to poor unsuspecting Rocky Goliath. In all likelihood, the last notice that Rocky received was from the Internal Revenue Service, assessing a tax deficiency. Before that, Uncle Sam claimed Rocky's body for the Army in a draft notice. No, Rocky ruminates, you never get good news in a notice. His nervous system is experiencing the first shock waves from the impact of a super threat.

Inching his way through the mine field of legalese, Goliath realizes that he might, just *might*, get into serious trouble if he ignores this notice. That's precisely the edge that Saul David worked for—that nasty little sliver of doubt, uncertainty, and fear now firmly lodged in Goliath's imagination.

Let's suppose, however, that Goliath is made of sterner stuff than the typical insecure bureaucrat or the shaky executive who just wants to play it safe. While he's still wavering, Rocky grabs the phone and calls his lawyers, Shirk, Shun and Shaft. He explains the contents of the notice to Mr. Shun.

"Can I really be held liable if some crook gets by that front door, Mr. Shun?" Rocky asks.

"Mr. Goliath, I would be much better equipped to answer your question if you were to make an appointment with my secretary and bring this notice down to my offices."

"Okay, Mr.—"

"But before you do that, Mr. Goliath, may I inquire how much it would cost you to repair this front-door lock?"

"I figure a new lock has to run at least twenty or thirty dollars, and the locksmith's labor would be about the same."

"To be perfectly candid, Mr. Goliath, your total expense of, say, sixty dollars is exactly what I will have to charge you for an office consultation."

"Oh..."

"Mr. Goliath, permit me to offer you some sound advice. This tenant, this Mr. David, definitely sounds like he knows what he's talking about. From what you've read me, it's clear that Mr. David is familiar with the rudiments of negligence law. He's even cited one of the leading cases in this area. It is generally true that you have a duty not to negligently increase the risk of danger to your tenants.

"Now, it may be that Mr. David is just bluffing, but from the gist of what you've read me, I seriously doubt it. Anyway, that's beside the point. The main issue here is: Do you want to risk a lot of money on legal fees and a potentially high jury verdict to find out if David's for real?"

"No, sir, I guess that doesn't make much sense."

"Take my advice, Mr. Goliath. Spend sixty dollars on a new lock. It's well worth the investment."

This imaginary conversation is the kind that may well occur after any super threat has landed. Three aspects of this conversation are worth remembering. First of all, legal advice is expensive. Just as you will resort to a super threat in the hope of avoiding the cost of a lawyer, your adversary, too, will discover (if he doesn't know already) that it can cost an arm and a leg just to get a professional appraisal of your super threat. So there will be a natural inclination on your adversary's part to settle your grievance without incurring legal expenses.

Second, if any attorney does happen to look at your super threat, he will not dismiss it as hot air or bluffing, because you are writing the same sort of letter that he would write were he in your position. Your language and citations will impress the attorney as being both authentic and persuasive.

Third, and most important, attorneys tend to be a conservative lot. They don't shoot from the hip and tell clients to run unnecessary risks; not only would such advice be irresponsible, but it could also backfire if the client later wound up in serious trouble and blamed the attorney. Any attorney who reads your super threat will have to admit to himself that, at a minimum, you may have an arguable case against his client. You've expressed a legitimate grievance;

you've cited real legal authority; you've left a reasonable escape hatch. Only a rash attorney is going to advise his client to ignore that escape hatch and pursue the risky course of continued resistance.

So, you see, your super threat can even gain the edge over an attorney—not so much for what it says, but because of the attorney's basic play-it-safe character. Ironically, the best possible enforcer of your super threat is probably your adversary's attorney.

2

How to Write a Super Threat

Having learned the general strategy behind the super threat, you are now ready for some basic tactics. So let's seek hard answers to these four questions:

1. How can you know whether a super threat may solve your particular problem?
2. Assuming a super threat may work, how do you know where your adversary's soft spot lies?
3. When should you send a super threat; or, to put it a bit differently, what steps should you take before sending a super threat?
4. Finally, and perhaps most important, what do you say in a super threat in order to sound like a lawyer and get your rights?

Will a Super Threat Work?

At the outset, let's be clear on one point: *Super threats are not magic.* They are not all-purpose infallible miracle-workers. Certain problems are just not solvable by means of a super threat—let alone a polite complaint letter or an SOS letter. Sometimes your adversary is utterly irresponsible—maybe even criminal in his conduct—and no amount of highfalutin legalese or citations of the Bill of Rights, the Declaration of Independence, and the Magna Charta will make him give in to you.

In other instances, there may be considerable money or a significant principle at stake, and your adversary will be determined to get a formal—that is to say, legal—resolution of your complaint. If so, you are going to need more firepower than even a super threat can muster. You're going to need a lawyer.

There are also situations which a super threat is simply not designed to alter. Remember, the whole point behind a super threat is to give you enough leverage to make your adversary budge. You are asking him to do something that is relatively reasonable and manageable (such as refund the $99.95 that you paid for a defective FM radio); by way of leverage to induce his compliance, you are threatening to subject him to some disproportionately large sanction (such as a treble-damages lawsuit in which he will also have to pay your attorney's fees and court costs). Your leverage derives from the lopsided relationship between what you're asking and what you're threatening. In effect, you are proposing a fair trade-off: "Give me my just deserts," you're saying, "make me whole again; in return, I will forgo my legal right to make you pay dearly."

When real leverage is lacking, you are in no position to offer such a trade-off. Suppose the apartment of Saul David, our friend from Chapter 1, is burglarized. Some thief enters Saul's building through the unlocked front door, breaks into Saul's apartment, and steals five thousand dollars' worth of valuables. Can Saul effectively threaten the landlord, Rocky Goliath, with a five-thousand-dollar lawsuit unless Rocky pays Saul five thousand dollars to cover the theft? Of course not. Such a threat would be totally ineffective, because the landlord has little or nothing to lose by ignoring Saul's demand. Saul is, after all, demanding the very thing that he is also threatening to take: namely, five thousand dollars. The threat, therefore, supplies Saul with no leverage at all. What is he offering Rocky in trade for the payment of five thousand dollars? Only forbearance from bringing a five-thousand-dollar lawsuit. That's hardly a trade anyone would jump at.

Fair enough, you may be saying to yourself, but how am I supposed to know when the law supplies me with sufficient leverage to make a credible super threat? The following chapters are a guide to a wide array of your legal rights and, more important, the legal remedies available whenever your rights are violated. Armed with knowledge of the legal remedies at your command, you will have enough leverage to horse-trade with the most ornery of varmints: negligent landlords, cheating car dealers, stubborn insurance companies, fly-by-night travel agents, and slipshod mail-order houses, to name a few. You will be able to offer trade-offs which your adversaries will find too compelling to refuse.

Where Is the Soft Spot?

Lawyers are particularly adept at detecting soft spots. Indeed, most of the games lawyers play center around either attacking or defending a soft spot. Where do these soft spots come from? They are basically the result of the law's many and varied attempts to control conduct.

Left to their own devices, most people and businesses would prefer to act purely in their own self-interest. Inevitably, however, such conduct calls for the sacrifice of someone else's interest—perhaps yours. So the law intervenes in an attempt to minimize hostility and promote social order. The law institutionalizes certain standards of conduct, which individuals and businesses may ignore only at their peril.

How does the law cope with violations of these standards of conduct? In part, through the creation of so-called *legal remedies*. For example, your next-door neighbor may feel perfectly fine about letting his Great Dane roam freely outdoors. You, however, object violently to the dog's constant barking, not to mention the little presents it deposits all over your lawn. How does the law deal with such festering disputes between neighbors? In a nutshell, the law honors your neighbor's right to enjoy his pet, but not to the point where his enjoyment becomes the bane of your existence. Once that point is reached, your neighbor has committed what the law calls a "nuisance," and the law affords you a legal remedy against your neighbor. You can sue him to collect money damages, which will compensate you for your suffering, and you can also obtain a court-ordered injunction prohibiting him from continuing the nuisance he has created.

The very fact that these legal remedies are available to you—regardless of whether you actually invoke them—makes your neighbor vulnerable to you. That Great Dane is already racking up a big enough bill in chopped meat without your neighbor also having to pay you damages on account of the dog. More important, your neighbor loves his dog and doesn't want to run the risk that some court might severely restrict his rights of pet ownership. So your neighbor has a definite soft spot. You can put pressure on that soft spot in a super threat and quite likely get what you want without actually having to sue.

This Great Dane example may seem elementary, but the principle involved applies to many of the bigger problems that you face. Suppose you're up against a huge insurance company that stubbornly and arbitrarily refuses to pay out on your legitimate claim. Does an insurance company with all its agents and computers, its gleaming corporate towers and miles of fine print, have a soft spot? Yes, and for reasons similar to those that make the Great Dane's owner vulnerable. The law says that an insurance company owes a high duty of care, a public trust, to people whom it serves. If your insurer violates this trust and wantonly disregards your claim, you have a potent legal remedy. You can sue to recover not only what's due you under the policy, but also to punish the insurer for malice. Punishment will be exacted by a jury (probably composed of disgruntled policyholders) in the form of so-called *punitive damages.* (In one case we'll read about later on, an insured man won a jury verdict of $180,000 in punitive damages from his insurance company.) An insurance company's uncertainty over just how much a generous jury might award is the soft spot here, and you can lean on it heavily in a super threat.

When Should You Send a Super Threat?

In terms of your personal arsenal, think of a super threat as the weapon of last resort. Other, less drastic, steps should be taken before you launch a super threat. Studied escalation is the best general policy, regardless of the particular problem that you face.

Each of the chapters that follows describes various initial steps, short of a super threat, which may solve your problem or at least make it less complicated. Some general observations about preliminary steps to take are in order at this point. Your two most frequently used preliminary steps will be the telephone call and the polite complaint letter. There are several basic dos and don'ts that apply regardless of whom you are calling or writing.

Telephone calls

Using the telephone to solve your problems can be a godsend or a curse: If you know what you're doing, you can get quick results; but if you're misguided or nervous or just plain unlucky, you can wind up inside a ball of red tape. While there is no ironclad formula for the successful phone call, the following pointers may help.

1. *Be prepared.* Before you dial the number, collect everything you'll need to carry on an intelligent conversation and arrange it next to the telephone. For example, you may have to refer to sales slips or canceled checks or monthly bills or newspaper advertisements. Have them handy. Also place some paper and a pencil by the phone, so that you can take notes on your conversation.

2. *Rehearse.* A telephone conversation is a performance, just like a lawyer's summation before a jury. You will be trying to persuade someone to help you out. Therefore, you should decide in advance exactly what it is that you want. Otherwise you'll just be throwing yourself on the mercy of the court.

For example, that self-cleaning oven you just bought decided to clean itself while you were cooking. Do you want the appliance dealer to refund your purchase price? Probably not, since you still want to have a self-cleaning oven. Do you want the entire unit replaced? That's asking for too much, at least initially. Most likely, what you want is a service visit by a representative from the store, and you want it before the weekend, when you'll be throwing a big dinner party.

3. *Speak to the proper person.* As a general rule, the proper person is one who has the authority to grant what you want. That person does not have to be the president of a company, or even the general manager. Someone in a "com-

plaint department" or a "customer-service department" may suffice.

How do you know whether you're speaking to the proper person? One way to find out is simply to ask the person directly. For example, you might open a conversation with "Hello, this is Jane Smith. I'm having trouble with a self-cleaning oven I bought at your store last week. Are you the person I should speak to about arranging for a service call?" By asking such a question at the outset, you'll avoid wasting time talking to someone who can't help you.

When you do get the proper person, be sure to ask his or her name and write it down. This will immediately make the person feel accountable to you, and perhaps to his or her superior as well. Besides, in subsequent correspondence you may have to refer to the person with whom you spoke.

4. *Be persistent.* You've heard the old consumer watchword, "Get it in writing!" In terms of telephone calls, this translates into "Get an oral promise." You want some concrete assurance from the person you speak to that specific steps will be taken to solve your problem and that they will be taken by a specific date. Don't settle for a vague "we'll-get-back-to-you" type of response.

With perseverance, you may succeed in getting the kind of response that you want from the person at the other end of the line. If you want a little added assurance that results will actually be forthcoming, you might write a *confirming letter* to the person whom you spoke to. In this brief letter you will simply state that you are writing to confirm the substance of the conversation you had on a specific date. Then you will summarize the gist of that conversation, laying emphasis on exactly what was agreed on over the telephone. Through the device of the confirming letter, you will be signaling to the other person that you fully intend to hold him to his word. You will also be manufacturing a written record of what transpired on the phone. Keep a copy of the confirming letter for yourself; it may prove handy later on if you have to substantiate what was said to you.

Suppose you can get no encouraging response over the phone, or the response that you do get turns out to be just hot air—in other words, promises that were made to you are never fulfilled. Then it's time to escalate.

The polite complaint letter

On page 13 we saw a good example of a polite complaint letter, namely, the one that Saul David wrote to his landlord. Referring back to that letter now will help to illustrate the following guidelines:

1. *Certified mail.* All polite complaint letters should be sent via *certified mail, return receipt requested.* Any clerk at the post office can explain to you how this simple, cheap, and extremely useful system works, and you will discover that it is well worth your while to use certified mail.

First of all, each piece of certified mail has a separately assigned number, which you can record at the top of your letter—for example, "Certified Letter No. 12345678." (Ask any post office clerk how these numbers are assigned.) From the start, this number adds a semiofficial flourish to your correspondence.

Second, when you use certified mail you get a validated slip from the post office showing when the item was mailed. This proof-of-mailing slip can be useful later on if you have to prove that you sent the letter on a certain date.

Third, when your certified letter is delivered someone will have to sign the return-receipt card presented by the mail carrier. That card will then be mailed back to you. Consequently, you will know when your letter was received and by whom; more important, *the recipient will know that you know.* So the recipient will tend to feel more accountable to you from the outset.

Be sure to preserve both the proof-of-mailing slip and

the return-receipt card with the records you keep on the progress of your complaint.

2. *Date of mailing.* Just below the certified-letter number, type the date on which your letter will be mailed.

3. *Your name and address.* In the upper right-hand corner, type your name and address. Sometimes it's helpful if you add your telephone numbers at work and at home, especially if you're expecting a prompt response or the opportunity to speak with someone.

4. *The addressee.* Below your name and to the left of it, you will type the name and address of the person to whom you're writing. In Saul David's case the identity of that person was obvious, but that may not be so in other situations. If you're in doubt about whom to address in your letter, you will generally fare better if you steer clear of underlings and shoot for someone in a position of authority. Frequently that person will be the president or general manager of the business that you're confronting. One direct way of learning this person's identity is to call the business and ask the receptionist. Simply say, "I'd like to address some correspondence to the president of your company. Will you please give me the correct spelling of the president's name?" Another source for the names and addresses of top executives at thousands of major American companies is Standard and Poor's *Register of Corporations, Directors and Executives,* available at any reference library. Even if your letter is not actually read by the top brass, it will be referred to someone else by the top brass, which automatically gives you a certain cachet.

5. *Caption.* If you look back at Saul David's letter, just below Rocky Goliath's name and to the right of it you will see "Re: Broken front-door lock." A brief caption such as this is useful to the recipient. It immediately alerts him to the gist of your complaint.

6. *The problem.* Get right to the point, as Saul David

did, in your very first paragraph. Supply the minimum number of facts necessary to explain what your problem is. If you purchased a product that performs only poorly and erratically, identify it by name, model, and serial number and describe what it does or does not do. For example: "On March 1, 1977, I purchased at your store a Whirlwind electric mixer, deluxe hand model, serial number DD38640. The mixer is defective in that it is totally incapable of performing the easiest mixing chores. It frequently slows to a halt even in relatively loose substances, such as whipping cream."

7. *Prior complaints.* Briefly review your unsuccessful attempts to solve your problem (over the phone, by personal visit).

8. *Special grievances.* Note any serious consequences you have suffered, which the recipient might not otherwise know about. For example, the recipient's conduct may be causing you great inconvenience, distress, and sleeplessness. If so, say so. In Saul David's case there was the critical element of criminal intrusions, which added urgency to the need for prompt repairs.

9. *The demand.* As in the case of your telephone call, request specific action (repair, replacement, refund, prompt payment of your claim, removal of a hazardous condition from your neighbor's property, et cetera).

Considering these nine points which you should cover, you will have to be succinct in order to fit everything onto a single page. That's right: one page. Don't tax your reader's patience; it's quick results you want, not heartfelt sympathy.

Sometimes you may want to submit documentation (sales slips, canceled checks, advertisements) to substantiate the grounds for your complaint. If so, *send only photostatic copies, not originals.* Retain all originals for your records.

Finally, and most important, *always make copies—at least two—of your polite complaint letter.* You will save one for your own records. Another can be enclosed with any super threat that you later send. (Having even more additional copies can prove useful, especially if you have to send one to a government official or a lawyer.)

What if your polite complaint letter produces no satisfactory results? In some instances, there may be one more step before launching a super threat. For instance, in Chapter 12 you will learn about writing a complaint letter to the Federal Trade Commission about any credit-reporting agency that ruins your credit rating; in Chapter 14 you will see how to complain to your State Commissioner of Insurance. Unless such pleas for outside intervention succeed, brace yourself for the launching of a super threat.

What Do You Say in a Super Threat?

There are basically two elements in a super threat: the facts and the law. We will be supplying you with the law, so don't worry about that angle. Your job will be to state the facts—"Just the facts, ma'am," as they used to say on *Dragnet*.

Later on we will give step-by-step instructions and samples for writing your own custom-made super threat. For the present, some general rules are in order. Let's consider a super threat's overall format; this aspect hardly ever varies, regardless of a super threat's individual contents. Stripped to its skeletal form, a super threat would look like this:

NOTICE

IN THE MATTER OF

Name of addressee
Mailing address
City, state, zip code

Date of mailing:
[Insert date here]

NOTICE OF _____

STATEMENT OF COMPLAINT

DEMAND FOR ACTION

ULTIMATUM

[Your signature]
Your name

Mailing address
City, state, zip code

Certified Mail No. 12345678

Here are some general rules for fleshing out the super threat's skeleton:

"*Notice.*" This word appears centered at the top of all super threats. "Notice" signals your offensive stance to the recipient; it says to him, "Pay attention. I'm talking to you!"

"*In the Matter of.*" Underneath "Notice" comes the

caption. Think of it as the title to your super threat. Frequently we will give you the words with which to complete the phrase "in the matter of." At other times we will tell you what sort of words to choose on your own. Whichever approach is taken, the caption adds a cool touch of formality; it suggests to the recipient that things have now become serious—why, they've turned into a "matter"!

Date of mailing. Opposite the heading you will record the date of mailing your super threat.

"Notice of..." Here comes the first of the legalese. Don't get nervous—we will supply you with the necessary legalistic boilerplate language. We will give you official citations to laws and cases and tell you what those authorities stand for.

"Statement of Complaint." In this second main part of the super threat, you get to show your wares. Obviously, we can't dictate the particular facts in your case; you'll have to do that.

You've already had some basic training in the concise recitation of facts—namely, in connection with composing a polite complaint letter. Indeed, if you have already sent your adversary a polite complaint letter (and kept copies for yourself), your task here may be easier than you would expect. Simply summarize the gist of your complaint in one introductory sentence; then, in a second sentence, refer to your polite complaint letter and say that a copy of it is enclosed.

For example: "On February 15, I sent you a check in the amount of $22.98 for the purchase of three knives, but you mailed me two salad servers instead. The difficulties which your mishandling of this order has caused me are more fully described in my letter of March 30, 1977, a copy of which is enclosed." The virtue of this approach is that it keeps the text of the super threat short and to the point.

Another approach that can be equally effective calls for the recitation of your facts in short, consecutively numbered paragraphs. Why the numbered paragraphs? Because they force you to organize your facts into a logical progression.

For example, you want to persuade the owners of a nearby gravel pit that the lack of a fence around their property endangers neighborhood children. You could state your complaint in one continuous paragraph: "On January 25, 1977, I observed seven children playing in the gravel pit. This pit is dangerous, since landslides can occur which can suffocate children. The children were playing on a particularly steep portion of the pit. There is no fencing around the pit to keep the children out. The playing of the children can cause a landslide to start. If an adequate fence were installed, the children would be prevented from entering."

There is nothing terribly wrong with this statement of complaint; it manages to get the point across, although it wanders a bit in doing so. But note the increased forcefulness that can be achieved when the same six sentences are rearranged into three numbered paragraphs:

1. On January 25, 1977, I observed seven children playing in the gravel pit. The children were playing on a particularly steep portion of the pit.

2. This pit is dangerous, since landslides can occur which can suffocate children. The playing of the children can cause a landslide to start.

3. There is no fencing around the pit to keep the children out. If an adequate fence were installed, the children would be prevented from entering.

Now the same six sentences form three logical units of thought: Children are at play; their play places them in peril; the peril can be eliminated. Presenting your facts in a rational step-by-step manner is an important element in any super threat, because the more organized you sound, the more of a threat you pose.

"*Demand for Action.*" In this third main part of the super threat, you will once again have to help out. After all, you're in the best position to know what you want the recipient to do for you. Just make sure that in demanding action you express yourself with precision; there's nothing less effective, or easier to wriggle out of, than a demand that's ambiguous or full of loopholes.

For example, if your neighbor's dog annoys you by constantly barking and howling at sirens, you should not simply demand the dog be kept quiet. Such a vague demand would leave room for too many differing subjective judgments (when is a dog "quiet"?) and thereby stir up future arguments—the very thing you'd like to avoid. A better demand in this situation would be that the dog not be let outdoors before eight A.M. or after eight P.M. Now there can be no doubt as to what your neighbor must do in order to comply with your demand.

Another important point to recall from Chapter 1 is that your demands should be reasonable. Don't be greedy and grab for the moon. Always provide your adversary with an escape hatch, which he should be willing to take in the face of your threat.

Finally, set a deadline for compliance. After an ambiguous demand, an open-ended one provides the greatest chance for evasion by the recipient. In the instructions leading up to most model super threats we will suggest appropriate time limits.

"*Ultimatum.*" In this fourth and final part of the super threat, you can pretty much relax. It's time for more legalistic boilerplate. All you do is attach it to your super threat.

Signature. Sign your name underneath the ultimatum. Then supply your name and address.

Certified mail number. Like a polite complaint letter,

a super threat should also be sent via certified mail, return receipt requested. To reinforce the psychological edge gained through the use of certified mail, you should record your certified mail number just below your name and address. Thus, your super threat will end with a fitting semiofficial flourish.

The appearance of a super threat is almost as important as its content. Remember, you are engaging in psychological warfare, and it must be waged on all fronts. Therefore, all super threats must be typed; handwriting, no matter how neat, undercuts the businesslike formality that you are trying to achieve. If you don't own a typewriter, borrow one or use one at somebody's office. Even if you have to pay a few dollars to a professional typist, the investment is worthwhile. (To play the super-threat game in real style, have your super threat typed on an electric typewriter equipped with a carbon ribbon, which yields a crisp impression that resembles print in a book.)

All super threats should be typed with double spacing. Unlike a polite complaint letter, a super threat can be longer than one page if necessary. Don't take this rule as a license to ramble and turn your super threat into a crank letter; more than one page may be needed, solely because the various captions, as well as our boilerplate legalese, may not all fit on one page when combined with your facts. So if you need two pages, fine; much beyond that, though, and you are probably rambling in your statement of complaint or your demand for action.

You will have to underline certain words in your typed super threat. Whenever we supply you with super threat language (e.g., the names of court cases) that is *italicized* in this book, type that language with underlining in your super threat.

Use plain white 8½-by-11-inch paper for all super threats. Never use colored paper or personal stationery or any other paper with a letterhead on it. (For you high rollers in the super-threat game, try 8-by-13-inch legal-size white paper to create an even more striking impression.)

Make at least two photocopies of your super threat. One you will keep in your own files; the other you may eventually supply to a lawyer.

3

Troublesome Neighbors

Bad Business Neighbors

Business and pleasure rarely mix well, and the mixture can become explosive when a business moves next door to someone's home. Too often what is good for business is bad for business's neighbors.

Usually the offending business activity is loud noises or nasty odors. An occasional problem is traffic congestion created by the business, and there are even a few cases in which bright lights turned a homeowner's night into day. In all of the cases, the courts have looked at the location of the business to determine the reasonableness of its activity. For example, if you decide to live in a commercial area with many factories, you will have a difficult time complaining about a business which emits smoke. However, if you live in a residential area and your neighbor opens up a cement factory, you've got a good case. Once again, the circumstances of the case will determine whether the business is acting reasonably.

A typical business nuisance case is *Mandell* v. *Pasquaretto*. Mr. Mandell and his wife lived in peace with their neighbor, the Hewlett House of Tires, for a number of years. In 1969 Hewlett decided to expand its house beyond tires into installing mufflers, brakes, and shock absorbers, selling used cars, and painting autos. Much of this activity took place outdoors, causing greater noise and fumes to the immediate neighbors.

The Mandells claimed that Hewlett had gone too far. The noise and soot were making their life miserable. They went to court. And the court agreed with them. In the course of rendering its decision, the court explained the general rules involved: "The common law doctrine of nuisance has received renewed vitality in recent times with the advent of modern environmental sensitivities. Emphasis on preservation of outdoor life qualities is not confined to wholly natural or biological wildlife. It serves to prevent destruction of the environment whether in remote national parks, inland waterways, or suburban residentia. The rules for permissible land use with direct impact on neighboring property have become far more strict, and the sensitivity to noxious intrusions far keener.... A private nuisance is generally anything that by its continuous use or existence works annoyance, harm, inconvenience or damage to another landowner in the enjoyment of his property." The court concluded that Hewlett was operating a nuisance. Hewlett was ordered to pay its neighbors two thousand dollars in damages and stop making a nuisance of itself.

This case is an example of the common problem of business in a residential neighborhood. There are also cases in which a business can be a nuisance even if it's operated in a commercial environment. In *Braddock* v. *Barbecue Cottage, Inc.* the offensive business was a drive-in fast-food restaurant. The problem was that orders from the autos were broadcast back to the restaurant over a loudspeaker. Mary Braddock, who lives some 150 feet from the restaurant, could hear the orders, which were broadcast right up until closing time—about one A.M. every day.

The restaurant was located in a commercial area next to a Sunoco service station. Nonetheless, the court found that the loudspeaker was a nuisance: "No man has a right to take from another the enjoyment of the reasonable and essential comforts of life and, consequently, cannot commit acts on his own premises calculated to interfere with the reasonable enjoyment by others of their homes. Even music, however elevating and enjoyable at times, and depending, of course, on its character, may be continued so long as to become an annoyance to those compelled to remain in the immediate vicinity. In fact, the general trend of decisions has been to hold that any noise, whether of musical instrument or the human voice, or by mechanical means, or however produced, may be a nuisance, especially if its tendency is to draw together in the vicinity of a person's residence or place of business large crowds of noisy and disorderly people." The court ordered the restaurant to stop using the loudspeaker and make various other changes to avoid being a nuisance.

A court confronted with a business which is a nuisance usually orders the business either to change its procedures to avoid the nuisance or to shut down entirely. In many cases the court will assess damages for the annoyance caused to neighbors. For example, a cement factory that made its neighbor's life miserable was assessed damages of over $150,000. In another case a man who raised mice (for scientific experiments) was ordered to pay $8,000 to a neighbor who was bothered by the "mousey odors" coming from the "mouse house."

Before launching a super threat against an offending business, you must decide what you want the business to do. You clearly won't have much success if you ask it to shut down entirely. We suggest that you aim for a remedy that the business can reasonably grant. The more you ask for, the less likely you are to get your way with a super threat. And remember, most likely the annoying practices of the business are good for the business.

Opening volleys

Contacting your local police may prove useful. If enough people are being annoyed, you might want to join together and get in touch with a local politician.

Launching a super threat

Soft spot. Here the soft spot lies in the possibility that a court will assess substantial damages against the offending business and/or shut the business down entirely.

"In the Matter of." Insert the name of the business.

Heading. Insert the name of the owner of the business, the name of the business, and the address.

"Notice to Abate Actionable Nuisance." This language remains constant for all such super threats.

NOTICE TO ABATE ACTIONABLE NUISANCE

PLEASE TAKE NOTICE: Pursuant to *Mandell* v. *Pasquaretto*, 76 Misc.2d 405, 350 NYS2d 561 (1973), and cases cited therein, NOTICE is hereby given to abate the nuisance described below.

"Statement of Complaint." Indicate what conditions are causing the nuisance. Do not indicate the steps you have already taken to remedy the problem. Thus, do *not* indicate that you contacted the police or a local politician and they would not help. Your previous failures will not be impressive.

"*Demand for Action.*" This is an extremely important portion of the super threat. Here you must spell out in some detail the steps you want the business to take to eliminate the nuisance. For example, you might demand that a particular blinking neon sign not be used after a certain hour at night. Try to avoid making unreasonable demands. Presumably, the business has a right to exist (if the area zoning permits). Reasonable demands are more likely to be met.

"*Ultimatum.*" While your demands should be reasonable, your ultimatum should pull no punches. The ultimatum we suggest can be used for all such super threats.

ULTIMATUM

In the event you fail to meet the above demands a legal action may be commenced to abate the nuisance. A successful action may result in the imposition of substantial damages (see *Kinley* v. *Atlantic Cement Co.*, 42 A.D.2d 496, 349 NYS2d 199 [1973]). Further, we will seek an injunction which may result in an order terminating your business (see, e.g., *Braddock* v. *Barbecue Cottage, Inc.*, 69 Dauphin Reports 221 [1956]).

Malicious Neighbors

Good fences, they say, make good neighbors. However, if your neighbor has determined to make you miserable, nothing short of a demilitarized zone will help you. And, going by a number of cases dealing with malicious neighbors, even a DMZ won't help much. Super threats may work. However, to be candid, if you're dealing with an irrational neighbor, nothing short of court-ordered psychiatric treatment is likely to do much good.

The case example which follows will show you what a court might do in the event that you sue your malicious neighbor. We have also included a super threat for those of you who want to take a long shot before hiring a lawyer.

In *Gorman* v. *Sabo,* two families, the Gormans and the Sabos, lived next door to each other. It is an understatement to report that they did not get along. Indeed, the Gormans undertook a strategy designed, it appears, to drive the Sabos out of their minds. First Mrs. Gorman set up a radio facing the Sabos. She played the radio at a loud volume several hours each day. Even during the winter she left the window open to allow the noise to blast away at the Sabos' house. Second, Mrs. Gorman ordered her children to beat with sticks and stones on metal furniture and cans at strategic times to annoy the Sabo children and Mrs. Sabo. Finally, Mrs. Gorman made her intentions very clear: According to the court record, "Mrs. Gorman told various neighbors that she intended to make the Sabos move, that she would make life miserable for Mrs. Sabo, that she hoped that Mr. Sabo would be struck down and never speak, and prayed that she would see Mrs. Sabo lie bleeding on the floor, that the Sabos would wish they were in hell before she was through with them, and on several occasions, with Mr. Gorman present, she said that she intended to see that Mrs. Sabo was carried out of the house either in a strait jacket or in a coffin."

As was said earlier, the Gormans and the Sabos did not get along.

The Sabos retaliated by going to court. They claimed the Gormans were maliciously interfering with their peace and quiet, and the court agreed. It awarded damages of $3,500.

Opening volleys

If neighbors are deliberately annoying you, your first remedy (after having asked your neighbors to cool it) should be the police. However, police are reluctant to enter into what they consider private arguments. Most likely, they will recommend that you file a criminal complaint. Certainly, discussing your problem with the local district attorney's office would be worthwhile.

Launching a super threat

Soft spot. If the police or district attorney can't or won't help, you are left on your own. Your ultimate remedy is a court action to compel your neighbors to leave you alone. Such action would seek an injunction to force your neighbors to stop bothering you in the future and pay money damages for the annoyance they have already caused. The soft spot, as we have already seen, is in the amount of damages which may be awarded. If your neighbor has any sense, he will see that you have a viable legal remedy and mean business. If he has no sense, he has no soft spot, and only a lawyer can help.

"In the Matter of." Insert your neighbor's name.

Heading. Insert your neighbor's name and address.

"Notice to Abate Actionable Nuisance." This language remains the same for all such super threats.

NOTICE TO ABATE ACTIONABLE NUISANCE

PLEASE TAKE NOTICE: Pursuant to *Gorman* v. *Sabo,* 210 Md. 155, 122 A.2d 475 (1956), notice is hereby given to abate the nuisance described below.

"Statement of Complaint." Indicate the facts of your case in a dispassionate manner. You may want to use numbered paragraphs to list the exact actions which your neighbor engaged in and when. If the police were called at any

time, note this fact. You may also want to indicate that the police have a record of your complaint.

"Demand for Action." This language remains constant for all such super threats.

DEMAND FOR ACTION

Forthwith discontinue the above-described nuisance, which has caused, and continues to cause, irreparable damage.

"Ultimatum." This language remains constant for all such super threats.

ULTIMATUM

You are hereby on notice that your activity described above may be the proximate cause of substantial damage including, but not limited to, personal injury. Your liability for nuisance, intentional infliction of mental distress, personal injury, and wrongful death by any improper activity on your part, including any activity after receipt of this NOTICE, may subject you to substantial liability.

4

Troublesome Animals

Noisy Animals

Noisy animals, dogs in particular, account for a large number of complaints from tenants and homeowners. A single dog in good voice can provide a steady stream of noise, which can annoy even the most patient neighbor. As one court has said: "It has been held that a pack of dogs may create a nuisance, and it follows that a constituent part of a pack, to wit, one dog, if sufficiently persistent, may make as much noise as a dozen barking seriatim...."

A typical nuisance case involving a dog is *Davoust* v. *Mitchell*. Richard Davoust had a son named Danny. Danny had a dog named Queenie. Queenie lived in a dog pen in the back yard, about ten feet from the house of the next-door neighbors, the Mitchells. Queenie did what dogs will do: She barked and defecated. The odor wafted up to the Mitchells' second-story bedroom. Neither doggie activity pleased the Mitchells, who went to court.

The attorneys for the Davousts probably saw defeat

ahead and pleaded to the court: "This is the saga of 'Queenie,' a small German shepherd dog, and her master, Danny Davoust, an eight-year-old boy, who lives with his mother, father, five brothers and sisters on a fifty-foot lot in the city of Evansville." This "Old Mother Hubbard" approach failed. The Davousts did not live in a shoe, they lived next door to the Mitchells. And the Mitchells were not amused. Neither was the court: "Anything offensive to the senses so as to essentially interfere with the comfortable enjoyment of life and property is a nuisance. Certainly, it would be offensive to the senses of the [Mitchells] or other persons of their social level to be required to refrain from looking out their living room window because the drapes had to be closed and, too, it would be offensive to look out their living room window at dog stools and an unkempt dog pen.... The writer of this opinion, in considering things that happen in ordinary affairs of life and men, has long since been of the opinion from such experience that the barking of a dog at night time which keeps one awake night after night is a nuisance on the part of the party harboring such a dog." In conclusion, the court ordered the Davousts to keep Queenie quiet or get rid of her.

While most noisy-animal problems involve dogs, there is no reason why any other kind of animal can't become a nuisance. In each case, however, the quantity and quality of the noise produced will determine whether the animal is a nuisance. After all, as one court has pointed out, "There is quite a difference between the crowing of a five or six pound chicken and the barking of a seventy or eighty pound dog insofar as the loudness or volume and tone of the noise is concerned."

Assuming you are in the unfortunate position of having a noisy animal for a neighbor, what can you do about it? The problem is especially severe because many pet owners treat their pets as members of the family. No super threat, regardless of how potent, is likely to get your neighbor to put a family member up for adoption.

The practical answer is that in most cases if a neighbor takes reasonable precautions his pet will likely not be a nuisance to you. For example, in the case of Danny and his dog, if Queenie had not been penned up outside, the problem of noise in the morning and odors during the summer would have been avoided. In other cases the problem could be remedied if the animal was not left home alone to pine for affection while the owner was away. Putting the dog in a kennel or hiring a "dog sitter" could also be a solution.

Thus, assuming you have a noisy animal for a neighbor and have found that polite requests to tone down the racket have not worked, a super threat is in order. And in order to give your super threat some punch, we will use those cases in which a court did take the drastic remedy of ordering the animal out of the house. Let's hope that your neighbor will choose to quiet his pet down, rather than risk losing it entirely.

Opening volleys

A call to the police may add emphasis to a polite request; however, there is not much the police can do to keep a dog quiet. Some communities have passed laws to control noisy dogs, and you might want to check for such a law. If nothing works then (short of a lawyer), a super threat is the only possible remedy.

Launching a super threat

Soft spot. Here the soft spot lies in the possibility of damages and/or a court order directing the removal of the dog.

"In the Matter of." Insert name of animal owner.

Heading. Insert the animal owner's name and address.

"Notice of Application for Removal." This language will

remain constant except for the type of animal which is creating the nuisance.

NOTICE OF APPLICATION FOR REMOVAL

PLEASE TAKE NOTICE: Pursuant to *Adams* v. *Hamilton Carhartt Overall Co.*, 293 Ky. 443, 169 SW2d 294 (Ct. of App. 1943), you are on NOTICE that failure to abate the nuisance described below will result in application for a permanent injunction requiring the removal of your [insert type of animal].

"Statement of Complaint." Insert the facts of your case. Describe the type of animal behavior which is causing the problem. Also indicate the effect of this behavior on your peace, quiet, and comfort. The use of numbered paragraphs will be especially helpful here, to avoid a rambling history of your misery.

"Demand for Action." We suggest that you provide a reasonable demand for action. For example, if a dog is causing a problem whenever it is let out into the yard, it may be unreasonable to demand that the dog *never* be permitted in the yard. If the dog bothers you only at night, then a demand that the dog not be permitted in the yard at night is a reasonable solution. Remember, the effect of a super threat is minimized if you do not provide the recipient with a viable escape hatch.

"Ultimatum." This language remains constant, with the exception of the insertion of the type of animal involved.

ULTIMATUM

In the event you fail to respond to this demand, action may be brought to permanently remove your [insert type of animal]. In addition to injunctive relief, a claim for damages shall be entered. See *Davoust v. Mitchell,* 146 Ind. App. 536, 257 N.E.2d 332 (1970).

Dangerous Animals

Noisy animals, as we have seen, can be a pain in the neck. Nasty animals can be a pain in the ankle, thigh, rear end, arm, or anywhere else they choose to bite. And sometimes a nasty animal can kill. If you've got a noisy animal next door, be thankful and give a moment of silence for those inflicted with a vicious animal as a neighbor.

Some animals are naturally dangerous. Lions and poisonous snakes, for example, are presumed to be vicious. The law calls them *ferae naturae.* Other animals are naturally friendly. Dogs and cats, for example, are presumed to be tame. The law calls them *domitae naturae.* As we will see, the distinction can be important.

The owner of a vicious animal is liable for any injury which that animal causes. For example, if your neighbor likes to have a monkey for a pet, and that monkey likes to have your ear for lunch, the pet owner will be liable to you for the damage his monkey causes. The mere fact that he has a dangerous pet makes him liable for any damage that pet causes. It is presumed that he knows that his pet can hurt people or damage property, and he keeps that pet at his own risk.

The owner of a tame animal is *not* presumed to know that his pet is or may be dangerous. Thus, if, for example, your dog bites someone, you will not be liable unless you should have had reason to know that your dog gets nasty and might bite someone. Only if you have reason to know that your "tame" pet does get vicious will you be liable.

Classically, it's the dog that bites the postman. However, cats can be vicious also. There are many cases in which a cat owner who should have known his pet scratched or bit people was held liable for the damage caused by his pet.

So far we have looked at injuries caused by vicious animals. However, injury can sometimes be caused by a friendly animal. That's exactly what happened in *Groner* v. *Hedrick*. According to the court, here is what happened: "First Friend, as Kipling called Wild Dog, was in this case a large Great Dane, named 'Sleepy.' It jumped upon the plaintiff who was seventy-four years old, five feet two in height and 150 pounds in weight, and knocked her down so that she broke her arm and leg...." Sleepy was not trying to hurt Bertha Groner. Sleepy was just being friendly in his own way. However, as the court noted, "A large, strong, and over-friendly dog may be as dangerous as a vicious one...." Since Sleepy's owner knew that his dog was overly friendly and liked to jump on people, he was held liable for the damage Sleepy caused—to the tune of $17,000.

As anyone who has read *The Hound of the Baskervilles* knows, you don't have to be bitten by a dog to suffer from a dog; being scared can be very painful. The courts have held that a person who suffers fright can have serious mental and physical consequences. And courts have also held that animals, including dogs, can scare people. Thus, for example, if a neighbor has a leashed dog which lunges at people, it's quite possible that the dog owner will be liable should somebody be frightened after being lunged at, even though the dog did not get close enough to bite. In many cases the damage will be mental. However, there are many cases in which the injury is physical.

In *Machacado* v. *City of New York*, Nilda Machacado was walking down the street on a snowy night and passed a yard enclosed by a high metal fence. Edward Davidson kept his German shepherd in the yard, and his dog lunged viciously at people who walked along the sidewalk. Nilda was no exception. When the dog lunged, Nilda slipped and fell. Edward knew the dog was vicious. The question was: Is Edward liable for Nilda's injury even though the dog never got its teeth into her? The court decided that he was: "The right to harbor animals must yield to the duty of containing them in a reasonable manner so as to avoid the harm that can befall an unsuspecting person, lack of physical contact notwithstanding. Owning and keeping a German shepherd in an urban area requires the highest standards to be employed in the protection of the innocent public."

The super threat we will use relies on the importance of informing an animal owner about the dangerous characteristic that the animal possesses. As we have seen, the owner of a normally tame pet is liable for the damage that his pet causes only if he knew, or should have known, that the pet had a mean streak. Our super threat will provide him with that notice.

In the case of naturally dangerous animals, the super threat will also rely upon the liability of the animal owner for injuries that his pet causes. However, in this case we will add on an additional factor.

Opening volleys

If the dangerous animal is *domitae naturae* (normally tame), you might try to tell your neighbor that he has a problem. He honestly may not realize it, and informing him would certainly be doing him a favor. However, if your neighbor has a *ferae naturae*, telling him he has a dangerous animal is telling him something he knows already. About the only opening volley which would do any good would come from a musket. You should consider contacting your health department to determine whether the *ferae naturae* is legal (in many states keeping dangerous animals as pets is forbidden). If nothing works, and you're willing to take the time to try a super threat before hiring a lawyer, here's the information you need. But please, don't remain in a seriously dangerous condition while waiting for a super threat to work.

Launching a super threat

In Appendix A you will find a sample super threat that follows the instructions given below.

Soft spot. The owner of a dangerous animal has a very soft spot: liability for any damage his animal causes. The possibility that the animal may injure or even kill a child is very real. Were this to happen, the liability to the animal owner could run into hundreds of thousands of dollars. In order to avoid a tragedy, the super threat will aim hard at the possibility of liability. Furthermore, in the case of *ferae naturae* the pet owner has *absolute* liability for any damage his animal causes.

"In the Matter of." Insert the name of the owner of the animal.

Heading. Insert the name and address of the owner of the animal.

"Notice of Liability for Possession of Dangerous Animal." This paragraph will remain the same for all super threats, with one exception. Insert the proper term, *ferae naturae* or *domitae naturae,* to describe the dangerous animal.

NOTICE OF LIABILITY FOR POSSESSION OF DANGEROUS ANIMAL

PLEASE TAKE NOTICE: Your possession of a [insert type of animal] constitutes a condition which is dangerous and may cause serious injury or death. Pursuant to *Maxwell* v. *Fraze* 344 S.W.2d 262 (Mo. App. 1961), this letter constitutes notice of the dangerous propensity of your animal.

"*Statement of Complaint.*" Describe the facts of your case. These facts must include the information you have which tends to show that the animal is dangerous. If the animal is *ferae naturae,* of course, the animal is presumed dangerous, but you should still include any instances which show that the owner of the animal is recklessly exposing people to danger.

"*Demand for Action.*" It's entirely up to you to decide what your demands are. You might settle for a muzzle on a dangerous dog or a leash on a monkey. On the other hand, you might want your neighbor's python to remain indoors at all times. Be sure to include a date by which your neighbor must fulfill your demand. Beginning the demand with, for example, "On or before June 1, 1977, you must..." is a good approach.

"*Ultimatum.*" We have provided two ultimatums; one is for situations involving *ferae naturae* and the other for *domitae naturae.* Use the ultimatum appropriate for your case. You will need to insert the particular type of animal in whichever ultimatum you choose.

ULTIMATUM

[For use with *ferae naturae.*] Possession of your dangerous animal subjects you to absolute liability for any injury which is proximately caused by said animal. See, e.g., *Copley v. Mills,* 152 S.W. 830 (1913). This injury may include death. Liability may be substantial and recent decisions indicate that awards may be over $200,000. In addition, your negligent failure to honor the demands contained herein will prove the necessary intent for possible criminal liability.

[For use with *domitae naturae.*] You are now on notice of the dangerous characteristics of your animal. Your failure to accept the reasonable demands contained herein will expose you to liability in the event your animal causes any injury. See *Groner* v. *Hedrick,* 403 Pa. 148, 169 A.2d 302 (1961) ($17,000 award). This liability may be substantial in the event your animal causes serious injury or death.

5

Neighborhood Hazards

Four years ago your neighbor built a swimming pool. Three years ago your son, Johnny, was born. Johnny doesn't know how to swim—but he does know how to walk. And now he can walk the 170 feet to that pool.

You know you've got a problem. Johnny's got a problem too, but he is too young to know it. The owner of the pool may have a problem, but he too may not know it. One way to avoid a tragedy is to get the owner of the pool to realize that he may have a serious problem and force him to do something about it, such as put up a fence, before it's too late. The answer is a super threat based upon the legal doctrine of "attractive nuisance."

The attractive-nuisance doctrine is based upon the realization that children, especially very young ones, are not safety-conscious. Indeed, dangers which an adult would naturally avoid can be appealing play opportunities to children. For example, if you were walking down the street and saw an open well, you would not jump into it. You know that you would get hurt. However, a four-year-old child might think that she was Alice in Wonderland (or the White Rabbit) and hop into it.

Who should be responsible if the child gets hurt in the well? The law may hold the parents responsible if they did not adequately supervise the child. However, in some circumstances the law will impose liability upon the owner of the land with the well on it. The theory behind this liability is that the owner of land accessible to young children has a duty to avoid creating any condition which might be dangerous to those children. In other words, he has a duty to avoid creating an attractive nuisance.

Now, in the case of the well and the child who thinks she is a White Rabbit, the child probably is trespassing on the land with the well on it. Is the owner of land responsible for injuries to trespassing children? The answer is yes. As we said earlier, children are not worldly-wise. Most young children probably can't even spell "trespasser," much less know what it means. The law requires a landowner who knows that children might trespass on his land to avoid creating a condition which might injure them.

Finally, and perhaps most important, a landowner is responsible to trespassing children only if he knows, or should have known, that a dangerous condition exists on his property. After all, it would not be very fair to hold a landowner liable for a danger that he had no reason to know existed.

There is no way to list all the situations in which an attractive nuisance exists. A great deal depends on the circumstances of each case. Broadly speaking, however, an attractive nuisance probably exists wherever you feel that a child might be exposed to danger on land belonging to someone else. It may be a swimming pool, a drainage ditch, an abandoned house, a rusting tractor, a quarry with falling rocks, a tower with electrical wires. The important questions to ask yourself are: (1) Are children likely to be near the dangerous condition? (2) Can the owner of the land on which the danger exists do something to eliminate the danger? If the answer to both questions is yes, then an attractive-nuisance super threat is in order.

Launching a super threat
    Soft spot. The soft spot is the very substantial liability for damages for any injury caused to a child. Any jury will award such damages when the victim is a child.
    "In the Matter of." Insert the name of the property owner. If the owner of the land is different from the people who are using the land, prepare two super threats and send one to each of the two parties.
    Heading. Insert the name and address of the owner of the land (or the person using the land).
    "Notice of Attractive Nuisance Condition." This language will remain constant.

NOTICE OF ATTRACTIVE NUISANCE CONDITION

PLEASE TAKE NOTICE: A condition of ATTRACTIVE NUISANCE exists on property owned [or used] by you.

    "Statement of Complaint." Insert a description of the condition which is causing the danger. Indicate that children are in the area of the dangerous condition, and use any facts you have to back this up. For example, if you have seen children playing in a neighboring gravel pit and fear the danger of a landslide, indicate in your statement when and where you saw the children playing. Also indicate that there is danger of a landslide.
    "Demand for Action." In most cases, all you will need to demand is "appropriate action to eliminate the danger."

However, if you feel there are specific steps which could be taken, you are free to make them part of your demand. We advise that any suggestions be inserted after the boilerplate language we have provided in the model "Demand for Action" that follows.

DEMAND FOR ACTION

Request is made for you to take immediate appropriate action to eliminate the ATTRACTIVE NUISANCE described above. [Insert any particular suggestions you might have.]

"Ultimatum." This language will remain constant for all such super threats.

ULTIMATUM

In the event you fail to eliminate the above condition you shall be liable for any injury or death which may result from this condition. See, e.g., *Mitchell* v. *Akers*, 401 S.W.2d 907 (1966). Since notice has been served on you, your failure to remedy the nuisance may be construed as an intentional maintenance of a dangerous condition with a consequent increase in liability before a jury.

6

Utility Companies

Many people hate public utilities. They may not be able to say why; they just don't like the electric company or the gas company or the water company. What accounts for this unusual show of passion may be the fact that utilities control our essential services. No one likes to be at the mercy of a large corporate enterprise. After all, if you don't like the electric service you're receiving, what can you do about it?

Most of the problems which arise with utilities do not involve the quality of the service but rather the cost. Utilities have a unique leverage to force payment: Pay up or live in the dark (or without heat or water). So what can you do when you receive a utility bill which you don't believe is correct? How can you contest the bill without having the utility company discontinue service? How can you force the utility to listen to you?

The answer lies in an 1871 federal law, called the 1871 Civil Rights Act. What has civil rights got to do with utilities? For an answer, we need to go back to the civil rights movement and see how this law was used. Civil rights lawyers of the 1950s and 1960s frequently battled with municipal and state governments in an effort to secure rights for clients who were poor or members of minority groups or both. These lawyers saw little hope of finding municipal or state laws to help their cause, so they turned to the federal government. Some lawyers lobbied for new laws. Others looked to the past to uncover old federal laws which could be used as the basis for a court action. Once in court, they hoped, a liberal judge would interpret the laws to establish hitherto unknown rights for their clients.

The lawyers looking to the past came across an 1871 statute which, though only one sentence long, seemed to be suited to their needs. The law was aptly called a Civil Rights Act. It turned out to be extremely useful. Indeed, the numerous victories achieved by civil rights lawyers using the 1871 Civil Rights Act have resulted in a body of law which everyone today can look to for assistance. As we shall see, this law is uniquely suited to be the basis for a super threat to limit the arbitrary power of utilities to shut off services in the event that a disputed bill is not paid.

Today, the 1871 Civil Rights Act is tucked away in Title 42, Section 1983 of the United States Code. It is marvelously short and, as laws go, simple: "Every person who, under color of any statute, ordinance, regulation, custom, or usage, of any State or Territory, subjects, or causes to be subjected, any citizen of the United States or other person within the jurisdiction thereof to the deprivation of any rights, privileges, or immunities secured by the Constitution and laws, shall be liable to the party injured in an action at law, suit in equity, or other proper proceeding for redress."

Even a simple law has a way of sounding confusing, so let's translate it into everyday language. The law says that any person, acting on behalf of state or local government, who takes away your constitutional rights is liable to you in damages. For example, if a police officer beats you up while giving you a parking ticket, that officer has violated this law. You have a constitutional right not to be wantonly beaten up, so the police officer is liable to you. Most likely, this liability will be in the form of money damages, which the court will assess against him.

So far this law appears interesting. What makes it really intriguing is that in the example we just gave you, the police officer would have to pay for any judgment against him *out of his own pocket*. Remember, this law protects you from persons acting for the state or local government. These people are civil servants—bureaucrats. They don't want trouble. However, under this law, civil servants and public officials cannot hide behind the state or local treasury. If they violate the law, they are *personally liable*. As one court interpreting this law put it: "This statute authorizes the recovery of compensatory and punitive damages against an individual defendant for the unjustifiable violation of the constitutional rights of an individual plaintiff 'under color' of state law. Thus, the liability is entirely personal in nature, intended to be satisfied out of the individual defendant's pocket." This law, therefore, provides a strong deterrent to state and local government officials and employees who might violate your constitutional rights.

There are innumerable situations in which quoting from Section 1983 may be useful. In general, whenever a state or local government employee acts to take away what you believe are your rights, a cry of "1983" is in order. Certainly, there isn't a police officer in the country who doesn't cringe at the mention of the numbers "1983." But the law does not apply only to the police. Every employee is covered, from the dog catcher to the mayor.

Why does this law apply to utilities? The courts have concluded that a utility is more like a branch of government than a private corporation. Indeed, most state governments control utilities in a number of ways. Thus, most courts have taken the view that the activities of a utility are essentially "under color" of a state law. Therefore, the practices of a utility fall under the scrutiny of Section 1983.

Now that we know that Section 1983 applies, what constitutional right is violated if a utility terminates your service? The answer is that a utility may terminate service only after having investigated your reason for not paying. Indeed, some courts require a hearing before service may be terminated when a customer refuses to pay a bill because he believes it is erroneous. This requirement of a hearing derives from the basic rule in the Constitution that no person may be deprived of property without due process of law. Courts have held that utility services are "property." Therefore, you cannot have your utility service terminated without due process. And most courts have held that due process requires a hearing prior to termination.

If you've received a turnoff threat from a utility, you have two choices: You can pay up and dispute the bill thereafter, or you can refuse to pay and use your nonpayment as leverage to settle the disputed bill. We are not recommending one course of action over the other. We don't want you cursing us in the dark or cold. We know that some utilities have disregarded contempt orders from a court. For us to suggest that a super threat is guaranteed to keep the heat or electricity coming would be irresponsible. However, if you've decided to fight a utility's threatening "pay up or else," you're going to need a super threat.

Opening volleys

There have been books written on dealing with utilities. They suggest everything from petitioning your local Public Service Commission to writing certified letters that you are in an electrically operated iron lung. In some cases these approaches work. However, most utilities are so used to receiving these kinds of letters that they will not be very impressed. They already know how to handle these claims. We don't think many utilities know what to do with our super threat.

Launching a super threat

Soft spot. The personal liability of the officers of the utility under Section 1983 is the soft spot. In addition, if the utility has not already been ordered by a court to institute due process into its service-termination procedures, your complaint will threaten to do so.

"In the Matter of." Insert your name and account number.

Heading. Insert the name of the president or chief operating officer of the utility. You should have no problem getting this information from the utility. However, if it balks, contact your state Public Service Commission. Also include the address of the main office of the utility.

"Notice of Violation of United States Code, Title 42, Section 1983." This language will remain the same for all such super threats.

NOTICE OF VIOLATION OF UNITED STATES CODE
Title 42, Section 1983

PLEASE TAKE NOTICE: Personal liability under Title 42, Section 1983, of the United States Code may result. You are hereby on NOTICE of the allegations and facts contained herein.

"Statement of Complaint." Here you should explain exactly why you dispute the bill that you have received. If your bill is unusually high, provide whatever information you have showing that previous bills were lower. If an open-

ing volley has resulted in some explanation from the utility, state why you are still not satisfied. Also, if any unusual damage might occur because of termination of service, spell this out. For example, if you have a heated greenhouse and termination of electrical service will kill the plants, put this fact in your statement.

"*Demand for Action.*" There is no basis under the law to demand that your bill be reduced. What you can and should demand is a proper hearing on your claim. You should also demand assurance that your service will not be terminated until there has been a proper opportunity for you to present your case.

"*Ultimatum.*" This language will remain constant for all such super threats.

ULTIMATUM

In the event you fail to provide the due process requirements demanded above you shall be in violation of Title 42, Section 1983, known as the Civil Rights Act. Liability under this act is personal (see *Collins* v. *Schoonfield*, 363 F. Supp. 1152 (D.C. Md. 1973)).

Further, any damage which may result from suspension of service on the above-captioned account may be assessed against you under the Act or under a tort theory, *Gilbert* v. *Duke Power Company*, 179 SE2d 720 (Sup. Ct. S.C. 1971), 112 ALR 232.

7

Tenant Problems

Common Tenant Gripes

Leaky pipes—crumbling plaster—central air conditioning that breaks down every summer—a refrigerator that won't defrost—a doorman who won't watch the door—hallways prowled by strangers—the litany of tenant woes is long and sad. It's repeated from Boston to L.A., from Seattle to Miami. Too many tenants are simply not getting what they're paying for, and what they're paying for is not merely four walls and a ceiling. In the words of Federal Judge J. Skelly Wright, "When American city dwellers, both rich and poor, seek 'shelter' today, they seek a well-known package of goods and services—a package which includes not merely walls and ceilings, but also adequate heat, light and ventilation, serviceable plumbing facilities, secure windows and doors, proper sanitation, and proper maintenance." Judge Wright's point is that tenants do not purchase an interest in real estate; they consume services, just like shoppers in the marketplace. To the extent that tenants don't receive the services for which they pay rent, they are being gypped.

Without a doubt, the two universal sources of complaint for tenants are lack of proper maintenance and repairs and the vulnerability of tenants to criminal intrusions. Lately, tenants have become increasingly militant about preserving both their comfort and their safety. State legislatures and courts have responded, especially in the 1970s, by radically changing outdated legal concepts which favored the landlord unfairly. We will be looking at a number of these new state statutes and state-court decisions. Together, they provide three fertile sources for super threats aimed at landlords.

1. *Repair-and-deduct laws.* In at least twenty-three states, the law lets you make your own repairs and deduct their cost from your rent.

2. *Warranty-of-habitability laws.* Landlords in at least twenty-seven states must warrant—in the same way that a manufacturer gives a warranty on his product—that your apartment will be maintained in habitable condition. For breach of this warranty, you can withhold payment of rent and even get your rent reduced by, say, 10 or 20 percent.

3. *Common-law negligence.* Landlords, like any other careless people, can be held personally liable for the consequences of their acts. So if your landlord neglects your complaints about some defect that he ought to fix, and as a result you get hurt or your furnishings are damaged or, as is increasingly the case, a stranger slips into your building and burglarizes your apartment, you can sue your landlord for money damages. Depending upon the severity of your loss or injury, the amount of a jury verdict here can be staggering.

As you may have gathered, the cutting edge of a super threat based upon any one of these three sources is *money.* You will be theatening to hurt the landlord in one of his softest spots: the wallet. Although the thrust of all super threats against your landlord is, therefore, similar, certain ones are most appropriate for specific problems. For example, if you're concerned with a relatively minor repair problem—a malfunctioning refrigerator, or a loose hinge on a door—and your state has a repair-and-deduct law, then the most logical and direct route for you to follow is a super threat based on the repair-and-deduct theory. Suppose, however, your problem is caused by a breakdown in some essential building service, like heat, hot water, electricity, elevators, air conditioning, or basic sanitation. Whenever the fundamental habitability of your building or apartment is adversely affected, your super threat should take advantage of the warranty-of-habitability laws.

Finally we come to common-law negligence. It can fill in the gaps in almost any state that lacks either repair-and-deduct laws or warranty-of-habitability laws. In particular, though, resorting to a negligence super threat is appropriate when the situation is one that might well deteriorate into a serious mishap. Examples are legion. Take that creaking floorboard in your living room. Is it just a little annoyance, or is it a sign that the beams underneath are giving way? Who can tell? Your landlord, that's who. If he neglects to do so, and you break a leg when the board unexpectedly collapses, you'll sue the landlord to recover for your medical expenses and your pain and suffering.

In the last few years courts have begun applying the negligence theory to crimes committed in apartment houses. So if security seems to be deteriorating in your building, try a super threat which relies on these modern court rulings.

Repair-and-Deduct

The philosophy behind repair-and-deduct laws is essentially: *Do it yourself and charge the landlord.* These laws afford the tenant a welcome form of self-help. If the landlord won't do his duty, despite the tenant's request for repairs and services, then the tenant ought to be able to take the initiative at the landlord's expense.

Repair-and-deduct statutes have been enacted in at least eighteen states: Alaska, Arizona, California, Delaware, Hawaii, Kentucky, Louisiana, Massachusetts, Michigan, Montana, Nebraska, North Dakota, Ohio, Oklahoma, Oregon, South Dakota, Virginia, and Washington. What's more, the repair-and-deduct remedy has been upheld by courts in five other states: Colorado, Georgia, Illinois, New Jersey, and New York. (Appendix B lists the law or case which establishes the repair-and-deduct remedy in each state.)

Although these laws and cases are not identical, they all follow one basic pattern. First, the repair-and-deduct remedy is generally designed to cover basic and necessary repairs—not frills. For instance, a tenant can use the law to fix a defective electrical socket, a clogged drain, or a broken appliance furnished by the landlord (such as stoves and refrigerators). Generally speaking, repair-and-deduct can't be used by a tenant who wants to repaint his apartment, install new window awnings, or perform some other nonessential work. Nor is repair-and-deduct available if the tenant caused the state of disrepair through his own negligent disregard for property.

Second, before a tenant attempts to repair-and-deduct, he must notify the landlord of the specific repairs that are needed. Notification should be in writing, and sending it via certified mail, return receipt requested, is advisable.

Third, the landlord is entitled to sufficient time after notification in which to make the repairs. How much time is "sufficient"? That varies from one state to another. Some statutes afford a landlord as much as thirty days; others provide only twenty days or fourteen or twelve; some make special provisions for emergencies. (Check Appendix B for the time allowed in your state.) Perhaps the most intelligent laws are those which provide a "reasonable time" for repairs (as in California and Ohio). Under such a flexible standard, the time allotment will be measured according to the situation at hand. For example, a few weeks might be reasonable for run-of-the-mill repairs, when a tenant is not seriously inconvenienced. In an emergency, however, twenty-four hours might be reasonable.

Fourth, after a landlord has failed to make timely repairs, the tenant can take the initiative. Rather than undertake the actual work himself, the tenant would be well advised in most cases to hire a professional. As a general rule, whatever repairs are performed will have to be done in a workmanlike manner. Many local building codes require repair work to meet certain specifications, both for durability and for safety. The repair-and-deduct statutes in Arizona and Washington require tenants to employ a licensed contractor.

Fifth, the state statutes vary widely on how much money a tenant can deduct from his rent to pay for the repairs. (Check Appendix B for the amount specified in your state.) Even in states that set no monetary limit or simply allow "reasonable" deductions, the tenant should bend every effort not to overspend, because he may have to justify his expenses later on in court.

Several good illustrations of repair-and-deduct in action have emerged from recent court cases. New Jersey's Supreme Court first adopted the repair-and-deduct remedy in 1970 in *Marini v. Ireland*. On June 25, 1969, Alice Ireland discovered that the toilet in her apartment was cracked and water was leaking onto the bathroom floor. Alice made repeated attempts to notify the landlord but could not reach him. So she hired a registered plumber, who repaired the toilet for $85.72. Alice deducted this expense from her next month's rent ($95) and sent the landlord a check for $9.28, together with a receipt for the plumbing repair. The landlord sought to evict Alice for nonpayment of rent. The Supreme Court upheld Alice's right to repair the toilet and deduct the cost from her rent.

In two New York cases, tenants used the repair-and-deduct theory to take the offensive by suing their landlords in Small Claims Court. José Garcia lived in an apartment that had been painted with dangerous lead-based paint. The paint was peeling off the walls, and Garcia's children were eating the flakes. When the landlord refused to repair this threatening situation, Garcia bought his own supplies and replastered and repainted the apartment. He then sued the landlord to recover his expenses. The Small Claims Court awarded Garcia not only $29.53 for his supplies but also $16 for his labor—based upon the minimum hourly wage for unskilled labor.

The tenants in Manhattan's Lincoln Square Apartments were inconvenienced during the summer of 1973, when the building's central air conditioning broke down for six weeks. Three of the tenants went out and rented their own air conditioners and then sued their landlord to recover the rental fees. The Small Claims Court awarded $101.65 to one of the tenants and $197.95 to each of the other two.

If your apartment needs some basic repairs and they can be performed competently by you or someone whom you hire, a super threat based upon your state's repair-and-deduct law will set you up for some do-it-yourself work, or else it will prod the landlord into saving you the trouble. Leading up to the super threat, you should initially pursue less drastic measures.

Preliminary skirmishes

At the first signs of trouble in your apartment, telephone the superintendent or building manager or the landlord himself—whoever is supposed to handle your complaints.

Opening volleys

If your phone calls don't produce prompt results, follow up with a polite complaint letter to the landlord. Describe clearly and succinctly the condition that needs repairing. Call the landlord's attention to your prior phone calls and the lack of any satisfactory response. Request that the landlord contact you immediately to let you know when the necessary work will be performed. To expedite this request, supply telephone numbers at which you can be reached at home and at work.

Don't let too much time slip by if you get no response to your letter, or if the response you do get is evasive. On the average, you can allow the landlord about fifteen days in which to respond positively; the more urgently repairs are needed, the less time you should wait. Bear in mind that you will be affording the landlord still more time in your super threat.

You may want to write a polite complaint letter to your local housing agency or department of buildings. You can usually find the address in your telephone directory, listed under the heading for municipal government. (Unfortunately, many such agencies are slow to respond, and the sanctions at their disposal, such as nominal fines, provide no incentive for landlords to comply with housing regulations.) In any letter to a housing agency, try to stress, if you can, the extent to which health, life, or safety is imperiled by the condition in your apartment. For example, faulty wiring poses a threat to safety; a clogged toilet threatens health. The housing agency is likely to respond more quickly, and perhaps with a more effective sanction, if your situation appears to be an emergency.

Here is a sample polite complaint letter to a housing agency.

Certified Letter No. 12345678

March 18, 1977

> Name of tenant
> Mailing address
> City, state, zip code

Housing agency
Mailing address
City, state, zip code

> Re: Rust-colored water supply

Dear Sirs:

The water flowing from my bathroom and kitchen faucets began appearing discolored several weeks ago, and it is now distinctly rust-colored. I believe that this condition threatens my health, since the water supply in my apartment can no longer be safely used.

I called the building's superintendent four weeks ago, and I wrote to the landlord on March 11, 1977. To date they have given me nothing but excuses.

Will you please send an inspector to my apartment immediately and take whatever steps are necessary to compel the landlord to repair this situation. Considering the health hazard posed, please treat this matter as an emergency.

> Sincerely,
>
> /s/ Name of tenant

If the housing agency's response is slow in coming or is ineffective, you'll be ready to act on your own.

Launching a super threat
The object here is to convince the landlord that you're fed up with waiting; if he won't act, then you will—according to the letter of the law.

Soft spot. If forced to make a choice, the landlord would prefer to oversee the performance of any maintenance or repairs. By hiring personnel whom he's used before, the landlord can be assured of getting what he wants at a price he can tolerate. Most landlords just don't like the idea of tenants bringing in strangers to work on the building, especially if the strangers charge higher rates. Besides, once a tenant has succeeded in diverting part of his rent check into repairs and maintenance, it may become a habit—a bad habit, from the landlord's point of view.

"In the Matter of." Finish this phrase with "authorized deductions from future payment of rent." Hit the landlord right up front with the bad news.

Heading. Give the name and address of the landlord.

"Notice of Final Opportunity for Compliance." Under this heading for the first paragraph, you will be notifying the landlord of his last opportunity to make necessary repairs. You will cite as authority the statute or case in your state (see Appendix B) that permits tenants to engage in repair-and-deduct.

For example, if you live in California you would write: "PLEASE TAKE NOTICE: Pursuant to Sections 1941 and 1942 of the California Civil Code, you are hereby provided with a final opportunity to comply with your legal obligations to perform certain repairs and/or maintenance, as hereinafter enumerated." If you live in Illinois you would write: "PLEASE TAKE NOTICE: Pursuant to *Jack Spring, Inc.* v. *Little*, 50 Ill.2d 351, 280 N.E.2d 208 (1972), you are hereby provided with a final opportunity to comply with your legal obligations to perform certain repairs and/or maintenance, as hereinafter enumerated."

"*Statement of Complaint.*" Under this heading for the second paragraph, you will briefly reiterate the nature of your repair or maintenance problem. Refer to your prior polite complaint letter to the landlord, and enclose a copy of it. Note the lack of any satisfactory response to your letter. For example: "The refrigerator that you supplied to me is malfunctioning, in that it cools erratically. This defect was more fully described to you in my letter of February 25, 1977, a copy of which is enclosed. To date you have still not sent over an authorized repairer to inspect and fix the refrigerator."

"*Demand for Action.*" Under this heading for the third paragraph, you will state precisely what you want the landlord to do, and you will set a specific date for compliance. Be reasonable when imposing a deadline; remember, you want to leave the landlord an escape hatch that he'll be willing to take in order to avoid the thrust of your ultimatum. Generally speaking, fifteen days should be sufficient, assuming the repair is not a major one, in which case more time might be necessary. (When you add this fifteen-day period to the one already consumed after your polite complaint letter, you will have waited sufficiently long under the statute or case that governs repair-and-deduct in your state.)

For example, if you were to mail your super threat on February 1, 1977, it could demand: "No later than February 15, 1977, you must repair in a workmanlike manner the defective tiling in my bathroom wall."

"*Ultimatum.*" Under this heading for the fourth paragraph, you will warn the landlord of your intention to exercise your right to the repair-and-deduct remedy if your demand is not met by the stated deadline. It's a good idea to cite once more the legal authority relied on in your first paragraph. Impress the landlord with the fact that you will be acting pursuant to the letter of the law.

For example, a Colorado tenant might give the following ultimatum: "If by March 1, 1977, you have not completed all necessary repairs and/or maintenance, then pursuant to *Shanahan* v. *Collins*, 539 P.2d 1261 (Colo. 1975), I shall invoke my legal right to cause the necessary repairs and/or maintenance to be performed and, further, to deduct the expense incurred from my rent."

To reinforce the earnestness of your intention, you might also use the ultimatum to inform the landlord of an estimate on the cost of necessary repairs. Solicit an estimate from a licensed contractor (electrician, plumber) and refer to it in your ultimatum. Tell the landlord that unless he makes the repairs by your deadline, you will direct the contractor to proceed at the landlord's expense. For example, the Colorado tenant might tack onto his ultimatum this sentence: "To that end, you will find enclosed a copy of a written estimate by a reputable contractor, whom I shall hire at your expense if the necessary repairs have not been performed by March 1, 1977." A copy of the estimate would then be enclosed with the super threat.

Before you send the super threat, you should be forewarned: If your super threat falls on deaf ears, you ought to consult a lawyer before actually going ahead with the repairs and deducting the expense from your rent. A landlord who didn't respond to your super threat may respond once you've taken a bite out of your rent check. His response will probably be a lawsuit for nonpayment of rent, which you can defend against successfully so long as you've followed the rules laid down by your state's repair-and-deduct law. To insure that you do abide by the letter of the law, you'd be smart to see a lawyer before you take the plunge.

Landlord's Liability for Negligence

The common law of negligence provides an indirect way of pressuring your landlord into making repairs. Negligence is the legal theory under which a careless person may be held personally liable for the consequences of his acts. This theory applies to myriad forms of carelessness, including the neglect of repairs and maintenance characteristic of many landlords. If the landlord's negligence causes you personal injury or property loss, you can sue him to recover money damages.

Of course, there is no predicting how grave a mishap may result from the landlord's negligence. For example, if the landlord neglects to replace burned-out bulbs in a dark hallway, a tenant may eventually bump into a wall. That's no big deal. The medical bills, if any, and the pain would probably be so minimal that the tenant wouldn't even think of suing. But suppose the tenant fell down the stairs because of the darkness. He broke a leg and fractured two ribs. He might even have broken his neck and died. Then the landlord is in for the lawsuit of his life. Depending on the severity of the tenant's fall, a jury may award tens or even hundreds of thousands of dollars. That's a huge bill to pay just for one lousy light bulb.

Now you may have some inkling of how a super threat can make creative use of negligence law: Your super threat will put the landlord on notice that a condition exists which he ought to repair. You will let him know that if he neglects his duty and damages result, he will be personally liable for however much harm is done. What you're really doing here is making an end run around the landlord's main line of defense: indifference. Unlike a repair-and-deduct super threat or one based upon the warranty of habitability, a negligence super threat poses no immediate challenge to the landlord. After all, you are not saying you will withhold rent. You're not even saying that the landlord's negligence is bound to lead to catastrophe. All you are saying is: Mr. Landlord, you're taking a big gamble. You may win it; you may not. But is the price of one light bulb (or screw or hinge or floorboard) worth the potential risk of a half-million-dollar lawsuit?

The negligence super threat is ideally suited to those situations where it doesn't take much imagination to see that disaster could result from a lack of maintenance or repairs. In order for a landlord to be held liable to a tenant for negligence, five basic factors must exist: (1) The landlord must have had a duty to repair the condition in question. (2) The landlord must have known—or at least should have known—that the condition in question needed repair work. (3) Neglecting to perform his duty, the landlord either failed to make repairs or made them in a careless manner. (4) As a result of this negligence on the landlord's part, the tenant suffered personal injury or property loss. (5) The injury or loss was a reasonably foreseeable consequence of the landlord's negligence.

Let's look at some cases in which landlords have been successfully sued by tenants. Two New York cases are illustrative of decisions reached by many other state courts. One involves personal injury to a tenant, the other property damage.

Yvette Acosta, a two-year-old infant, lived with her mother and father in an apartment in Manhattan's East Village. The walls of the apartment were cracked, and paint and plaster would peel off the walls onto the floor. Little Yvette was in the habit of eating the paint chips that she found on the floor. Unfortunately, the paint had a high enough lead content to make Yvette dangerously ill. She had to be admitted to Bellevue Hospital, where her condition was diagnosed as lead poisoning and she was treated for over two months.

Yvette's father sued the landlord to recover for the hospital bills as well as to compensate Yvette for her personal injury. Judge Emilio Nunez held that the landlord had a clear duty to repair the cracked and crumbling wall. Furthermore, the landlord had been aware of the dangerous condition for at least three months prior to Yvette's hospitalization, but he made no repairs.

Was it reasonably foreseeable that Yvette would get lead poisoning as a result of the landlord's failure to make necessary repairs? Yes, decided Judge Nunez: "That small children go around the house picking up everything within their reach and placing it in their mouths and attempting to eat it is well known. They often have a craving to put in their mouths and eat most unusual things. It would not be unreasonable therefore, to foresee that Yvette would pick up pieces of plaster and paint if they were lying around and eat them...

"I find that in the setting and surrounding circumstances which existed at the premises in question, the hazard which the broken walls presented should have been reasonably foreseeable to the landlord. Given the broken walls and plaster, the lead contents in the paint... the child in the apartment, the known propensities of children and the results that followed, I find that Yvette became ill with lead poisoning as a direct result of the [landlord's] negligence in failing to keep the premises... in proper repair."

The tenants were awarded $1,820 to cover Yvette's hospital bills plus $2,500 to compensate her for the personal injury she had suffered. Needless to say, it would have been a lot cheaper for the landlord to have repaired the walls in the first place.

In another New York case, two tenants won money from their landlord because his negligence resulted in damage to their furnishings and personal belongings. One of the tenants, Mr. Lobell, lived directly beneath the other, Mr. Mendelsohn. Lobell noticed a patch of wet plaster high on the wall of his closet, and he showed it to the building's superintendent. Neither the super nor the landlord made any effort to discover the cause of the wetness.

Three weeks went by. Then the cause became apparent. A water pipe burst inside one of Mendelsohn's walls—just above Lobell's closet. Both apartments were flooded, causing substantial property damage to the tenants.

The court held that the landlord, having been put on notice of the wet plaster, had a duty to inspect the wall and open it up to learn why the plaster was wet. Had he done so, the landlord would have observed water trickling from a slow leak somewhere above. At that point, the landlord could not have closed his eyes to the obvious direction of the danger. The landlord's duty would have been to continue a reasonable inspection, following the water up to its source—a corroded water pipe inside Mendelsohn's wall. Failure to perform this inspection and make the necessary repairs amounted to negligence. Both tenants recovered their property losses from the landlord.

As you can see, a negligence super threat will be most appropriate in situations where the lack of maintenance or repairs can lead to drastic results. Before you resort to a super threat, you should exhaust the usual initial procedures.

Preliminary skirmishes

As always, contact the superintendent, building manager, or landlord at the first signs of deterioration in your apartment or building.

Opening volleys
If whomever you call belittles the seriousness of the situation, put yourself on record in a polite complaint letter. Describe the need for repairs in clear, succinct terms. Reiterate your belief that the landlord ought to take the precautionary measure of making repairs.

Launching a super threat
The strategy here is to persuade the landlord that a stitch in time saves nine.

Soft spot. The landlord will be vulnerable if he worries enough about the range of accidents that may be caused by his failure to act. Once he begins to worry, it's only a short step to fear of financial liability.

"In the Matter of." Complete this phrase with "personal liability for negligence."

Heading. Give the name and address of the landlord.

"Notice of Negligence." Under this heading for the first paragraph, you will alert the landlord to the fact that he is carelessly overlooking a potentially risky situation. By way of authority, you will cite two representative court cases; both uphold the legal principle that a landlord must not subject other persons to an unreasonable risk of harm. In one of these cases, *Sargent* v. *Ross,* a New Hampshire court held a landlord liable for the death of a child who had fallen from a stairway that the landlord had neglected to supply with an adequate railing. In the other case, *Canfield* v. *Howard,* a Georgia court held that a tenant who was injured when part of a leaking ceiling collapsed could recover damages for the landlord's failure to make repairs.

Your first paragraph will read:

NOTICE OF NEGLIGENCE

PLEASE TAKE NOTICE: Pursuant to *Sargent v. Ross*, 113 N.H. 388, 308 A.2d 528 (1973), and *Canfield v. Howard*, 109 Ga. App. 566, 136 S.E.2d 431 (1964), you are presently subjecting both persons and property to an unreasonable risk of harm by reason of your negligent failure to perform certain repairs and/or maintenance as hereinafter enumerated.

"Statement of Complaint." Under this heading for the second paragraph, you will briefly describe the repair or maintenance problem that creates a potential risk. Refer to your prior complaint letter to the landlord and enclose a copy of it. For example, "Whenever there is a rainstorm, the ceiling in my living room begins to leak. This condition was more fully described to you in my letter of March 1, 1977, a copy of which is enclosed."

"Demand for Action." Under this heading for the third paragraph, you will state precisely what steps you want the landlord to take. In doing so, you will adopt some of the highfalutin language that lawyers use.

DEMAND FOR ACTION

In order that you may cease and desist as soon as possible from subjecting both persons and property to the risk of harm, it is incumbent upon you to repair forthwith, and in a workmanlike manner, the aforementioned [conclude by specifying in a few words the condition described in the "Statement of Complaint": e.g., "leaking ceiling," "broken window," "loose stair tread."]

Notice that you will set no specific deadline for compliance; instead, you'll call for repairs "forthwith." Let the landlord fret about how long he can afford to gamble; that's part of the strategy behind this type of super threat.

"*Ultimatum.*" Under this heading for the fourth paragraph, you will be using some boilerplate legalese to warn the landlord that he will be personally liable for the consequences of his negligent failure to make repairs.

ULTIMATUM

If you negligently fail to satisfy the above demand, and your negligence is the proximate cause of any reasonably foreseeable harm to persons and/or property, you shall be held personally liable in money damages to the full extent of any losses sustained by tenants or their lawful invitees.

This legalese is broad enough to encompass any personal injuries or property damage which the landlord's negligence causes you or your guests (the "lawful invitees").

Warranty of Habitability

The so-called warranty of habitability is a revolutionary new safeguard for tenants. It's similar in concept to the warranty you might expect on any new product. If you're a smart shopper, you probably never buy an appliance or other "big ticket" item without first asking the merchant, "How good is the warranty?" You want to make certain that the merchant or manufacturer will stand behind the product if it breaks down.

Logically, the same demands that you make of merchants ought to be leveled at your landlord. Before you sign a lease, you might reasonably inquire, "How good is the warranty of this apartment?" Chances are the landlord would reply, "Warranty? You kidding? I'm not General Motors. This apartment rents 'as is,' no guarantees on maintenance or repairs." In a growing majority of states, such a take-it-or-leave-it response is now contrary to the law.

At least twenty-seven states and the District of Columbia have adopted the new warranty-of-habitability law, either through their state legislatures or through state-court decisions. These states are: Alaska, Arizona, California, Connecticut, Delaware, Florida, Hawaii, Illinois, Iowa, Kansas, Kentucky, Maine, Maryland, Massachusetts, Michigan, Minnesota, Missouri, Nebraska, New Hampshire, New Jersey, New York, Ohio, Oregon, Pennsylvania, Virginia, Washington, and Wisconsin. (Appendix C lists the appropriate citation for each of these jurisdictions.)

Although warranty-of-habitability laws aren't identical, they do share many common attributes. In general, the whole thrust of the warranty is to make a landlord accountable to tenants for basic maintenance of their apartments and the building they live in. The landlord is obligated to keep the apartments and "common areas" (e.g., halls, stairs, lobbies) in a habitable condition. This obligation automatically accompanies the rental of an apartment, and it lasts throughout the tenant's term of occupancy.

The concept of habitability is, of course, critical to the amount of protection afforded by the warranty law. Just what does habitability include in the way of repairs and essential building services? There is no hard answer. State courts are busy developing the concept of habitability on a case-by-case basis. At a minimum, most courts seem to agree that a building or apartment which endangers a tenant's life, health, or safety is not habitable. To determine whether such a deteriorated condition exists, courts commonly apply the standards established in local housing codes. Thus, the landlord would breach the warranty if he allowed any serious violation of the housing code: for example, failure to supply essential services like heat, light, hot and cold water would breach the warranty. Similarly, failure to maintain basic facilities such as sinks, toilets, plumbing, wiring, and major appliances supplied by the landlord (e.g., refrigerators, stoves) would be contrary to the terms of the warranty. Add to these items the landlord's duty to keep the halls and stairways clean, to provide for refuse removal, and to exterminate rats and roaches, and you have a pretty good idea of the basic coverage of the warranty of habitability.

As a general rule, courts don't look on the absence of certain minor amenities as detracting from the habitability of an apartment. Thus, the lack of a fresh paint job (unless the walls are really grimy) or the presence of a few ceiling cracks (unless the ceiling is sagging dangerously) would most likely not breach the warranty of habitability.

Between basic necessities and minor amenities is a wide array of building services that may or may not affect habitability. It all depends on the facts in each case and the court making the decision. Lately there have been some encouraging signs that a more expansive interpretation of habitability is emerging. Two New York courts have found that the warranty may be breached if a landlord fails to silence an inconsiderate neighbor who persistently throws boisterous parties or vacuums at odd hours or pounds away at a piano, all to the distress of other tenants. In another case, the maintenance of elevator service in an apartment high-rise was considered to be essential to the habitability of the building. It is also entirely likely that courts are prepared to classify breakdowns in central air conditioning and buildingwide security systems as violations of the warranty of habitability.

In a 1975 New Jersey case, *Timber Ridge Town House*

v. *Dietz*, the tenants, James and Mary Dietz, won a major victory for all tenants affected by the warranty of habitability. The Dietzes rented a three-bedroom, two-and-a-half-bath, two-story townhouse apartment—the kind that has become fashionable in many suburban developments. This apartment was the highest-priced apartment in the surrounding community. The rental brochure had described the apartment as "quietly nestled in a gently rolling glen ... [offering] serene living in a beautiful country setting with ... individual patio facing a spacious landscaped courtyard." For several months after moving in, the Dietzes were unable to enjoy the sylvan paradise portrayed in the brochure. It seems that construction work caused mud and water to overflow the patio constantly; for the same reason, the "spacious landscaped courtyard" was nonexistent.

Had the warranty of habitability been breached? We might well assume that the answer would be no. After all, the Dietzes were not complaining about the lack of any basic necessities, like heat or hot water or a weathertight roof over their heads. In essence, the Dietzes were being deprived only of an amenity—and an outdoor one, at that!

The New Jersey court, however, ruled that the landlord had breached the warranty of habitability by denying the Dietzes the pure pleasure that their patio might have afforded them. "Tenants had a reasonable expectancy of a decent exterior environment from the sales promotion, the initial condition of the premises, and the higher price of the apartment compared to others in the community, whether the expectancy be characterized as one of amenity or necessity."

The *Dietz* case is part of a judicial trend toward evaluating a tenant's reasonable expectations instead of just his bare necessities for living. When this realistic approach is taken, the concept of habitability expands greatly; it is measured by such factors as the apartment's setting and the amount of rent being paid. For tenants in a particularly luxurious apartment house, habitability might include regular cleaning of the rooftop swimming pool and lavish furnishings in the lobby. The point is: Habitability is a flexible legal standard, still very much in a state of judicial development. Courts are likely to adapt it in order to fulfill the varying levels of expectation which tenants legitimately have.

What legal recourse does a tenant have when the warranty of habitability is breached? The most commonly accepted remedy is *withholding rent from the landlord.* This remedy is generally approved by state laws and courts, because, under the legal theory of the warranty of habitability, a tenant's duty to pay rent is dependent upon the landlord's duty to maintain the apartment building. So if the landlord doesn't perform, then, theoretically, the tenant doesn't have to either.

As a practical matter, when a tenant withholds rent, the landlord tries to evict the tenant by means of a nonpayment lawsuit, sometimes called a "dispossess." The tenant can then raise the defense of breach of warranty. If he fails to prove his case, he will have to pay the back rent or face eviction. However, if a breach of warranty is proven, the court may authorize the tenant to deposit his rent with the court, and the amount of rent due each month may be reduced to reflect the decrease in habitability. The payment of a reduced rent into court will generally continue so long as the landlord fails to maintain habitable conditions.

In the *Dietz* case, the Dietzes withheld their rent, and the landlord brought a dispossess action. They defended themselves successfully on the grounds of breach of the warranty of habitability. The court reduced the Dietzes' rent by 15 percent: "From observing the conditions the court feels at least 15% of the general livability of the premises is affected." This rent reduction was calculated from the time the Dietzes first withheld their rent, and it was ordered to continue until the landlord corrected the mud overflow on the outdoor patio.

A New York warranty case, *Morbeth Realty Corporation* v. *Rosenshine,* resulted in a 20 percent rent reduction. For two months the tenant had withheld rent because of the landlord's failure to make some fundamental repairs: The toilet was leaking onto the bathroom floor; an upstairs shower was leaking through the ceiling; several windows were broken; and the walls needed replastering and painting. The tenant had been withholding her seventy-dollar-a-month rent. She was ordered by the court to pay her rent into court—her new rent, that is, of fifty-six dollars a month —until the necessary repairs were completed.

If you believe that the basic habitability of your apartment or your building has been impaired by the lack of maintenance and repairs, you may have to resort to a super threat based on your state's warranty-of-habitability law.

Preliminary skirmishes

Telephone your superintendent or landlord at the first signs of deterioration and breakdown in your apartment or building.

Opening volleys

Follow up any fruitless phone calls with polite complaint letters. One will go to your landlord or the managing agent for your building. Another might go to the local government agency that regulates housing conditions in your locale.

If the decline in habitability affects other tenants besides you—for example, inadequate water pressure or constant elevator breakdowns—contact the other tenants in your building and see if they are prepared to join in pressuring the landlord. You should also try to locate any established tenants' organization in your locale. Ask this organization for advice on how the tenants in your building can best act as a group.

The news media can often be helpful in arousing public and official indignation over nonhabitable housing conditions. Action reporters on local television are usually receptive to covering the plight of tenants, because there is such great visual potential in these stories. Through the television camera's eye, viewers can be shown dramatic evidence of how "other people" live. Therefore, you may want to check with your local TV stations to see whether any of them will do a news story on your building.

Launching a super threat

A warranty-of-habitability super threat will have greatest impact if it issues from a solid group of tenants in your building. So before you act on your own, check around your buiding to see who else objects to the decrease in habitability and will sign the super threat with you.

Soft spot. The soft spot here is the landlord's inability to count on meeting his financial obligations as they become due. Your super threat poses the prospect that future rent checks may be withheld, and their dollar amount may even be reduced by court order.

"In the Matter of." Finish this phrase with "breach of implied standards of habitability." That's legalese for the landlord's failure to maintain those minimum requirements for decent living which your state's warranty law reads into your lease.

Heading. Give the name and address of the landlord.

"Notice of Breach of Warranty." Under this heading for the first paragraph, you will be citing the warranty law (see Appendix C) that your landlord has allegedly breached. For example, if you're a Florida tenant, your first paragraph will read: "PLEASE TAKE NOTICE: Pursuant to Florida Statutes Annotated, Secs. 83.51, 83.56 (1973), you are in

breach of the warranty of habitability." If you're a Michigan tenant, the first paragraph will read: "PLEASE TAKE NOTICE: Pursuant to Michigan Compiled Laws Annotated, Sec. 554.139 (1967–77 Supp.), and *Rome* v. *Walker*, 38 Mich. App. 458, 196 N.W.2d 850 (1972), you are in breach of the warranty of habitability."

"Statement of Complaint." Under this heading for your second paragraph, you will briefly describe the condition in your apartment or building which impairs habitability. The simplest way to do this is to refer to your prior polite complaint letter to the landlord and enclose a copy of it.

For example: "The incinerator in this building is malfunctioning, causing noxious fumes to permeate the public hallways and the elevator shaft. This condition was more fully described to you in my letter of [insert date of mailing], a copy of which is enclosed." To this brief recitation you may wish to add a one-sentence allegation regarding the degree to which habitability is impaired. Continuing the present example, you might allege, "Said condition jeopardizes health, safety, and/or comfort, because it irritates and offends all of the tenants in this building."

"Demand for Action." Under this heading for the third paragraph, state exactly what you want the landlord to do. Remember, you're asking basically for a restoration of facilities or services to an acceptable level. You are not asking for, nor are you entitled to, a lavish upgrading of things.

For example, if the self-service elevators in your building are always on the blink, you could demand, "No later than [insert specific date], you must have the self-service elevators thoroughly inspected and serviced so that they operate continuously, smoothly, and safely." You could not, however, realistically or legally demand, "No later than [insert specific date], you must have the self-service elevators converted to manual operation and staffed around the clock by uniformed attendants, who will insure continuous and smooth operation." If such an excessive demand were made, you would be denying the landlord a reasonable escape hatch and foiling the chances of your super threat.

When setting the deadline for compliance with your demand, use common sense. Buildingwide improvements may require more time (e.g., sixty to ninety days) than improvements in your apartment alone (e.g., fifteen to thirty days). Of course, if the situation is urgent (e.g., inadequate heat in winter), set a much tighter deadline (such as twenty-four to forty-eight hours).

"Ultimatum." Under this heading for the fourth paragraph, you will warn the landlord that if he does not meet your demand, you (and the other tenants) intend to withhold your rent and seek a court order for "retroactive and prospective rent abatement." That's legalese for a reduction in the amount of rent owed each month, dating back to the time when conditions first breached the warranty of habitability and stretching forward to the time when these conditions have been adequately corrected. You may want to suggest a percentage reduction in rent which you will also seek, based upon the percentage reduction in habitability. (Remember the 15-percent reduction in the *Dietz* case.) If you tack on such a suggestion, make it believable. For example, cockroach infestation may decrease the habitability of your apartment by 10 or 15 percent, but not 50 or 60 percent.

Your ultimatum will look like this:

ULTIMATUM

If the above demand for action has not been satisfied in full by the date specified, then I [substitute "we" if several tenants are signing the super threat] shall withhold future payment of rent and seek legal counsel in order to secure retroactive and prospective rent abatement by court order.

That order shall, if the court so determines, reduce whatever rental payments may become due by [insert percentage] to reflect the prevailing percentage of decrease in overall habitability.

A word of caution is in order as you prepare your super threat for mailing. If the landlord is not moved by your super threat, you should consult a lawyer before you actually begin to withhold rent. By withholding rent, you really force the landlord's hand; he will either comply with your demands or sue you for nonpayment of rent. You can defend against the latter action on the grounds of breach of warranty. To do so successfully, however, requires advance consultation with an attorney to make sure that the ice is thick enough before you walk out on it.

Landlord's Liability for Crime

ELDERLY TENANT MUGGED IN HALLWAY
BURGLARS RANSACK BAY AREA DUPLEX
COED RAPED IN OFF-CAMPUS APARTMENT

Hardly a day goes by when city dwellers aren't bombarded with another shocking headline about the perils of apartment living. If you live in an apartment building, the truth behind these headlines may be a little too close for comfort. All around you are signs that the security in your building is deteriorating. The night doorman, for example, was fired by the landlord in an economy move. Down in the garage, the parking attendant usually sleeps in his booth, allowing strangers to enter and prey on tenants. On your own floor, the hall lights have been burned out for more than a week, giving any mugger the drop on his victims.

Of course, the person ultimately responsible for these

lapses in security is your landlord. He has control over building personnel, locks, lights, and other security devices, such as bell-and-buzzer systems, TV surveillance, or even as simple a thing as convex mirrors in elevators to let you see who's inside while you're still outside. Some states and cities even have specific laws requiring the landlord to adopt anticrime devices. For example, New York City landlords must install peepholes, heavy-duty dead-bolt locks, and chain guards on all apartment doors.

To jar your landlord into beefing up security, you may want to try a super threat based on negligence. We've already seen how a negligent landlord can be held liable for injuries he caused to tenants. An increasing number of state courts have recently been imposing the same kind of liability on landlords who expose their tenants to criminal intrusions. These courts have not generally held that a landlord has a duty to prevent crimes in his building. The courts have held, however, that a landlord has a duty *not to enhance the risk of crime.* The difference is important. It means that while the landlord is no insurer of your safety, neither is he an idle bystander. He must not overlook conditions which, to any reasonable man, increase the danger that some tenant will be mugged or robbed or even murdered. If the landlord does blink at these conditions, and they facilitate criminal entries, the landlord will face an expensive lawsuit. That is exactly the kind of consequence on which good super threats are built.

Let's look at some recent cases in which the victims of of crime successfully sued their landlords. In a 1975 New Jersey case, *Braitman* v. *Overlook Terrace,* the landlord got hit with a $6,100 judgment just because of a simple door lock which he failed to fix. The tenants, Nathan and Olga Braitman, moved into Overlook Terrace, a New Jersey high-rise complex, in 1971. The door to their apartment was equipped with two locks: a relatively ineffective slip lock, controlled by means of two buttons on the edge of the door, and a much more formidable dead-bolt lock, operated by means of a knob on the inside of the door. On moving into the apartment, Nathan Braitman noticed that the dead-bolt lock was not working. He immediately complained to the management office, where he was assured that the matter would be "taken care of." No action was taken, however, so Nathan complained several more times, without any better luck. Shortly thereafter, a thief easily bypassed the Braitmans' slip lock and looted their apartment, stealing mostly jewelry. (Ironically, the landlord repaired the dead-bolt lock two days after the burglary.)

The Braitmans sued their landlord for negligence. There had been prior break-ins in the vicinity of Overlook Terrace. In light of these crimes, any reasonable man in the landlord's position would have recognized the enhanced risk of crime that a defective lock would create. Criminal entry was eminently foreseeable. By failing to make the necessary repairs, the landlord had negligently heightened the peril to which the Braitmans were exposed. "A residential tenant can recover damages from his landlord," ruled New Jersey's highest court, "upon proper proof that the latter unreasonably enhanced the risk of loss due to theft by failing to supply adequate locks to safeguard the tenant's premises after suitable notice of the defect." The Braitmans were awarded $6,100 to cover their loss.

The *Braitman* case is in agreement with a 1972 decision handed down by the Supreme Court of Michigan, *Johnston v. Harris*. Reese Johnston was an elderly tenant who lived in a Detroit apartment building. Returning home one October night at about 7:30 P.M., Johnston reached for the knob to the vestibule door. As he did, the door was jerked open by a young thug, who had been lurking in the dimly lit, unlocked vestibule. Johnston was assaulted and robbed by the youth.

Johnston sued his landlord for negligence. At the trial,

Johnston offered proof of the dim lighting and continuously unlocked door in the vestibule. Through the testimony of a public-lighting expert, Johnston established the relationship between poor lighting and the high incidence of night crime. Johnston also showed that his neighborhood in Detroit was a high-crime area.

The gist of Reese Johnston's case was that the landlord had, in effect, set a trap for the tenants. In a high-crime area, it is reasonably foreseeable that poor lighting and unlocked doors will attract criminals, who will prey on tenants. Michigan's highest court bought this argument. It ruled that Johnston's landlord could be held liable for his negligence in creating a condition conducive to assaults and robberies.

High courts in Georgia have come to the same basic conclusion as the New Jersey and Michigan courts. And in New York, where crime in the streets seems to have been replaced by crime in the halls, two courts have nailed landlords who negligently exposed tenants to crime. One of the New York cases arose because the tenants' apartment was burglarized while they were vacationing. During that period, the next-door neighbor's refrigerator went on the blink. Being a generous fellow, the landlord gave the neighbor a key to the vacationing tenants' apartment. No harm in letting one tenant use another's refrigerator, is there? You bet there is. Keys have a way of floating around, and this one landed in the itchy palm of a thief, who was less interested in a working refrigerator than in a full clothes closet. The thief let himself into the apartment empty-handed and walked out with an armful of clothes. The landlord was held liable for $1,300 in damages, because he had negligently created the risk of a crime.

A similar but much more tragic case from Washington, D.C., illustrates how a landlord can create an unsafe condition through the employees whom he hires. Codie Whitman was a young single woman who lived alone in the capital's

Ritz Apartments. Her apartment was due for a painting. The building manager employed a painter without bothering to make any check into his credentials, family, or personal background. This complete oversight was regrettable, for the painter was insane.

Virtually no supervision was exerted over the painter's work habits at the Ritz. He was given the key to Codie Whitman's apartment and told to paint it. That he did. He also strangled Miss Whitman to death. The court wisely decided that the landlord could be held liable for his negligent hiring practices. Referring to tenants in the nation's capital, the court observed, "Thousands of them are government women employees, like Miss Whitman, living, often alone, in small apartments where they have a right to think they are not to be molested as a result of the reckless ignorance of their landlords in the selection of apartment employees."

Most lawyers agree that the legal landmark in this whole area of tenant security was established in the 1970 case *Kline* v. *1500 Massachusetts Avenue Apartment Corporation*. It was decided in Washington, D.C., by the United States Court of Appeals, a federal court that ranks just below the Supreme Court. Sarah Kline moved into a 585-unit high-rise building in Washington in 1959. At that time, the building had extensive security measures: A doorman was stationed at the main entrance twenty-four hours a day; an attendant manned the lobby desk around the clock and watched all persons using the elevators; there were two garage attendants, whose duties were arranged so that one of them could always observe people using the side entrance to the building; a third entrance to the building was routinely locked after 9 P.M.

By mid-1966, however, there was no longer any doorman watching the main entrance. Much of the time, the lobby desk was left unattended. The side entrance was generally unguarded because of a decrease in garage personnel, and the third entrance was frequently left unlocked all night. In seven years, security had declined sharply, despite an indoor crime wave in which various tenants were burglarized, assaulted, and robbed. The landlord was well aware of the perils faced by his tenants.

On November 17, 1966, Sarah Kline was assaulted and robbed in the first-floor hallway just outside her apartment door. She sued the landlord for negligence. The court held flatly that a landlord has a duty to minimize the predictable risk of crime in his building. "There is implied in the contract [i.e., lease] between landlord and tenant an obligation on the landlord to provide those protective measures which are within his reasonable capacity." This implied obligation has become known in legal circles as the "implied warranty of security." That's simply legalese for a landlord's duty to warrant that his tenants will be kept reasonably safe.

Specifically, the court ruled that Sarah Kline's landlord should have preserved the level of security which existed when she first moved in. "The tenant was led to expect that she could rely upon this degree of protection. While we do not say that the precise measures for security which were then in vogue should have been kept up (e.g., the number of people at the main entrances might have been reduced if a tenant-controlled intercom–automatic latch system had been installed in the common entryways), we do hold that the same relative degree of security should have been maintained." Since Kline's landlord had not lived up to his responsibilities, she was entitled to collect damages for her losses and injury.

You may recall the sample super threat in Chapter 1, where hypothetical tenant Saul David sent a super threat to his landlord, Rocky Goliath. That super threat relied heavily on *Kline* v. *1500 Massachusetts Avenue* and the implied warranty of security. Your super threat will follow identical lines, but first let's consider some initial steps worth taking.

Preliminary skirmishes

Whenever a condition develops in your building which poses a possible threat to security, contact the building manager or landlord immediately. That condition may be one that requires repair work (e.g., a broken lock, a nonfunctioning front-door intercom, a poorly lit doorway), or it may call for closer supervision of building personnel (e.g., a doorman who sleeps on the job, a superintendent who makes passes at women in the laundry room). Contact other tenants in your building to see if they too are upset by the breach in security. Ask them to join in your complaint.

Opening volleys

Don't wait too long if your initial complaint proves ineffectual; remember, your security is at stake. Write a polite complaint letter to the landlord. Describe the condition that concerns you. Explain why that condition detracts from your personal security or overall building security. In this regard, call the landlord's attention to any crimes (or attempted crimes) that have already occurred in the building. Point out, if you can, how the condition that you are complaining about contributed to or facilitated the commission of these crimes. Even if there have been no crimes yet, your building may be located in a high-crime area. If so, your letter should alert the landlord to any local criminal element that may take advantage of a breach in your building's security. Try to convince other tenants in your building to add their signatures to yours on the complaint letter.

Launching a super threat

If the landlord has not been sufficiently alarmed by your polite complaint letter to restore tighter security, you'll probably need a super threat to scare him into acting. The object here is to sober the landlord to the legal reality that he may be held personally responsible—at least in terms of compensating crime victims—for crimes committed by unknown third parties. Your super threat will, in a sense, cast the landlord as an accessory before the fact, in that his negligence is setting up tenants as crime targets.

Soft spot. The landlord will be vulnerable to your demands once you've made him worry enough about the calamitous crimes that might occur and the amount of money damages that he might have to pay to a victim of crime.

"In the Matter of." Finish this phrase with "personal tort liability for the commission of third-party crimes."

Heading. Give the name and address of the landlord.

"Notice of Negligent Breach of Security." Under this heading for the first paragraph, you will warn the landlord that his carelessness is increasing the likelihood that crimes will be committed in your building. By way of authority you will cite the *Kline* case.

NOTICE OF NEGLIGENT BREACH OF SECURITY

PLEASE TAKE NOTICE: Pursuant to *Kline* v. *1500 Massachusetts Avenue Apartment Corporation*, 439 F.2d 477 (D.C. Cir. 1970), you are in open breach of the implied warranty of security and are negligently enhancing the risk of criminal intrusions at [give address of building where you live].

"Statement of Complaint." Under this heading for the second paragraph, briefly describe the condition that detracts from security in your building. Refer to your prior complaint letter to the landlord and enclose a copy of it. For example: "The lighting system in the garage and basement is so weak that intruders can and do hide there, waiting to prey on unsuspecting tenants. This serious breach in building secu-

rity was more fully described to you in my letter of March 10, 1977, a copy of which is enclosed."

"*Demand for Action.*" Under this heading for the third paragraph, use some boilerplate legalese to introduce your demands:

DEMAND FOR ACTION

In order that you may cease and desist from negligently enhancing the risk of criminal intrusions in the aforementioned premises, it is incumbent upon you to forthwith [specify those steps which the landlord must take in order to correct the condition described in the "Statement of Complaint"].

As this sample paragraph indicates, you will insert specifications regarding, for example, repairs or the supervision of building employees; if your specifications are numerous, list them in brief, consecutively numbered sentences. Notice that you will be telling the landlord to act "forthwith"; that's legalese for "without delay."

"*Ultimatum.*" More legalese; with it you will warn the landlord of his potential personal liability:

ULTIMATUM

If you negligently fail to satisfy the above demand and, as is reasonably foreseeable to any ordinarily prudent man, your negligence is the proximate cause of any unauthorized person or persons gaining access to the aforementioned premises and therein committing any crimes against person or property, including but not limited to burglaries, robberies, assaults, rapes, and homicides, then you shall be held personally liable in money damages to the full extent of any jury verdict based on the personal injuries or property losses sustained by tenants or their lawful invitees.

This language is sweeping enough to encompass both personal injuries (e.g., muggings) and property losses (e.g., thefts) which the landlord's negligence causes you or your guests.

8

Product Warranties

How do you know that a product you buy will do those things that the seller or manufacturer said it would? For example, how do you know that a $39.95 coffee maker will make coffee? The answer is you don't. You *hope* that it will make coffee. And why do you have any hope? Because the seller or manufacturer said that the machine would make coffee. Legally speaking, what the seller or manufacturer did was *promise* that your coffee maker would make coffee, and that promise is called a "warranty" or a "guarantee" (they're the same thing). This chapter will look at how to make sellers and manufacturers keep their promises.

There are two basic types of warranties: express and implied. Express warranties are given by the manufacturer or serviceperson and are in writing, usually on a card or as part of the instructions packed with the product. In the express warranty the manufacturer makes various promises regarding the quality of the product or the terms and conditions under which the product will be repaired. Repairpersons frequently make promises regarding the quality of the repair and terms under which a repair will be made at no charge. Exactly what the manufacturer or repairperson promises in the express warranty is entirely up to him.

If you read almost any express warranty, you will find a curious clause that reads: "This warranty is expressly in lieu of all other warranties and representations, expressed or implied, including, but not limited to, the implied warranty of merchantability or fitness for a particular purpose." Have you ever asked yourself why manufacturers and repairpersons insert this clause in their warranties? Could it be perhaps that this thing called an "implied warranty" is so good for you that it is necessary to use legal gobbledygook to make sure that you don't get it? We believe that the answer is a rousing yes! In fact, this little clause in your express warranty takes more rights away from you than the express warranty probably gave you to begin with.

It would seem then, that this "implied warranty" is strong stuff. It is. Basically, the implied warranty guarantees you the right to receive what you expected to get—not a bad guarantee. If you could just find a way to stop manufacturers and repairpersons from taking it away from you, you might have quite a weapon in the battle against defective merchandise. Well, we have found the way! And we feel that the implied warranty is a potential goldmine for you.

What is an implied warranty and why is it so important? Well, for one thing, it is *not* in writing. Rather, it is imposed by state laws on *anyone* selling products. These state laws tell sellers and manufacturers: "If you want to sell or repair products, fine. When you do, however, the law is going to require you to make certain promises to the buying public. Even if you don't make these promises in writing, the law will force you to honor them anyway." These promises comprise the so-called implied warranty. Exactly what the manufacturer promises in the implied warranty is determined entirely by state law.

Manufacturers don't like to make any more promises than are absolutely necessary. So long as manufacturers can decide for themselves what promises they will make, they can cleverly word their express warranties in such a way as to sound great but promise little. Not so with the implied warranty, however, which the state writes in its law books and enforces in its courts. Naturally, manufacturers don't like the legal device of the implied warranty, for it forces them to make promises that can be costly to keep.

Express warranties can be useful. In the event that a manufacturer or repairperson refuses to honor an express warranty, asserting your rights through a letter may get results. However, we believe the implied warranty possesses the type of broad protection which covers most problems. And, most important, you can now demand the rights of the implied warranty *even if the manufacturer tries to take them away.*

The source of this new protection is a federal law passed in 1975, the Magnuson-Moss Warranty Act. This Act deals squarely with the problems of manufacturers who try to eliminate the implied warranty. The Act simply says that if you receive *any* written warranty at all from the manufacturer or seller for a product costing fifteen dollars or more, then it is illegal under state law for the warrantor to eliminate your rights to the implied warranty. The Act also defines a written warranty to include (1) *any* statement regarding the nature or workmanship of the product or any statement to the effect that it is defect-free, and (2) any promise to repair, refund, replace, or take any other remedial action in the event that the product does not meet its specifications. Thus, the Act will apply to most consumer products that you are likely to buy. (While the Act also improves your rights to enforce the written warranty itself, these rights will not be fully in effect for a few years.)

The effect of the federal law on the implied warranty is rather startling. If you are given *any* written warranty, you also have an implied warranty, and this implied warranty cannot be eliminated by the manufacturer. And if you don't have any express warranty, then state law automatically imposes the implied warranty. Thus, there remain only two situations in which you will not have an implied warranty: (1) *If there is no express warranty and the manufacturer simply eliminates the implied warranty in writing.* For example, if the only promise accompanying the product you buy reads something like "The manufacturer expressly disclaims any and all implied warranties," then you have no implied warranty. Since there is no express warranty, the federal law does not apply. Under most state laws, a manufacturer can eliminate his obligations under the implied warranty by providing the buyer with this written disclaimer of the implied warranty. (2) *If all that accompanies the product is the term "as is."* This term means that all you are getting is what you see before you without any promises. If you bought something "as is" you got it "as is."

Thus, aside from these two exceptions, all products you buy have an implied warranty. Now we can get into the heart of the problem: What is an implied warranty and where does it come from?

Every state (with the exception of Louisiana) has adopted the Uniform Commercial Code. Sections 2-314 and 2-315 of this law provide buyers with the implied warranty.

Section 2-314 requires all goods sold to be "merchantable." While the law contains an elaborate explanation of what "merchantable" means, for our purposes we can simplify the definition. If what you buy does not meet the reasonable expectations of a reasonable person (such as you), then it is not merchantable.

Section 2-315 adds another, more specific promise to the implied warranty under certain circumstances. This section applies when you rely on a salesperson's judgment that a particular product is fit for a particular purpose. In such cases the product is implicitly warranted to be able to perform that particular purpose.

A good simple example of the implied warranty is the case of *Mindell v. Raleigh Rug Company.* Mindell bought some floor tiles from the Raleigh Rug Company. The tiles were made by the GAF Corporation. After the tiles were put down, they started yellowing. The court decided that "a product, such as tile, which discolors shortly after installation, is not . . . as required by the warranty of merchantability. . . . It must not only be durable but also hold its pattern and color for a reasonable length of time consistent with the degree of quality selected." The yellowing of the tile, the court concluded, was a breach of the implied warranty, which the Raleigh Rug Company was required to give to Mindell.

In *General Electric Credit Corporation v. Hoey* the disappointing purchase didn't turn yellow; the problem was that it didn't turn on. Benjamin Hoey bought a General Electric TV set on time for $177.04. The set arrived in a factory carton but immediately began to break down. Benjamin claimed that the set was not new but was, in fact, a floor sample. In any case, $177.04 is a lot of money for something that doesn't work.

The Best Gift Shop, where Benjamin had purchased the set, was unable to make the necessary repairs, so Benjamin stopped making payments for the set. General Electric Credit Corporation, which had financed Benjamin's purchase, sued him for payment. The credit corporation apparently did not care that the set was out of order. It was interested simply in collecting its money.

The court gave G.E. Credit Corporation a lesson in the

law and provided us with a good example of the implied warranty: "Defendant Hoey contends that the television set did not function properly and was inadequate for the use for which is was intended at the time it was purchased and that this constitutes a breach of the implied warranty of merchantability.... Even though the television set is purchased in a sealed package from a dealer in that brand of goods, the sale is covered by the implied warranty of merchantable quality.... From the evidence before it, the court concludes that the set did not function properly at the time it was purchased; that it was not fit for the ordinary purpose for which it was to be used, and that despite repeated requests by defendant Hoey that it be repaired and be made suitable and fit for its intended use, nothing was done to remedy the condition and make the set merchantable within the meaning of Section 2-314 of the Uniform Commercial Code. The court finds that the seller, Best Gift Shop, breached the implied warranty of merchantability and, despite numerous requests, has failed to remedy it."

Tiles that turn yellow and TV sets that don't work are typical breaches of the implied warranty. These problems involved relatively small amounts of money. Does the implied warranty apply when you make a bigger purchase, such as a boat or a car? You bet it does.

Gabriel Rudolf bought a boat from Boe Huchman Marine. Boe wrote on the bill of sale that it was a "new boat." Maybe it was new; maybe it wasn't. New or used, it certainly was a miserable boat. Gabriel went to court to complain. And the court lent a sympathetic ear: "The ... question in this case is whether a new boat with a defective steering wheel, windshield wiper, depth finder, throttle linkage, toilet, binnacle light, outrigger and electric anchor, in which the seats have fallen apart and excessive leakage has been experienced and whose engine has become severely but unexplainably damaged and inoperable after only fifty-one hours of operation, is of merchantable quality. The circumstances of the sale of the boat in this case give rise to an implied warranty that the boat was of merchantable quality. Given these defects, it is this Court's opinion that the boat was not of merchantable quality and that defendant has accordingly breached its implied warranty."

While boats are expensive, cars can cost even more—especially when you buy the car Ward Melby wanted. Ward bought a new Maserati Ghibli from Hawkins Pontiac. The car cost $22,750. For that kind of money you expect a car that works. The one Ward bought did not. He invoked the same law that had helped the woman with the yellowing floor tiles.

The case of *Melby* v. *Hawkins Pontiac,* however, is interesting not because it involves an expensive car, but because the case raises the question of whether the seller of defective goods should have an opportunity to repair the goods before the implied warranty is considered to have been breached.

The court had no problem finding that the Maserati was defective. The problem was whether Hawkins Pontiac had been given an adequate opportunity to make the necessary repairs: "[A] new automobile is impliedly warranted to perform with reasonable efficiency, safety and comfort.... It seems, however, that whether or not the length of time necessary for repairs is reasonable depends upon the facts and circumstances of the case."

Thus, the general rule put forward by the court is that the seller must have a reasonable opportunity to remedy the problem before there is a breach of the implied warranty. This rule was carried into the Magnuson-Moss Warranty Law. Thus, before Ward (or you) can claim a breach of the implied warranty, he must show that he gave Hawkins Pontiac a chance to repair the Maserati. In fact, Ward did just that. For the first 197 days he owned the car it was in for repairs on 191 days. Under anyone's definition of a "reasonable" opportunity to correct a defect, 191 days was enough time. However, in any case you must give the seller a reasonable opportunity to correct the problem. He may do this by fixing the product or by replacing it. The important point is that he must be given a chance to make amends before the law will recognize a breach of the implied warranty.

So far we have seen that the implied warranty is breached when you buy a product which any normal person would consider defective. We have also seen that there is a breach when a product does not do what it was clearly intended to do. Finally, we examined a case which showed us that before there can be a breach of the implied warranty, you must give the seller a reasonable opportunity to correct the problem by repairing the product or replacing it.

There may be many cases in which you buy a product with a particular purpose in mind and are assured by an advertisement or a salesperson that the product can serve that purpose. In these cases the implied warranty is not limited to what a normal person would reasonably expect of the product. As we said earlier, the warranty is extended by Section 2-315 of the Uniform Commercial Code to include what you were led to believe by the advertisement or salesperson. Let's consider an example of this important point.

Edis Ziskin was an interior decorator. She designed a wooden platform with six back and seat cushions for Mr. Goldberg's living room. The cushions were not quite up to par. As the court described them: "[T]hey are not the same length; they were not uniformly stuffed; after they were filled with kapok, they were re-stuffed with polyurethane [shredded foam], yet the contour of the shredded foam shows as bumps through the heavy vinyl covers; one pillow was inadvertently not restuffed; and the underfilled four corners are flat sharp points, indicating either that the vinyl was not properly cut or else not properly stuffed; and contrary to their specifications, they remain limp after use."

Now, limp pillows may have a place in somebody's apartment, but these were to be used as cushions for a seating arrangement. Who wants a limp seating arrangement? Goldberg certainly did not. But who is to say that a limp pillow is not merchantable? In this case, the court. It pointed out that the pillows were designed for a specific use: as cushions in a seating arrangement. *For this particular purpose* they could not be limp. The seller, Edis Ziskin, knew this. Therefore, under Section 2-315 of the Uniform Commercial Code, the pillows breached the implied warranty. As the court said: "There was implied, as a matter of law, in this sale transaction, a warranty by the decorator that the cushions would be suitable for their specific use on the platform." In this case the warranty was breached.

We all recognize the special skills of an interior decorator and can understand why Goldberg relied upon Edis's judgment. But what about the more typical situation of the salesperson making promises when you buy something in a store? Let's consider two cases.

The first case is *Gates* v. *Abernathy*. The court's decision speaks for itself:

Dr. Paul Gates wished to purchase some clothes to give his wife for a Christmas present. Dr. Gates had never before bought any clothing for his wife and was ignorant of what size she wore. He was aware, however, that his wife had frequently shopped at "Penelope's," a shop owned by [Abernathy], and that she had been waited on there by the store manager, Penny. Therefore, he went to "Penelope's," spoke to Penny and explained to her that he wished to buy some clothes to give to his wife as a Christmas present.

Penny showed Dr. Gates certain items in sizes that she said was certain would be proper for Mrs. Gates. Dr. Gates picked out three pants suits in the size that Penny had recommended and purchased them.

... When she received the gifts Mrs. Gates tried them on and discovered that they were much too big. Shortly after Christmas Dr. Gates returned the pants suits to "Penelope's" and received a credit slip. When Mrs. Gates came to the shop with the credit slip she was unable to find anything in her size. She was directed to another store owned by [Abernathy] but found nothing acceptable in her size. She demanded the money back but this was refused.

You can probably guess what claim Dr. and Mrs. Gates made. Here's what the court thought of their argument:

It is hard to imagine a case which fits into the outline of [Section 2-315 of the Uniform Commercial Code] as well as does this one. It is uncontested that the buyer here was relying upon the judgment of the seller to furnish the kind of goods he wanted, nor is there any question that the seller was aware that seller's expertise was being relied on by the buyer. [Dr. Gates] did not sue on the basis that the clothes were not merchantable or useable as clothes. Rather, [Dr. Gates] claimed that they were not useable for the particular purpose for which they were bought, that is, for Mrs. Gates to wear. ... In the case at bar, the clothes were good clothes but they did not fit Mrs. Gates as the seller had represented. We conclude that the instant case is controlled by section 2-315.

Thus, the court concluded that Abernathy had breached the implied warranty. While the case is rather unusual, the reasoning is impeccable.

Our second case should fully clarify the usefulness of the implied warranty when the seller is aware of the particular use you have for the product. Michael Catania asked Mr. Brown, a man engaged in the retail paint business, what sort of paint he should use for the exterior stucco walls of his house. Brown recommended "Pierce's shingle and shake paint." He told Michael how to put the paint on and sold him a couple of gallons.

Michael followed the instructions and painted his house. Six months later the paint began to peel, flake, and blister. Michael complained to Brown. Brown must have said, in effect, "Sue me," so Michael did.

The court found Brown had breached the implied warranty. "[T]he buyer, being ignorant of the fitness of the article offered by the seller, justifiably relied on the superior information, skill and judgment of the seller and not on his own knowledge or judgment, and under such circumstances an implied warranty of fitness could properly be claimed by the purchaser."

By now you should realize that the implied warranty applies to many of the problems which arise from buying a product. So what? What can you accomplish by using the implied warranty? Until recently the answer was "not much." A lawyer might use the warranty if you were injured by a defective product. The problem for the individual buyer was that the Uniform Commercial Code did not provide very effective remedies for a breach of the implied warranty. You could demand your money back, but if the seller refused you were forced to go to court. Regardless of the outcome of the case, you would have to pay for the lawyer. Who wants to pay two hundred dollars to an attorney to get your money back on two gallons of paint? (Of course, if your problem is a $27,000 Maserati, it might be worth it.)

The situation remained bleak until the Magnuson-Moss Warranty Act was passed in 1975. You know already that this law applies to any situation in which you buy a product which has a written warranty. What you don't know is that the law provides you with an important remedy in the event that the implied warranty is breached: *attorney's fees.* Thus, if you have to sue to get your rights and you win, it won't cost you a penny. But it will cost the person who sold you the defective merchandise. He may not know about this law—but our super threat will take care of that.

If you have no written warranty, the Magnuson-Moss Warranty Act will not help you. Your only remedy is the Uniform Commercial Code itself and, frankly, that remedy is not very good. Before resorting to it you should remember that *any* written warranty qualifies you for the benefits of the Magnuson-Moss Warranty Law. What is a written warranty? Basically, it is a statement in writing on or accompanying the product which (1) relates to the nature of the material or workmanship and promises that it is defect-free or will meet a specified level of performance over a specified period of time, or (2) promises to refund, repair, replace, or take other remedial action regarding the product in the event that such product fails to meet the specifications accompanying it.

While it is not entirely clear how far the concept of a "written warranty" was intended to be extended, one conclusion is certain: The seller is not sure either. Therefore, if the product you bought has *any* statement in writing accompanying it which makes any promises regarding its quality, you have a written warranty. And if there is any statement promising replacement or repair in the event of dissatisfaction, you have a written warranty.

Since there are different remedies available to you, depending on whether you have a written warranty, we will provide you with two different super threats. (Remember, however, that *any* problems with a product costing less than fifteen dollars should be dealt with as if there were no written warranty, since the Magnuson-Moss Warranty Law applies in these situations.) In both cases you will be relying on state law; see Appendix D for relevant citations to be inserted in your super threat where indicated.

Launching a super threat (written warranty)

Soft spot. Here it's attorney's fees. The importance of this soft spot should not be underestimated. After all, if you can collect attorney's fees, you certainly will have no problem finding an attorney willing to handle your case on a contingency basis (the lawyer collects his fee from the other side). Thus, your threat of a legal action is very real. Further, if you win, the cost of legal fees can run into the thousands of dollars—a soft spot for any merchant or repairperson.

"*In the Matter of.*" Insert a description of the product which is causing the problem. Use the sales-receipt number and date of purchase if they are available.

Heading. Insert name and address of the business which sold or repaired the product.

"*Notice of . . .*" Insert the appropriate reference to the Uniform Commercial Code for your state from Appendix D.

NOTICE OF VIOLATION OF [insert reference to state law]

PLEASE TAKE NOTICE: You are in violation of the Magnuson-Moss Federal Trade Commission Improvement Act.

"*Statement of Complaint.*" There are no special rules for the statement. Simply describe exactly what you thought you were getting and why. Then indicate exactly what you did get. Include a description of your efforts to get the product repaired or replaced.

"*Demand for Action.*" Decide whether you want the product repaired or replaced or your money refunded. In your demand indicate which alternative you have chosen, and be sure to provide a date by which the demand must be met.

"*Ultimatum.*" Insert in the ultimatum the appropriate reference to the Uniform Commercial Code for your state (the same reference used in "Notice of Violation"). The remainder of the ultimatum remains the same for all such super threats.

ULTIMATUM

In the event of your failure to accept the requests made above, I shall seek legal counsel with the intention of commencing civil proceedings pursuant to [insert citation] and Section 110(d)(2) of the Act. You will be liable for attorney's fees.

Launching a super threat (no written warranty)

As we pointed out earlier, a super threat designed to remedy problems with products having no written warranty cannot use the Federal Trade Commission Improvement Act. Does that mean that you have no remedy for breach of the implied warranty in these cases? The answer is that you have a remedy but it is not very potent. The law gives you the right to return the product and get your money back. But what if the seller refuses to follow the law? Do we have a super threat to *compel* him to give you your money back? The answer is no. The law simply gives you the right to sue the seller; there is no provision for attorney's fees. Thus, only by suing in Small Claims Court (where you don't need an attorney) are you likely to avoid a hollow victory (paying more for legal fees than the amount you recover from the seller).

And now for the good news: We have provided you with a super threat despite the fact that no true soft spot exists. The super threat will rely upon some provisions of the Uniform Commercial Code which give you the right to collect damages under certain limited circumstances. We know, and now you know, that as a practical matter the most you are entitled to is getting your money back. However, our super threat should raise some doubts in the seller's mind. He will certainly realize that you know what you are talking about. Hopefully, he'll want to satisfy you rather than pay his own attorney a large fee only to find out that you have a legitimate claim.

Soft spot. This is the seller's prospect of having to pay his own attorney to defend against your legitimate claim. No business wants to throw away money on an attorney. Neither do you. If you can convince the seller that you sincerely intend to sue (and win), he should give in rather than spend fifty bucks on an attorney only to test your sincerity. In order to add credibility to your threat to sue we have included a reference to Small Claims Court. These courts are available to any person who wants to sue without a lawyer. The seller may believe you are more likely to sue if you don't have the expense of a lawyer.

"In the Matter of." Insert a description of the product which is causing the problem. Use the sales-receipt number and date of purchase if they are available.

Heading. Insert the name and address of the business which sold or repaired the product.

"Notice of..." Insert the appropriate reference to the Uniform Commercial Code for your state from Appendix D.

NOTICE OF VIOLATION OF [insert reference to state law]

PLEASE TAKE NOTICE: Pursuant to *Cova v. Harley Davidson Motor Co.,* 182 N.W.2d 800 (Mich. 1971), you are in violation of Section 2-314 and/or 2-315 of the above-captioned law.

"*Statement of Complaint.*" There are no special rules for the statement. Simply describe exactly what you thought you were getting and why. Then indicate exactly what you did get. Include a description of your efforts to get the product repaired or replaced.

"*Demand for Action.*" Decide whether you want the product repaired or replaced or your money refunded. In your demand indicate which alternative you have chosen, and be sure to provide a date by which the demand must be met.

"*Ultimatum.*" Insert in the ultimatum the appropriate reference to the Uniform Commercial Code for your state (the same reference used in the "Notice of Violation"). The remainder of the ultimatum remains the same for all such super threats.

ULTIMATUM

In the event of your failure to accept the requests made above I shall seek legal counsel with the intention of commencing civil proceedings pursuant to Section 2-314 and/or 2-315 and Sections 2-712, 2-714, and 2-715 of [insert citation] in either civil court or Small Claims Court.

9

Deceptive Trade Practices

All of us feel gypped when we get less than we bargained for. Our resentment is particularly intense if the product or service or repair work that we purchased was represented to be one thing but turned out to be quite another. That's just the sort of switcheroo that Floyd G. Scott experienced a few years ago in Eugene, Oregon. Floyd's son was looking for a tent to take on backpacking trips. The tent was going to be used in snowy weather, so it had to have two important features: a window with a flap that could be securely fastened, and eaves—that is, flaps which would overhang the tent's sides and form an extension of its roof.

Floyd and his son visited the Eugene Surplus Sales Store. There they found what appeared to be a suitable tent. It was in a sealed plastic package, but an attached card stated, "Nylon Net Rear Window with ZIPPERED flap." A diagram on the card pictured the sealable flap, as well as a tent equipped with eaves—perfect on both counts! Floyd paid $38.86 for the tent and took it home.

The moment of bitter truth came when Floyd and his

son took the tent out of its sealed package. The tent had neither of the two features that were described on the card. Immediately Floyd took the tent back to Eugene Surplus Sales and tried to return it. The store, however, would not give Floyd a refund, and he refused credit for $38.86, because the only item he wanted was a satisfactory tent.

Put yourself in Floyd's shoes. Would you go to the trouble and expense of suing the store for a measly thirty-eight bucks? (Chances are a lawyer would charge that much just to listen to your story.) Well, Floyd did sue. And in the 1973 case of *Scott v. Western International Sales, Inc.*, the Oregon Supreme Court decided that Floyd was entitled to collect two hundred dollars as minimum damages, plus punitive damages, plus his attorney's fees.

How is it that Floyd Scott came into such a neat little windfall when he had paid only $38.86 for the tent? The answer lies in the Oregon Unlawful Trade Practices Act, which Eugene Surplus had violated. Under the Act, an unlawful (or deceptive) trade practice occurs if the characteristics which a product possesses are misrepresented to the customer. Just such a misrepresentation occurred when the tent was sold to Floyd as being equipped with a sealable flap and eaves.

For violation of the Oregon Act, Eugene Surplus had to pay Floyd minimum damages of two hundred dollars. (The Act provides for the award of either the actual amount of a consumer's loss or two hundred dollars, whichever sum is larger.) Also, Eugene Surplus got stung with punitive damages, because the store's personnel should have known about the discrepancies between the representations on the card and the actual characteristics of the tent. "The defendant sold so many tents," explained Supreme Court Justice Denecke, "that it had one employee designated as tent manager. One of his duties was to familiarize himself with the various tents offered for sale. Defendant had sold a substantial number of tents of the model sold plaintiff [Floyd Scott]. Defendant had a separate tent display area in which a tent of the kind purchased by plaintiff was set up for display. (This display area was not shown plaintiff nor was he told of its existence.) In the displayed tent defendant placed another tent of the same kind, wrapped in its plastic package." In short, store personnel should have known better than to sell Floyd a tent that could not live up to his justifiable expectations. As if to put icing on Floyd's cake, the court awarded him attorney's fees—in other words, Eugene Surplus got stuck with the bill—which is authorized under the Oregon Act.

Hurray for Floyd Scott, you're probably saying, but what about consumers who live in Los Angeles or Miami or Chicago, rather than in Eugene, Oregon? What law can they turn to when they don't get what they've paid for? The answer, in at least thirty-nine other jurisdictions, lies in the local "deceptive trade practices statute." Basically, these thirty-nine statutes resemble the Oregon Act; indeed, some of them provide even stiffer penalties than those in Oregon.

Frustrated consumers can bring the kind of lawsuit that Floyd Scott did in the following jurisdictions: Alaska, Arizona, California, Colorado, Connecticut, District of Columbia, Florida, Georgia, Hawaii, Idaho, Illinois, Indiana, Kansas, Kentucky, Louisiana, Maine, Maryland, Massachusetts, Minnesota, Mississippi, Missouri, Montana, Nebraska, New Hampshire, New Jersey, New Mexico, North Carolina, Ohio, Oregon, Rhode Island, South Carolina, South Dakota, Texas, Utah, Vermont, Virginia, Washington, West Virginia, Wisconsin, and Wyoming. (If your state is not included in this list, you still enjoy substantial protection against deception under the common-law doctrine of fraud, which is explained in Chapter 10.) Thus, we have a total of forty laws under which a consumer has a so-called *private right of action*. That's legalese for the right to bring a lawsuit on your own, without having to rely upon some government agency (e.g., the state attorney general's office, the department of consumer affairs) to crank its bureaucratic wheels into motion on your behalf.

Armed with a private right of action, you can sue a merchant who sold you goods that fell short of the representations which were made to you. A large number of the forty deceptive-practices statutes allow you to win punitive damages—sometimes double or treble damages—over and above your actual loss. What's more, virtually all of these laws authorize a judge to award you attorney's fees. (No doubt you can already see the makings of a potent super threat.)

The forty deceptive-practices statutes apply to a wide range of consumer transactions. The sale of goods is, of course, covered. So is the leasing of goods; for instance, a rented air conditioner or television set. Significantly, providing a service is also covered (e.g., repair work, vocational training, house painting). There is one broad qualification, regardless of whether goods or services are involved: The consumer transaction must be for purposes that are primarily personal—that is, for your family or your household.

The basic thrust of all forty statutes is to outlaw deceptive trade practices. These practices contribute substantially to the number of consumers who get gypped. A deceptive trade practice generally occurs whenever a false representation of fact is made by a merchant about the characteristics, quality, or price, et cetera, of a product. False representations, or "misrepresentations," as they're sometimes called, take many different forms. The sale of a product, after all, is normally not a cursory event; it's more like a process. It begins with the come-on: You see an ad or some brochure or salesperson solicits your business directly. During this initial stage, you will be reading or hearing a number of factual representations about the product. For example, it uses less electricity than all of its competitors; or it's so lightweight you can carry it in a coat pocket; or you can have it in eight new decorator colors.

The next stage usually involves a visit to a store or showroom. A salesperson will tell you about the product's many virtues. He will answer your specific questions regarding the product's capabilities and uses. You may read descriptive literature or display packaging. The product itself, or a model of it, is likely to be on display. Frequently the product will be demonstrated; indeed, you may be given the opportunity to try it out for yourself. At all of these steps in the sales process, you are being bombarded with further factual representations about the product. Some are made orally, others are printed, and still others are purely visual, such as what you perceive when you inspect a floor model or sample.

Finally you decide to buy the product. Presumably the salesperson has discussed the price with you. He may have told you that it's the lowest price in town or 20 percent off the regular price. These are factual representations, too. You will probably ask about the warranty, in which case expect still more representations; the salesperson may explain to you his company's policy on servicing products, or he may show you a printed warranty.

The whole point is: A dozen factual representations may have been made to you during the process in which you buy a product. (The same holds true for the process in which you buy a service or repair work.) If any one of these representations was false or misleading or deceptive—in short, a misrepresentation—you will probably find yourself with less than your money's worth.

For example, you paid fifty-nine dollars for an electric blender guaranteed to stir, whip, purée, grind, shred, chop, mince, blend, and liquefy. However, when you get the blender home and unwrap it, you see that it has settings only for stirring, grinding, and blending. Unless the fifty-nine dollars you forked over includes the services of a kitchen helper to do your whipping, puréeing, shredding, chopping, mincing, and liquefying, you've clearly been gypped out of part of the purchase price. Your loss resulted from a factual representation about the product's capabilities—namely, that it would perform nine functions—which turned out to be false. It is this kind of loss that can be remedied under a deceptive-practices statute.

Broadly speaking, there are a half dozen major categories of misrepresentation that are outlawed under all deceptive-trade-practice statutes. In reading the list that follows, you will probably recognize the bait for some consumer trap you've fallen into in the past:

Used goods. A deceptive practice occurs when goods that are not new are palmed off on you as if they were new. The goods may actually be secondhand or reconditioned or altered in some way inconsistent with a claim of newness. For instance, you buy a home freezer that has been represented to be brand new; in fact, it was repossessed from a prior customer who couldn't keep up payments on the freezer.

Price cuts. How many stores do you know that make a business of going out of business? Prices are slashed for absolutely the last time . . . month after month after month. Generally speaking, it's deceptive to misrepresent the reason for a reduction in prices. The same holds true for the amount of a price reduction. Thus, if a three-piece dinette set is on sale at an advertised reduction of 30 percent, but it used to sell for only 10 percent above the sale price, the store is engaging in a deceptive practice.

Sponsorship or affiliation. Suppose you want to get your three-hundred-dollar waterproof, dustproof, shockproof Alpiner watch cleaned and repaired. The chap in the watch store on the corner assures you that he is an authorized Alpiner representative—indeed, the only one within fifty miles. Unfortunately, your trusty Alpiner is not deception-proof; the corner store has no affiliation with the manufacturers of your watch. It is, in general, a deceptive practice to falsely represent that a store or product or service enjoys some sponsorship, affiliation, or approval which it does not in fact enjoy.

Characteristics. If a merchant or repairperson misrepresents the model or grade of goods or services, there's been a deceptive practice. For example, you buy a Zaftik-2000 radio after the salesperson tells you that the 2000 is Zaftik's transoceanic model. "It'll pick up London, Moscow—you name it!" he declares. Moscow my eye. In fact, the 2000 is strictly a domestic receiver, and one with a limited range at that. The salesperson engaged in a deceptive act. (See Appendix A for a sample super threat aimed at a television repairman who misrepresented the characteristics of his repair service.)

Quality. Deceptive practices commonly involve misrepresentations about the quality or characteristics of consumer goods. Suppose a furniture dealer claims that the wall unit you're buying is solid walnut when it's really just walnut veneer. Or the appliance salesperson assures you that the broiler-oven you're selecting runs on ordinary AC household current, but the truth is that you have to get a whole new 220-volt line installed in your kitchen. In both instances, the product was misrepresented, as to either its quality or its characteristics.

Bad-mouthing. A deceptive practice occurs when a merchant disparages the goods or services of some other merchant by making factual misrepresentations. Say you're considering taking driving lessons. You visit a driver-training school, where an instructor explains why the school's rates are higher than those charged at competing schools. According to him, none of the other schools owns demonstrator cars in which to take students out on the road; instead, these cheaper schools rely on classroom equipment to simulate actual driving conditions. In fact, all the other schools do take students out in demonstrator cars. Unfortunately, you've stumbled into an overly expensive school which also happens to be dishonest.

These half dozen common misrepresentations do not comprise an exclusive list. Many state statutes make no attempt to proscribe a long "laundry list" of illegal misrepresentations. Instead, these statutes broadly prohibit "unfair or deceptive acts or practices," leaving specific enforcement up to the courts and administrative agencies. The point is: Never presume that some deception is beyond the reach of the law just because it seems so novel. Chances are the practice is unlawful under the general or "catchall" language written into your state's deceptive-practices statute.

Now let's look at some practical steps to follow if you want to take advantage of your state's deceptive-trade-practices law. (Appendix E lists the major provisions of each such law.)

Preliminary skirmishes

What is the first thing you should do if some product or service you've purchased doesn't measure up to the representations which were made to you? Go back to the place of purchase (or service location), just as Floyd Scott went back to Eugene Surplus Sales. (If a return visit is impractical, because of time, distance, or perhaps the unwieldiness of the product, call the place of purchase rather than going there in person.) Explain to the management the discrepancy between representations which were made to you about the product and the actual nature of the product. Be firm but friendly, as though it were all an innocent misunderstanding that can easily be cleared up.

Try to resolve the problem in the way that's best for you. Floyd Scott wanted a refund of his $38.86, but you might be happy with full credit for your purchase price, or perhaps an exchange for a more suitable product. Don't settle for less than you deserve; remember, you're the one who was misled into buying something that you really didn't want.

Opening volleys

Suppose you meet with an unsympathetic response, as Floyd Scott did at Eugene Surplus. Then you should write a polite complaint letter to the business. Not only does this step make practical sense, but it also sets you up for resorting to the deceptive-practices law, should that become necessary. A number of these laws require the consumer to notify the business of any alleged deceptive practice. The business is then entitled to an opportunity to straighten matters out. Only after such an opportunity has been offered and either declined or taken advantage of in an unsatisfactory manner does the consumer's private right of action arise. So a polite complaint letter is a prerequisite to a credible super threat as well as the right to bring a lawsuit.

In your polite complaint letter, briefly review the consumer transaction and point out the way in which facts were misrepresented to you. For example, you went shopping for a room air conditioner. A salesperson at the local appliance store told you that a particular model comes equipped with an automatic thermostat. According to the salesperson, this device turns the cooling unit on whenever the air indoors rises to a certain temperature. Through this automatic control, the salesperson explained, a constant level of cooling is maintained. Unfortunately, the salesperson misrepresented the air conditioner's capabilities—as you learned only after you purchased the unit, took it home, and turned it on. The thermostat operates on a regular timed cycle, rather than on a sensitivity to room temperature. As a result, instead of steadily maintained cooling, there are uncomfortable fluctuations in temperature. When the thermostat's on, your room is suddenly cooled, but when the thermostat stays in its off cycle, your room heats up—and so do you. Given such a mess-up, your polite complaint letter to the appliance store would go like this:

Certified Letter No. 12345678

[Date of mailing here]

Your name
Mailing address
City, state, zip code

Name of store manager
Name of store
Mailing address
City, state, zip code

Re: Misrepresentation in sale of air conditioner

Dear [name of manager]:

I purchased a [give the manufacturer's name, the model, and the serial number of the air conditioner] at your store on [give date of purchase].

This air conditioner's performance does not measure up to the factual representations which were made to me at the time of purchase by your salesperson [supply the salesperson's name if you know it].

Your salesperson said to me that the air conditioner would maintain a constant level of cooling, because the thermostat automatically responds to rising room temperature. This statement was not, in fact, true. The thermostat works on its own timed cycle, regardless of room temperature. Consequently, room temperature fluctuates regularly and by wide margins.

Because of this misrepresentation by your salesperson, I have been deprived of an important feature which I was led to believe the air conditioner possessed.

Kindly rectify this situation, by [insert what you want done: e.g., refunding my $239 purchase price and picking up the air conditioner at my home or picking up the air conditioner at my home and giving me full credit, namely $239, toward the purchase of an air conditioner equipped with a truly automatic thermostat].

Sincerely,

/s/ Your name

Make extra copies of any polite complaint letter such as this, because you may need to send a copy along, should you resort to a super threat.

Allow the merchant about fifteen days in which to comply with your polite complaint letter. (In any super threat that may follow, you'll allow another fifteen days; if, after a total of thirty days, the merchant has not responded satisfactorily, you can fairly safely assume that you have earned a private right of action against him.) If politeness doesn't work, you'll have to abandon such relatively gentle terms as "misrepresentation" and charge the merchant with an "unlawful deceptive trade practice." For that kind of hard-nosed legalese, you'll need an authoritative vehicle—namely, a super threat.

Launching a super threat

Your super threat will dispel any notion which the merchant may have that you are merely chiding him for poor business ethics. He has violated a state statute, and you intend to hold him accountable. (See Appendix A for a sample super threat that follows the instructions given below.)

Soft spot. Here it's money, as well as the realization that you won't be reluctant to retain an attorney whose fees will be included in the judgment.

"In the Matter of." Continue this phrase with the words "violation of," and then insert the official title of your state's deceptive-trade-practices statute (from Appendix E). For example, if you live in Connecticut, your full caption would read: "IN THE MATTER OF violation of Connecticut Unfair Trade Practices Act."

Heading. Give the name of the president or manager of the business that you patronized. Also supply the address of the business.

"Notice of Deceptive Trade Practice." Under this heading for the first paragraph, you will charge the recipient with an unlawful deceptive trade practice and zing him right between the eyes with the official citation to your state's statute (from Appendix E). For example, if you live in Minnesota you would write: "PLEASE TAKE NOTICE: Pursuant to Minn. Stat. Ann. Secs. 325.79–325.80, 325.907 (1976 Cumm. Supp.), you have committed an unlawful deceptive trade practice."

"Statement of Complaint." Under this heading for the second paragraph, give a bare-bones recitation of the deceptive practice that you are complaining about. Refer to your prior polite complaint letter to the business, and enclose a copy of it. For example, "On March 1, 1977, I purchased from your store a three-piece living-room set, upholstered in 'Grade A' fabric, which your salesperson, Jane

Slick, told me was the highest quality and most durable fabric. I have since discovered that 'Grade A' is, in fact, the lowest quality rating, 'Grade Z' being the highest. The deceptive trade practice in which your salesperson engaged was more fully described to you in my letter of March 20, 1977, a copy of which is enclosed."

"Demand for Action." Under this heading for the third paragraph, you will state precisely what steps you want the business to take. In most instances you will request a full cash refund, an exchange, or credit toward a new purchase. Don't forget to include a request that the product be picked up and removed from your home. Set a deadline for compliance that falls fifteen days after your date of mailing.

For example, the slippery folks down at Fly-By Appliances sold you a $439 color TV set, which was supposed to be brand new but which you later discovered was a poorly reconditioned floor sample. Your super threat mailed on April 1, 1977, might contain this demand: "No later than April 15, 1977, Fly-By Appliances must perform the following steps: (1) refund in full the $439 I paid for the color TV set; and (2) pick up and remove said TV set from my home."

"Ultimatum." Under this heading for the fourth paragraph, you will state your resolve to file suit, if necessary, for violation of your state's deceptive-practices statute. You will let the recipient know what he stands to lose in the way of damages, attorney's fees, and court costs. To do this, you'll have to consult Appendix E for the monetary provisions of your statute and then insert this information as indicated below:

ULTIMATUM

If the above demand for action has not been satisfied in full by the date specified, then I shall seek legal counsel with the intention of commencing a civil action against you for the willful and wanton commission of an unlawful deceptive trade practice. Under the [insert official title of your state's statute], you may be subjected to liability for [insert the full measure of damages and attorney's fees available under your state's statute].

Lest you have any trouble inserting the necessary information, here is an example. The ultimatum of a Kansas consumer would conclude with: "Under the Kansas Consumer Protection Act, you may be subjected to liability for a civil penalty of $2,000 per violation as well as the amount of my attorney's fees."

10

Fraud

We all use the word "cheated" freely. If, for example, Reggie Jackson snares a line drive headed for a home run, we say the batter was "cheated." And if we put two dollars on Gallant Dream in the fourth at Aqueduct and Gallant Dream is edged out by a nose, we were "cheated." You can't do much about these problems, because being cheated is part of the game. But if you're buying products or services and the other guy isn't playing with a full deck, cheating is a definite violation of the rules of the game. The law gives a technical name to this kind of cheating: *fraud*.

Webster defines fraud as "an instance or an act of trickery or deceit esp. when involving misrepresentation." The legal definition of fraud is much lengthier, but it's really just an elaboration on the dictionary. Basically, if someone intentionally deceives you about a product or service and as a result you suffer a loss, a common-law fraud has been committed. Your legal remedy is a lawsuit for money damages, both compensatory and punitive.

Compensatory damages repay you for what you lost—for example, the purchase price of a used refrigerator which was fraudulently sold to you as new. Punitive damages, on the other hand, are not to compensate you, but to punish the person who defrauded you. From our point of view—always looking for the soft spot—the availability of punitive damages makes common-law fraud a rich source of super threats. Punitive-damage awards can run into tens of thousands of dollars. (We will shortly see how an elderly widow, defrauded by the Arthur Murray Dance Studios, won forty thousand dollars in punitive damages.)

In a nutshell, common-law fraud consists of five basic elements:

1. *A lie.* Some sharp operator misrepresents the product or service he's trying to sell you. This deception may be accomplished through words or deeds. For example, a salesperson lies to you that the shoes you're trying on were imported from Italy; in fact, he knows that they were manufactured in New Jersey. Or a used watch is displayed in a new red velvet case with a new-watch warranty. Even the nondisclosure of information can be a basis for fraud, especially when the person who's tight-lipped is an expert in what he's selling and you are a rank amateur.

2. *Scienter.* "Scienter" is legalese for a liar's state of mind. In order for there to be fraud, the person who lies to you must know or believe that what he is saying is false. Determining whether the necessary scienter exists is usually a question for the jury.

In *Holland Furnace Company* v. *Robson,* Mary Jane Robson was a seventy-seven-year-old woman with an ailing heart. On a cold, damp November day, Mrs. Robson hired the Holland Furnace folks to clean her furnace. Two men from Holland showed up and dismantled the furnace. While it lay in pieces on the basement floor, one of the Holland men called Mrs. Robson to the basement. He explained to her in rather technical terms that defects in the furnace would cause gas to escape, and therefore the furnace was dangerous and should be replaced. Extremely distraught and unnerved by this news, Mrs. Robson decided that she had to purchase a new furnace from Holland. The Holland men took the pieces of the old furnace and left.

On these facts, can scienter on the part of the Holland men be established? Clearly, we have no idea whether the old furnace really needed replacement, because it no longer exists (the pieces were thrown away). There was thus no way for Mrs. Robson to prove conclusively that the Holland men had lied. All she could do was present the cold facts, testify that "I didn't know what I was doing," and hope that a jury would find in her favor. A jury did. Confronted by a seventy-seven-year-old woman versus a furnace company, the jury found for Mrs. Robson. They concluded that Holland knew it was lying when it told Mrs. Robson that a new furnace was needed.

3. *Intention to deceive.* The liar must also intend to lead you on, so that you will act—or refrain from acting—in reliance on his lie. Obviously it's as difficult to pin down a person's intent as it is to establish scienter. In fraud cases, intent is usually proven through circumstantial evidence. For example, if a car dealer turns back the odometer to zero on a used car, there is a logical inference that he intended to deceive a buyer who is shopping for a new car.

4. *Reliance.* Legally speaking, reliance is the critical link between the defrauder's lie and your downfall. You must have relied upon the lie to your detriment. Your reliance may have led you to act in a specific way. For example, you paid $285 for a sport coat tagged as cashmere which the salesperson knew was really camel's hair. Or you may have refrained from acting in reliance upon the defrauder's lie. For example, you don't cancel your membership in a bogus diet clinic because the instructor assures you that weight loss

will begin suddenly after six more months of eating the clinic's special foods.

Your reliance must have been justifiable. Assuming that you possess reasonable intelligence, you cannot fall for patently outlandish lies and then cry fraud; reliance upon such lies would not be justifiable. This is not to say, however, that the law judges you by some unattainable ideal of the savvy consumer, who carefully checks and double-checks all representations before making a move. Only if there is some apparent reason why you should be on guard will your reliance on a lie be viewed as unjustifiable. Courts are generally solicitous of consumers who relied upon representations that were made under circumstances arousing no undue suspicion. Even gullible people and those who are downright stupid can recover for fraud if the defrauder purposely played on their weaknesses. (We shall shortly see this principle at work in the Arthur Murray case.)

5. *Damages.* The final prerequisite for any fraud case is damages: You must have suffered some loss because of your reliance on the lies that you heard. In most courts your loss will be measured by the fact that you were defrauded out of the value which you bargained for. The difference between that value and the actual value (if any) that you received is your measure of so-called compensatory damages.

Besides compensatory damages, you may also be able to collect punitive damages. If the defrauder was calculating in his lies to you, or callous in his disregard for your rights, it is likely that a jury will return a verdict including a sizable award of punitive damages. Such an award will not be overturned by a judge unless it is plainly the result of passion rather than reason. Judges recognize that awarding punitive damages has a prospective deterrent effect; not only does the defrauder learn his lesson, but others who might be tempted to engage in similar fraudulent practices are forewarned that the costs can be high. A New York judge has described this deterrent effect well: "Those who deliberately and coolly engage in a far-flung fraudulent scheme, systematically conducted for profit, are very much more likely to pause and consider the consequences if they have to pay more than the actual loss suffered by an individual [consumer]. In the calculation of his expected profits, the wrongdoer is likely to allow for a certain amount of money which will have to be returned to those victims who object too vigorously, and he will be perfectly content to bear the additional cost of litigation as the price for continuing his illicit business. It stands to reason that the chances of deterring him are materially increased by subjecting him to payment of punitive damages."

With these judicious thoughts fresh in our minds, let's see how the Arthur Murray dance studio in Des Moines, Iowa, got stung by an award of $40,000 in punitive damages. In the 1965 case of *Syester* v. *Banta,* Agnes Syester sued the studio for fraud. Agnes was a lonely elderly widow, whose first class was a gift from a friend in 1954. After this initial visit, Agnes apparently fell for the blandishments and flattery of those who saw a way to make some easy money. In the next six years, the studio mounted a staggeringly successful selling campaign, which resulted in Agnes's purchasing 4,057 hours of dance instruction for $29,174.30!

Included in Agnes's purchases were *three* lifetime memberships. At the trial Agnes testified that the studio manager had sold her the first of her three lifetime memberships: "He promised me all the privileges of the studio and I would be a professional dancer." Needless to say, such a promise to someone Agnes's age was ridiculous.

Agnes's regular instructor at the studio, a Mr. Carey, lavished attention, inducements, promises, and lies on Agnes. (He admitted as much at the trial.) Carey was about twenty-five years old, and apparently quite charming and fascinating to Agnes. On his birthday in 1960, she gave him a diamond ring.

At one point, to induce Agnes to buy further instruction, the studio showed her a film on so-called Gold Star dancing. The dancers in the film were imported from Europe by Arthur Murray. They performed an "English quick step," the kind of dancing Fred Astaire did with Ginger Rogers—only about twice as difficult. Agnes was easily sold a Gold Star course of 625 hours for more than $6,000.

Finally the bubble burst. Carey was discharged from the studio, and shortly thereafter Agnes abandoned her courses, even though she still had hundreds of hours of unused time. In 1961 Agnes sued the studio. To counter this action, the studio reinstated Carey and told him to persuade Agnes to drop her lawsuit and return to the studio. This he managed to do by constantly visiting Agnes at work, inviting her to a studio party, and promising to save her some waltzes. (He knew that the waltz was her favorite dance.) Agnes signed a release of all claims against the studio in return for $6,090 (out of the total of $29,174.30 she had paid).

Apparently things didn't work out at the studio, for within a year Agnes again dragged the studio into court, this time alleging fraud not only in selling the dance courses but also in obtaining the release and the dismissal of her first lawsuit. The jury returned a verdict of $14,300 in compensatory damages and $40,000 in punitive damages.

On appeal by the studio, the case was affirmed. "Since the beginning of recorded history," wrote Iowa Supreme Court Justice Snell, "men and women have persisted in selling their birthrights for a mess of pottage and courts cannot protect against the folly of bad judgment. We can, however, insist on honesty in selling. The old doctrine of caveat emptor is no longer the pole star for business...."

After reviewing the evidence, Justice Snell concluded

that Agnes Syester had been the victim of a calculated course of intentional misrepresentations. "The fact that she was so gullible as to be an easy victim," ruled Justice Snell, "does not justify taking over $29,000 of her money. She may have been willing and easily sold but nevertheless a victim." This ruling is a good example of the general principle we discussed earlier—namely, that even gullible people can recover for fraud, despite the foolhardiness of their conduct.

Regarding the release that Agnes had signed for six thousand dollars, Justice Snell observed: "That plaintiff was easily influenced appears without question. The consideration for the ... release was wholly inadequate. It was only a partial return of an unconscionable overcharge. ... The evidence was such that the jury could find that there was such a concerted effort, lacking propriety, to obtain the release as to constitute fraudulent overreaching. The jury obviously concluded that there was a predatory play on the vanity and credulity of an old lady. We find no reason for interfering with that conclusion."

While the award of forty thousand dollars in punitive damages was admittedly large, Justice Snell refused to reverse it. "The evidence of greed and avarice on the part of defendants is shocking to our sense of justice as it obviously was to the jury."

While the elderly are frequent victims of fraud, the young may also be illegally duped. In one case a young woman was sold a set of pots and pans after having been convinced that the set she had would surely cause cancer for herself and her children. While the woman may have been gullible, she was not completely stupid. She got an attorney and sued for fraud. Her reward was twenty-five hundred dollars in punitive damages. She also recouped the cost of the pots and pans that she had been coerced into buying.

Not all frauds require a gullible victim. Consider the

case of *Ahmed* v. *Collins*. Constance Collins needed an orthopedic bed. Ortho Comfort Stores told her they could provide her with such a bed for $1,366. Constance told Ortho that she didn't have that kind of money. Ortho told her that they would arrange for financing. All that was required was a deposit of $366. The bed would be delivered in two weeks. Constance paid the deposit but received no bed. Instead, Ortho told her that they needed another $328 to show her "good faith," in order to secure financing. Constance objected, since she had been told that she would receive financing for a deposit of $366. Ortho explained that they needed the money only for a few days and would deliver a small "loaner" bed in the meanwhile. She paid the $328 and got the "loaner" bed, and that was about all that happened. The result was that Constance had paid $694 for a small "loaner" bed. So far as Ortho was concerned, they were even.

Constance went to court claiming foul. She thought Ortho had acted fraudulently when they told her that they would get her financing with a deposit of only $366. Ortho told the jury that they had tried to get financing but were unable to do so. The jury chose to believe Constance. They awarded her compensatory damages of $694. In addition, they gave her $15,000 in punitive damages. Thus, Ortho was out $15,694 because it had tried to lure Constance into buying a bed by promising financing that it could not deliver.

Automobile frauds can cheat even an alert buyer. These frauds all have one aspect in common: They rely on the fact that automobiles are complicated instruments. For example, how can you tell whether new piston rings have really been installed in your car's engine? You rely on the repairperson who did the work. Dishonest repairpersons know your handicap and take advantage of it. Automobile-repair frauds are difficult to fight, because it's so hard to detect whether you've been defrauded. The only way you are likely to find out is if another repairperson tells you so. That's exactly what happened in the case of *Bowen* v. *Johnson*.

Mrs. Bowen's Dodge had some transmission problems. She went to Red Johnson Dodge to have the car repaired. Red said that the car's transmission had to be replaced. Red Johnson Dodge could install a rebuilt transmission for $135.24. Mrs. Bowen agreed and paid the amount by check. She was told to return the following Friday afternoon to pick up the car. When Friday came she went to Red's and picked up her car. She drove two blocks with the "repaired" car and found that the gears would not shift. She immediately returned to Red, but found that his shop was closed.

Mrs. Bowen's husband, who, it appears, knew something about cars, discovered that Red had installed a badly worn transmission instead of a rebuilt one. Mrs. Bowen called her bank to stop payment on the $135.24 check. Red's wife, however, had beat Mrs. Bowen to the bank and had already cashed the check.

The Bowens took their car (in first gear, presumably) to another service station, which confirmed Mr. Bowen's diagnosis. The Bowens had their car properly repaired and then tried to repair the damage done to their checking account by Red Johnson. They got more than they had bargained for (and so did Red): The jury decided that the Bowens were entitled to receive their $135.24 back from Red plus punitive damages of $3,500. Thus, the Bowens not only got a repaired transmission, they got enough money to buy a new car. Red's trick had clearly backfired on him.

While repair frauds account for many of the complaints regarding automobiles, there is a surprisingly large number of problems with buying used and new cars. A frequent fraud problem in the automobile-sales area is the sale of a used car under the misrepresentation that it is new. The unsophisticated buyer is hard pressed to distinguish a well-restored used car from a new one, and the desire for a good deal can often blur what might otherwise be sound judgment. The case of *J. Truett Payne Company, Inc. v. Jackson* should stop dishonest automobile dealers in their tracks.

Jackson bought a 1964 Oldsmobile from the J. Truett Payne Company. The dealer told him that it was a new car, and Jackson paid the sticker price, $4,980. The car ran for about five hundred miles before it started developing mechanical problems. Jackson brought the car in for repairs, and the mechanic told him that it had at least several thousand miles on it.

Buying a lemon is one problem, but buying a half-squeezed lemon is worse. Jackson claimed that he had been defrauded. The facts showed that he was right. The car was hardly new. In fact, it was a used demonstrator. Jackson went to court, claiming that the J. Truett Payne Company was guilty of fraud.

The company must have had a difficult time coming up with a defense, since the facts clearly showed that the company had tried to sell a used car by claiming it was new. The judge charged the jury: "You gentlemen consider all of the facts, you decide whether punitive damages ought to be awarded. You are the sole judges about that, considering the nature and the purpose of punitive damages." The jury, after listening to the judge's advice, imposed punitive damages of twenty thousand dollars.

Opening volleys

If you have been defrauded you may consider contacting your state attorney general or local office of consumer affairs. You may be able to file a complaint and, at the same time, find out if any actions are pending against the people who took you for a ride. Filing the complaint may prompt an investigation which could help prevent further frauds. Also, if you discover that other people have been defrauded, you can use this information in your super threat and raise the specter of a class action.

Launching a super threat
    Soft spot. This is money. Jury verdicts in fraud cases may result in extraordinarily high judgments. After all, juries have very little sympathy for defrauders. In addition, if you discover that others have suffered the same fate as you, the threat of a class action will only tend to tenderize the soft spot.
    "In the Matter of." Provide sufficient information to identify the fraudulent transaction. If a sales slip was used, indicate its number. If you remember the date of the purchase, insert it in the caption. For example, a typical caption might read: "IN THE MATTER of purchase of 'gold watch' on March 23, 1977, under sales slip number A23456."
    Heading. Insert the name of the president of the business which defrauded you. Underneath this name insert the following: "individually and as an officer of." Then insert the trade name of the business. For example, a typical heading might be:

John Smith
individually and as an
officer of
Best Widgets, Inc.

The purpose of using this language is to alert John Smith to the fact that he may be personally liable for any judgment you secure. Also be sure to give the address of the business.
    "Notice of Tortious Fraud." This is standard language which will remain constant. We have included a reference to "Prosser," which is the leading legal treatise on the subject of torts.

NOTICE OF TORTIOUS FRAUD

PLEASE TAKE NOTICE: Pursuant to *Ahmed* v. *Collins*, 23 Ariz. App. 54, 530 P.2d 900 (1975) (see also Prosser, *Law of Torts*, Sec. 105), your activity in the above matter may constitute actionable fraud.

"Statement of Complaint." Insert the facts of your case in a simple, straightforward manner. If you were at a particular disadvantage which facilitated the fraud, be sure to mention these facts. For example, if you are elderly indicate your age. If you do not understand English well, point this fact out. Finally, be sure to avoid the temptation to blast away.

"Demand for Action." Because of the wide variety of fraud situations which exist, there is no way to standardize a demand for action. In some cases you will want your money back on a purchase; in other cases you might want to get out of a contractual agreement. In any case, write your demand simply and specifically, and be sure to include a date by which you expect compliance. For example, a typical demand for action might be: "On or before June 12, 1977, return to me the sum of $450 made as down payment on the automobile. I will arrange to return the automobile on receipt of the money."

"Ultimatum." This is standard language. We could have chosen any of a number of cases to cite, but the ones chosen have particularly large awards of damages. If you have discovered that other people have been victims of the fraud perpetrated on you, you might add the following sentence to the end of your ultimatum: "Since an investigation has determined that other people have been victimized by your

fraud, a class action with multiple damage awards is being considered."

ULTIMATUM

In the event you fail to respond to my demand, I shall seek legal counsel with the intention of commencing a civil action against you for fraud. I shall seek a jury verdict large enough to encompass both compensatory damages and punitive damages based on your willful, wanton, and reckless misconduct. Personal liability for commission of a fraudulent act may result. Awards of punitive damages may be substantial: *Syester* v. *Banta*, 257 Iowa 613, 133 NW2d 666 (1965) (award of $40,000 punitive damages); *J. Truett Payne Company* v. *Jackson*, 281 Ala. 426, 203 So.2d 43 (1967) (award of $20,000 punitive damages).

11

Buying by Mail

Mail-order Merchandise

According to the Federal Trade Commission, the mail-order industry has annual sales of about forty billion dollars. That is the amount that consumers spend each year. How much they receive in merchandise each year is another story. Indeed, few industries are capable of causing as much frustration for the consumer as the mail-order industry, and, except for automobiles, no industry causes more consumer complaints.

The two largest categories of complaints can be summarized with the following pleas: (1) "I ordered a Whizbang pie cutter six months ago, and all I've received is my canceled check"; and (2) "I ordered my Christmas decorations in October, but they didn't arrive until January."

What aggravates these situations is the simple fact that you usually buy a product by mail because the business is far enough away to make it inconvenient for you to visit the seller and buy the product directly. A business which is inconvenient to visit for a purchase is also inconvenient to visit for a complaint. So you are left to complain by mail. And why should a business that didn't send your Whizbang pie cutter when you enclosed $2.98 respond when you send a complaint letter with no money inside?

The answer lies in Title 16, Section 435 of the Code of Federal Regulations. This section contains a Trade Regulation Rule promulgated by the Federal Trade Commission, which deals with problems encountered in the mail-order merchandise industry. The rule became effective on February 2, 1976.

The basic requirement of the rule is that a mail-order seller must ship ordered merchandise within the time period promised by him in any solicitation for sale or, if no time limit was specified, then within thirty days. Thus, if you order a product through an advertisement which promised that the product would be shipped within seven days, the seller must ship within seven days. However, if the seller made no promises to you, the rule requires that he ship within thirty days.

In the event that the seller cannot ship the merchandise within the required time period, he must inform you of the length of the delay. He must also offer you the option of a refund of your money and provide you with a postpaid card with which to accept the offer.

If the delay is thirty days or less, and you do *not* inform the seller that you want the order canceled, the rule allows the seller to ship the merchandise on a delayed schedule. However, if the delay is more than thirty days and you do not respond to the seller's offer to refund the money, the seller must assume that you want a refund and promptly send it to you.

When the seller knows there is going to be a delay in

shipping but has no idea how long the delay is going to be, what is he supposed to do? (The question is quite likely to arise since, according to an attorney for several mail-order companies, "It is a widespread business practice not to have an item in stock when advertised.") The answer is that the seller must inform you that there will be an "indefinite delay." If you still want the merchandise, you must notify the seller; otherwise, he must cancel the order and refund your money. If you do consent to the indefinite delay (and good luck to you), you can still change your mind later on and cancel the order. So long as the product has not been sent before the shipper receives your cancellation, he must send a refund.

There are additional nuances to the rule. However, the basic provisions which we have discussed will cover the problems most consumers are likely to confront.

Opening volleys
Prior to launching a super threat, you should consider sending a copy of your polite complaint letter to:

> Mail Order Action Line
> Direct Mail Advertising Association
> 230 Park Avenue
> New York, N.Y. 10017

This organization is composed of direct-mail-sales businesses. If the business you are having problems with belongs to this organization, you might find that a letter to the organization will help. They have a good track record. However, if they cannot help or if the business you are dealing with is not a member of the organization, you will have to consider a super threat.

Launching a super threat

In order to show that you mean business, your super threat will incorporate a petition to the Federal Trade Commission requesting action under Section 205 of the Federal Trade Commission Improvement Act.

This section provides that any business which violates a Trade Regulation Rule may be fined $10,000. While the Commission does not routinely act on every petition, there still is a distinct possibility of such action. In the event that the super threat does not produce satisfactory results, you may want to send off the petition. The petition should then be sent to your regional office of the Federal Trade Commission (see Appendix F).

Soft spot. The possible liability of ten thousand dollars per instance of violation of the Federal Trade Commission Improvement Act is enough to make any direct-mail outfit queasy. This is a new law, and no one is quite certain how effective its enforcement will actually be. We believe a prudent business will not want to find out.

"In the Matter of." Provide sufficient information to identify the particular purchase you made which did not arrive. Indicate when you sent the order in and what it was for.

Heading. Insert the name of the business you sent the order to. If you happen to know the name of an officer of the business, put it down.

"Notice under Section 205." This is standard language, which remains the same in all such super threats.

NOTICE UNDER SECTION 205

PLEASE TAKE NOTICE: Pursuant to Section 205 of the Federal Trade Commission Improvement Act, you are in violation of Part 435 of Title 16 of the Code of Federal Regulations. This letter constitutes notice under said section and title.

"*Statement of Complaint.*" There will be no statement of complaint, since you will be enclosing a petition which recites the facts.

"*Demand for Action.*" Insert here exactly what it is you want the mail-order business to do. If you still want the merchandise, you can include the following: "On or before [insert date] send me the merchandise I ordered or a refund of the full amount sent to you." Of course, if you no longer want the product, simply demand a refund.

"*Ultimatum.*" This is standard language for all such super threats.

ULTIMATUM

In the event you fail to satisfy the foregoing demand, the enclosed petition will be filed with the Regional Office of the Federal Trade Commission. Since you have been served with NOTICE pursuant to Section 205, you are liable for a fine of up to $10,000 for each violation of Title 16, Part 435.

Petition. On a separate piece of paper type out the petition using the form which follows. Under the "Date of mailing" be sure to put in the same date used in your demand for action: the date by which you are demanding satisfaction. Simply attach a copy of the petition to your super-threat letter.

PETITION

FEDERAL TRADE COMMISSION
            AND   Date of mailing:
[insert name of business]

    PETITIONER requests implementation of Section 205 of the Federal Trade Commission Improvement Act as expressed in Title 16, Part 435 of the Code of Federal Regulations. PETITIONER has provided the above-captioned business with actual NOTICE that its activities constitute an unfair and deceptive practice as is required under said Section 205.
    PETITIONER avers the following:
[insert facts using numbered paragraphs]
    PETITIONER claims the mail-order-merchandise business captioned above is in violation of Section 205 and implementing rules and requests the Federal Trade Commission to seek the maximum penalty mandated by law.

[Your signature]

Your name

Mailing address
City, state, zip code

    If your super threat does not get action, you may send the petition to your Federal Trade Commission Regional Office (see Appendix F).

Negative-option Plans

In 1927 Max Sackheim and Harry Scherman had a good idea for their book-club business: Send a book to people every month. If they don't want the book, they can send it back. You can sell a lot of books that way. You can also get a lot of books back. So in 1928 Max and Harry got a better idea: Don't send books to people. Instead, send them an announcement telling them that if they *don't* want a particular book they should send a card back. If they do want the book they should do nothing. A lot of people clearly found it easier to do nothing than send in a card, and the Book-of-the-Month Club was born, the first of hundreds of companies to use the idea that Max and Harry originated.

Forty years later, Raymond Sawyer of the University of New Mexico School of Law had a good idea. He decided to join the Columbia Stereo Tape Club. He thought he would get a tape machine and some prerecorded tape cartridges. What he got was aggravation.

Sawyer began receiving monthly announcements about specific tapes. If he didn't send back an enclosed card quickly (paying the postage himself), Columbia would send the tape and bill him. Sawyer didn't know that was part of the deal and told Columbia so. His next letter to Columbia, a few months later, should be familiar to many of you:

> You are getting off to a miserable start with me. After I ordered your Stereo 8 Tape Cartridge Player, you sent me a card on December 6 that your "supply has been depleted." Now, on December 23 you had nerve enough to send me an American Express Charge Record billing me for $39.95 although I have not received either the player or the three tapes which were a required part of my order.

As a result of this letter, Sawyer received a cute "Columbia Collect-O-Gram" saying that his account was in the collection department. Twice he tried to resign from the Club, but it appears that, like the Mafia, once you join you can never quit. Sawyer's last letter reported that "the tapes keep coming."

We don't know whether Sawyer was ever able to turn off the spigot and stop the tapes and Columbia Collect-O-Grams from arriving. We do know that he wrote to the Federal Trade Commission. Partly as a result of his effort, you can avoid the fate that he was forced to endure.

Section 425 of Title 16 of the Code of Federal Regulations contains a Federal Trade Commission rule which regulates so-called negative-option plans. Under these plans you periodically receive an announcement that a product will be shipped to you unless you notify the company within a certain number of days that you don't want the product. Usually you are offered a special bonus deal (free books, a cheap tape machine) for joining the "club." And you obligate yourself to buy a minimum amount of the product over a particular period of time.

The term "negative option" comes from the fact that you are never asked if you want a product. Instead, you are asked if you *don't* want it. Silence means you bought it.

Many businesses use these plans. The Book-of-the-Month Club is perhaps the most famous and most reputable. However, there are millions of consumers buying cheese, flowers, records, bibles, wine, dogs, dolls, and dresses on negative-option plans. And these plans not only generate sales, they generate problems.

Part 425 of Title 16 of the Code of Federal Regulations regulates these plans by establishing the following rules:

1. Any promotional material for the plan must clearly spell out the plan's terms, such as the amount of merchandise you must buy, whether there are billing or shipping charges, and your right to return unwanted merchandise. Thus, for example, Raymond Sawyer would have learned what he was

getting into before joining Columbia if the law had been in effect then.

2. You must have at least ten days in which to review the announcement and decide whether you want to refuse the product by returning the card. Previously, many consumers would receive an announcement on, say, October 10 that unless the card was returned by October 9 the product would be shipped.

3. A seller cannot substitute a different product for the one which was offered to you. For example, the prior practice of Doubleday and Company (which runs a large book club) was to use "book substitution": In the event that you wanted a book which was out of stock, Doubleday simply sent you another book, "as near as possible to the selection which the member anticipated receiving."

4. If you receive merchandise which you have refused (by sending in the card within the specified period), you can return the merchandise, and the postage must be paid by the seller.

5. Once you have purchased all the products required under the plan, you can quit the club at any time. If you do quit and thereafter receive a product, you can refuse to accept it or can return it at the seller's expense. If, thereafter, you receive still another product for any reason, you are entitled to keep it as a gift. Assume, for example, that you have purchased all twelve records required of you under the Singsong Record Club plan, and now you want out. You send a letter to Singsong clearly terminating your relationship. A week later Singsong sends you Errol Garner's *Concert by the Sea*. You have the right to send the record back, and Singsong must pay the postage. If an announcement arrives the next month (you throw it away) and three weeks later a record arrives, you can keep the record (and any others that arrive) as a gift.

6. A seller must ship any introductory or bonus mer-

chandise within four weeks of receiving your initial order. If the seller can't meet the four-week deadline, he must let you know and give you the chance to quit the plan or take alternative merchandise. If you decide to quit you must return any portion of the bonus offering which you have received.

Opening volleys
Aside from a polite complaint letter, there is no special opening volley available.

Launching a super threat
In order to show that you mean business, your super threat will incorporate a petition to the Federal Trade Commission requesting action under Section 205; this is similar to the one on page 159.

Soft spot. The soft spot here is the same one that applies to mail order: the possible liability of ten thousand dollars per violation of the Federal Trade Commission Improvement Act.

"In the Matter of." Provide sufficient information to identify the particular negative-option plan you belong to. Indicate any account number you have been assigned as well as your name. For example, a caption might read: "IN THE MATTER OF Account #23456 of Randy Brooks in Singsong Record Club, Inc."

Heading. Insert the name of the business operating the plan. If you happen to know the name of an officer of the business, use it.

"Notice under Section 205." This is standard boilerplate, which remains the same in all such super threats.

NOTICE UNDER SECTION 205

PLEASE TAKE NOTICE: Pursuant to Section 205 of the Federal Trade Commission Improvement Act, you are in violation of Part 425 of Title 16 of the Code of Federal Regulations. This letter constitutes notice under said section and title.

"*Statement of Complaint.*" There will be no statement of complaint, since we will be enclosing a petition which will recite the facts.

"*Demand for Action.*" Insert here exactly what it is you want the negative-option-plan company to do for you.

"*Ultimatum.*" This is standard language.

ULTIMATUM

In the event you fail to satisfy the foregoing demand, the enclosed petition will be filed with the Regional Office of the Federal Trade Commission. Since you have been served with NOTICE pursuant to Section 205, you are liable for a fine of up to $10,000 for each violation of Title 16, Part 425.

Petition. This is handled exactly as explained on page 158.

PETITION

FEDERAL TRADE COMMISSION
              AND   Date of mailing:
[insert name of business here]

PETITIONER requests implementation of Section 205 of the Federal Trade Commission Improvement Act as expressed in Title 16, Part 425, of the Code of Federal Regulations. PETITIONER has provided the above-captioned business with actual NOTICE that its activities constitute an unfair and deceptive practice as is required under said Section 205.

PETITIONER avers the following:
[insert facts of your case]

PETITIONER claims the negative-option-plan operator captioned above is in violation of Section 205 and implementing rules and requests the Federal Trade Commission to seek the maximum penalty mandated by said law.

[Your signature]
Your name

Mailing address
City, state, zip code

Mail Fraud

In 1973 the Outpost Development Corporation advertised a product by stating that " 'My Secret' [is the] safest, fastest most effective fat destroyer in the world—this amazing tonic which I call 'My Secret.' " This "tonic" would allow you to lose weight without dieting. However, if you sent in the required charge for the tonic, what you received was a short booklet entitled "My Secret." The booklet, it appears, worked like a tonic.

Over thirty-five years earlier, a Mr. Simmons advertised in pulp magazines a booklet called "Art of Love—thirty actual photos, Montmartre Type, of men and women in different affectionate poses, also including women models alone in various poses." If you sent in the money for "Art of Love," however, you received "worthless matter not of an obscene, lewd, or lascivious character."

Both the Outpost Development Corporation and Mr. Simmons had one trait in common: They wanted to deceive someone into buying a product through the mails. They had something else in common: Both were prosecuted under Title 39, Section 3005 of the United States Code.

What can you do when, relying on an advertisement, you buy something only to find that what you bought is not what was advertised? In part it depends upon how far the advertisement strayed from reality. If the advertisement merely did a little "puffing," then you have succumbed to the instincts which make the advertising business a billion-dollar industry. But if the advertisement went beyond mere puffing and was designed to "deceive persons of ordinary prudence and comprehension," then you may be able to do something about it.

Any business which relies on the mails to secure orders is most vulnerable if its mail service is cut off. Certainly, the soft spot of a mail-order business is its use of the mails. Thus, the most effective super threat would indicate that mail service may be terminated. Fortunately, Title 39, Section 3005 of the United States Code is just the law we need.

Section 3005 provides that the Postal Service may terminate mail delivery to any person or business that is "conducting a scheme or device for obtaining money or property through the mail by means of false representations. . . ." If Section 3005 is violated, the Postal Service can direct "the postmaster of the post office at which mail arrives, addressed to such person or his representative, to return such mail to the sender appropriately marked as in violation of this section. . . ." Furthermore, the Postal Service can order that any money orders or postal notes payable to the company or person engaged in false representations be returned unpaid to the drawer.

Clearly, an order to stop mail delivery under Section 3005 can have a devastating effect. The full impact of Section 3005 was felt by both the Outpost Development Corporation and Mr. Simmons. In the *Outpost* case, the decision of the Postal Service was upheld with a rather cryptic observation by the court that "it can hardly be said that the printed word is a fat destroyer." A tonic was advertised, and a booklet is not a tonic.

In the case of Simmons, the court also upheld the decision of the Postal Service to stop mail service. What makes the case rather extraordinary is that the Postal Service had suspended mail delivery because obscene material had been promised but only tame material was provided. As the court pointed out, "The Postmaster General was entitled to consider the whole advertisement, and it was not unreasonable for him to conclude that ... obscene material was being promised.... It is without dispute that the material furnished by [Simmons] was of a non-salacious and non-obscene nature.... We think it clear upon the evidence in the case that [Simmons] was carrying on a scheme calculated fraudulently to prey upon the curiosity of the salacious minded. They, as well as the innocent, are entitled to the protection of the laws against fraud."

Thus, it is clear that the Postal Service is prepared to stop mail service to anybody engaged in false representations who utilizes the mails, even if the representation is to supply obscene material. Our super threat will, therefore, be based upon the possibility that the Postal Service will act upon your complaint.

However, before we outline the super threat we should examine another remedy which is similar to a mail stop-order but is a bit more drastic. There is a federal criminal law entitled "mail fraud." A violation of this law does not result in a stoppage of mail service. Rather, the perpetrator of the mail fraud can go to prison. (Once in prison, he is still entitled to receive mail.)

The mail-fraud statute (Title 18, Section 1341 of the United States Code) is remarkably similar to the law which gives the Postal Service authority to stop mail delivery. The mail-fraud law provides that any person "having devised or intending to devise any scheme or artifice to defraud, or for obtaining money or property by means of false or fraudulent pretenses, representations, or promises... shall be fined not more than $1000 or imprisoned not more than five years, or both." The only additional requirement is that the mails must have been used in some way to assist in the completion of the fraud.

Surprisingly, in cases in which mail fraud has been prosecuted, the patterns are similar to those in the stoppage-of-mail-delivery cases. For example, in *United States* v. *Uhrig*, Joseph Uhrig was the prime mover behind an executive recruitment company. The company, World Executive, Inc., advertised that its founder "had been 'in the business' for fifteen years, had offices in every major city in the United States and in foreign cities; dealt with over 25,000 companies in the United States and more than a hundred overseas; had 'personal contact with top executives in many major firms and dealt directly at the top level with most major firms'; placed applicants 'on almost daily basis,' and refunded application fees upon placement, with companies served paying [the company] the requisite commission." Sounds like a good executive-recruitment organization.

However, the business, in truth, was not as good as it sounded. In fact, World Executive, Inc., had been in business for only one year. It did not have offices in every major United States city, and it had no foreign offices. World's only dealing with companies or top executives in this country or abroad was through reading traditional business directories such as *Standard and Poor's* and *Moody's,* and sending résumés to, and placing telephone calls with, company executives listed in the directories. Furthermore, World had placed a grand total of only five executives during its entire existence.

Uhrig was charged with mail fraud and was convicted on eight counts; that's a total of up to forty years in prison. His appeals proved fruitless. While you may have little sympathy for him, there are other mail-fraud cases in which it's harder to find a clear villain. Consider, for example, the case of *United States* v. *Hannigan.*

William Hannigan was the president of a corporation which sold movie equipment to the public. He offered a deal too good to refuse. He would give you free of charge a whole package of movie-making equipment, which sold for between five hundred and six hundred dollars, if you agreed to buy six hundred rolls of Technicolor film at a reduced price of one dollar per roll. The total cost was six hundred dollars. It sounded like a good deal.

In fact, however, the movie equipment was worth only about two hundred and eighty dollars. Furthermore, you received only one roll of film. When you had that roll processed at an inflated cost, you received another roll free of charge. That, of course, is not exactly what the offer appeared to be saying.

Hannigan claimed that he had been merely "puffing" and that the case should not go to a jury, since the government had no case at all (and juries are made up of consumers who don't like fraud). The court disagreed. Hannigan had not said, for example, that the movie equipment was "worth up to" six hundred dollars. That might have been considered puffing, a mere statement of subjective fact or opinion. Rather, he had said the equipment "sells for" about six hundred dollars. That was not puffing. That was a statement of an objective fact which, the government claimed, Hannigan knew was false. Furthermore, the clear implication that a purchaser would receive six hundred rolls of film was a false representation, since the purchaser received only one roll of film. The jury, the court concluded, must decide the question of guilt.

We can see, therefore, that trying to deceive purchasers into buying a product or service, and using the mails in the process, can be a very risky business. You can make it an even riskier business by knowing what to do if you are bilked. The answer is a super threat. Since we have two good theories on which to base the super threat, we will use both in one letter.

Opening volleys

Businesses which use the mails to practice fraud usually know exactly what they are doing. They certainly are used to receiving complaint letters. We believe a polite complaint letter is always in order. However, those businesses which practice fraud would not stay in business long if they cared about simple complaint letters. We recommend sending a copy of a complaint letter to your local department of consumer affairs and the state attorney general's office. If there is an ongoing investigation of the business, your letter may add fuel to the fire. However, when it comes to getting back what you've lost as a result of the fraud, a super threat is your best bet, short of hiring a lawyer.

Launching a super threat

In Appendix A you will find a sample super threat that follows the instructions given below.

Soft spot. Our super threat will press on two soft spots by utilizing the prospect of a mail stop-order as well as criminal liability. The mail stop-order is a particularly devastating remedy for any business which receives orders through the mail. The danger of criminal prosecution would touch a soft spot in anyone. As a practical matter, however, criminal prosecutions are entirely in the hands of district attorneys, who may or may not respond.

"In the Matter of." Provide sufficient information to identify the fraudulent transaction. Indicate the date you sent your order in, and identify what it was you were buying.

Heading. Insert the name of the president of the business, if you can find it out. If you cannot get the name, insert instead "John Doe" and keep the quotation marks. Underneath the name of the president (or "John Doe") write: "individually and as an officer of" followed by the trade name of the business. Then give the address of the business.

"Notice of Violation." This is standard language, which can be used in any such super threat. The citations are to two sections of the United States Code which deal with mail stop-orders and mail fraud.

NOTICE OF VIOLATION

PLEASE TAKE NOTICE: You are in violation of Title 39, Section 3005 of the United States Code (see *United States* v. *Outpost Development Corp.,* 369 F. Supp. 399 (D.C. Cir.), aff'd, 414 US 1105 (1973)), and Title 18, Section 1341 of the United States Code (see *United States* v. *Uhrig,* 443 F.2d 239 (7th Cir.), cert. denied, 404 US 832 (1971)).

"Statement of Complaint." Insert the facts of your case. Indicate what you were led to believe you were receiving and how you were led to this belief. Indicate what you actually received.

"Demand for Action." With very few exceptions, the only remedy you can seek for a fraud committed through

the mail is return of your money. Therefore, we have standardized the demand for action. You need only insert the amount of money you want returned and the date by which you demand compliance.

DEMAND FOR ACTION

On or before [insert date] return to me the sum of [insert amount]. This amount reflects the payment made to you as a result of your false representations. Include instruction for return of any goods I have received from you, said return to be at your expense.

"*Ultimatum.*" This is standard language. Because of the wide variety of types of fraud perpetrated through the mails, we have used more than one legal action.

ULTIMATUM

In the event you fail to respond to my demand in a timely manner, I shall file a formal petition with the Postal Service, Inspection Division, pursuant to Title 39, Section 3005 of the United States Code. This may result in a stop-order being issued against your receipt of any mail. Further, a "Request for Investigation" may be filed with the United States Attorney, which may result in criminal penalties, *United States* v. *Uhrig, supra.*

If it becomes necessary to follow through on your ultimatum, you should send a polite complaint to: Chief Postal Inspector, United States Postal Service, Washington, D.C. 20260.

12

Credit Problems

There is an old adage that goes, "You get what you pay for." The previous chapters dealt with the problem of getting. This chapter deals with the problem of paying. Most of these problems arise in the area of credit, that wonderful system which allows you to get something now and pay for it later. However, we will also look at what you can do when you bought something but don't want to pay for it and are therefore confronted by the bill collector.

We will begin by looking at credit-reporting agencies, those businesses that survive by telling other businesses how likely you are to pay your debts. This is a logical place to start, since without a good credit rating you're not likely to get credit. And without credit you won't be able to have the problems discussed in the rest of this chapter.

Upholding Your Credit Rating

James Millstone was a White House correspondent for the St. Louis *Post-Dispatch*. In 1971 he left Washington and returned to the newspaper's home office to work as an editor. On returning, Millstone applied for auto insurance on his Volkswagen bus. The policy went into effect on November 15, 1971, but on December 20 the insurance company informed Millstone that the policy would be canceled.

Why this sudden turnaround? The insurance company had retained the services of a company called O'Hanlon Reports, Inc., to investigate Millstone's background. O'Hanlon sent an investigator into Millstone's old neighborhood in Washington. The investigator's findings were rife with innuendo, misstatement, and slander:

A poll of four of local neighbors at the former address proved that the assureds were very much dislike [sic] here by all informants, mainly because of the attitute [sic] and by the non-discipline of their four children. Mrs. Millstone would allow her children to run free in the area, and they frequently played ball in neighbor's yards, and even gardens, and tore them up on several occasions. When confronted with this Mrs. Millstone was quoted to have said "they will play ball where they please, and no one will stop them." In addition, both assureds were reported to be the "hippie" type by all neighbors and participated in many demonstrations here in Washington and also housed out of town demonstrators in their house during these demonstrations, and these demonstrators slept on the floors, in the basement and any where [sic] else they could on assured's property. Assureds were strongly suspected to be drug users by all neighbors, however this could not be positively substantiated by any of our informants. Assured is reported to have shoulder length hair and a beard on one occasion while living here. The risk, a late VW Bus, was used to transport out of town demonstrators to and from the demonstrations here in Washington informats [sic] also stated. Rumors thru [sic] this neighborhood was [sic] that the assureds had lived in three other places in Washinvgton [sic] and were evicted by neighbors from each prior to coming here. Assureds were alos [sic] criticisised [sic] in their utter lack of reasoning and judgement [sic] by all informants in this neighborhood.

On the basis of this data, O'Hanlon reported back to Millstone's insurance company. Not surprisingly, the company's immediate reaction was a negative one.

The predicament James Millstone found himself in is not unique. Consider the fact that O'Hanlon Reports is only one of more than two thousand so-called credit-reporting agencies busy in America today. Together these agencies turn out over one hundred million reports annually. Whenever someone like Millstone—or, for that matter, you—applies for insurance or a loan, time-payment plan, credit card, charge account, or job, the company receiving the application usually hires a credit-reporting agency to investigate the creditworthiness and often the personal life of the applicant.

Considering the massive volume of credit reporting, it's not surprising that errors frequently occur. An agency may pass along unsubstantiated gossip, as in James Millstone's situation. One consumer may be mistaken for another with the same name, so that hard-working, bill-paying Phil Forward gets tagged with the shoddy past of Phil Forward, deadbeat. An agency may dig up an old lawsuit that was filed against a consumer out of spite ten years earlier but never got to first base. If errors like these stain your record, you may find yourself unable to qualify for credit, insurance, or employment.

What can you do to fight back when a credit agency slanders your good name? Up until April 26, 1971, there was little in the way of remedy. On that date, however, the federal Fair Credit Reporting Act (FCRA) went into effect, and it improves the consumer's lot considerably. Under the FCRA, you have the right to discover what's in your file at the credit-agency office and who's been receiving reports on you; you can correct or clarify material in your file; and you can compel renotification of people who have received inaccurate reports about you. Enforcement of the Act rests primarily with the Federal Trade Commission (FTC) and you, the private citizen.

Under the FCRA you must be notified when a credit-type decision goes against you because of a credit-agency report. For example, you're turned down for a new job because a credit agency informs your prospective employer that you perfected the three-hour four-martini lunch at your last job. Your application for a credit card is rejected after the agency digs up a forty-dollar hospital bill you never paid. So long as the adverse decision relates to a denial of employment, credit, or insurance—or an increase in your rates for credit or insurance—you must be notified by the decision-maker. You're entitled to know the name and address of the credit agency whose report played a part in the decision.

Contact the agency immediately. Request an appointment to review the file that the agency is keeping on you. Under the FCRA, the agency must set up a personal interview with you during normal business hours. (If it suits you better, arrange for a telephone interview between yourself and an agency representative. Bear in mind, however, that any toll charge for the call will have to be paid by you.)

Let's assume you opt for a personal interview at the agency office. You have a right to be accompanied by another person of your choosing; this is advisable, because you can focus your attention on questioning the agency's representative while your friend concentrates on taking notes.

Unfortunately, the FCRA does not give you the right to actually touch your file or even see it; nor can you demand a copy of it. The Act does require that agency personnel "clearly and accurately" disclose to you the "nature and substance" of everything that's in your file, except medical information. Don't let the agency representative breeze by with a ten-second summary of what's in your file. You're entitled to an explanation of each item, so be pushy and ask questions.

You are also entitled to learn the names of any parties who have received agency reports on you for employment purposes within the past two years, and for any other purpose (such as credit or insurance) within the past six months.

When you hear all the bad news the agency has dug up on you, what can you do about it? In a word: protest. If you dispute the completeness or accuracy of any item in your file, yell foul and demand that the agency reinvestigate. Legally, the agency must honor your demand, unless it has good reason to believe that the dispute you're raising is either frivolous or irrelevant. The FTC has warned agencies not to use the excuse of frivolousness as a ploy for avoiding reinvestigation.

For example, the agency's file might indicate that you're behind in your rent payments, but you know that's not so. The whole problem arose out of a computer error, which you've complained about to the apartment-house management. Explain this to the agency representative and insist on a reinvestigation.

If, after reinvestigation, the disputed information is found to be inaccurate, or if it can no longer be verified, the agency must promptly delete that information from your file.

But suppose the reinvestigation doesn't resolve the dispute. The FCRA gives you the right to insert a brief statement (a hundred words or so) in your file, explaining the nature of your disagreement with the agency's findings.

Now we come to a final important step in your confrontation with the agency, namely, *renotification.* The agency has a legal duty to set the record straight with people who have been fed bogus information about you. You may designate anyone who received the information in a report for employment purposes within the past two years or for any other purpose within the past six months. These parties must be notified by the agency about any deletion from your file or any explanatory statement you've added.

Some of you may be asking yourselves, What's all this interview-reinvestigation-renotification rigmarole going to cost me? In most cases, nothing. The FCRA does allow an agency to make a "reasonable charge" for your personal interview if you failed to request it within thirty days after you received notification that you were turned down for credit, insurance, or employment. Even then, the charge can't be sprung on you at your interview; it must be disclosed in advance.

You may have gathered by now that the credit-reporting industry is not exactly a tea-and-crumpets society. Fortunately, the FCRA not only gives you valuable rights when dealing with agencies, but it also supplies you with a powerful sanction if an agency steps too far out of line. Under the "civil liability" sections of the FCRA (Sections 616 and 617), you can sue any credit-reporting agency that negligently or willfully violates the Act. Why should the agency be apprehensive about the prospect of such a lawsuit? Because of what it stands to lose: first, any actual damages you've suffered—for instance, the loss of credit or insurance coverage or a job; even your anguish and wasted time in fighting the agency can be grounds for an award of damages. Second, if the agency's violation was willful, the court can assess punitive damages ("sting money"), without any ceiling. Third, and here's the real kicker, as part of any judgment in your favor the agency may be held liable to you for your attorney's fees. So the agency realizes that you will have little reluctance to sue, since you fully intend to sock the agency with your legal fees.

One of the most successful lawsuits against an agency was *Millstone v. O'Hanlon Reports, Inc.* As you can tell from the name of the case, it was brought by our old friend James Millstone, whose good name was tarred by the O'Hanlon credit agency. For months Millstone fought O'Hanlon's reluctance to disclose the file information that he was entitled to under the FCRA. He was forced to visit the agency's office several times and argue on the phone repeatedly. Millstone protested the inaccuracy of virtually everything that was dribbled out to him from his file. And, indeed, a reinvestigation revealed that every allegation in the original investigation was untrue. O'Hanlon's investigator in Washington had depended solely on one biased informant in Millstone's old neighborhood; no attempt had been made to verify this gossip by checking with other sources.

The court held that O'Hanlon had willfully violated the FCRA because of its slovenly investigation techniques and its withholding of information from Millstone. The court awarded Millstone $2,500 in actual damages to compensate him for the worry, frustration, sleeplessness, and general inconvenience that be suffered. Because O'Hanlon's violation had been willful, the court awarded Millstone another $25,000 in punitive damages. To top it all off, our hero collected still another $12,500 for his attorney's fees—making a grand total of forty grand.

Another successful consumer, Louis Nitti, won a big judgment against a Rochester, New York, credit agency in *Nitti v. Credit Bureau of Rochester, Inc.* Like James Millstone, Louis Nitti was given the royal runaround by an agency that refused to cooperate. The judge described Nitti's plight: "Time and again plaintiff came to the defendant's office and went over the same credit information with the defendant's employees, pointing out the errors, all to no purpose. Time and again he tried to have the defendant update and correct its report on him; he pleaded, he lost his temper, all to no avail. Like a character in Kafka, he was totally powerless to move or penetrate the implacable presence brooding, like some stone moloch, within the castle." The Rochester agency was finally moved in court, however. It got a stiff kick from the FCRA: ten thousand dollars in punitive damages, plus another eight thousand dollars to cover Louis Nitti's attorney's fees.

Preliminary skirmishes

We've already had a preview of some likely skirmishes as we learned about the operation of the FCRA. These skirmishes will usually occur at the office of the credit agency or over the phone when you talk to agency personnel. Be firm. Don't let the agency evade your demands for disclosure or reinvestigation or correction or renotification. Without sounding blustery, let the agency know that you insist upon all your rights under the FCRA being fulfilled.

Opening volleys

If you're up against a particularly stubborn agency, you might try to soften it up with a polite complaint letter. Briefly describe the way in which the agency is causing you difficulty. Inform the agency that if the matter is not cleared up within, say, fifteen days, you intend to file a complaint with the FTC, requesting that the agency's operations be investigated.

Should a complaint to the FTC become necessary, consult Appendix F for the address of the Regional Office with jurisdiction over your state. Write a polite complaint letter to the Regional Director; a form letter that you can adapt to suit your particular purposes follows.

Certified Letter No. 12345678

[Date of mailing here]

Your name
Mailing address
City, state, zip code

Name of Regional Director
Regional Director
Federal Trade Commission
Mailing address
City, state, zip code

Re: Noncompliance
with Fair Credit
Reporting Act

Dear [Director's name]:

I believe that the Fair Credit Reporting Act is presently being violated by [name the credit agency] located at [supply the address].

Under the Act, this agency has the duty to [briefly specify what the agency should be doing: e.g., "clearly and accurately disclose to me the substance of my file," "reinvestigate the accuracy of disputed items in my file"]. The agency is not performing its duty for the following reasons. [Briefly list those things that the agency has done, or failed to do, which comprise its breach of duty.]

Kindly investigate the operations of [name the agency] to determine what violations of the Act have occurred and what sanctions ought to be imposed in order to bring this agency into compliance with the Act.

Sincerely,

[Your signature]
Your name

cc: [name the agency]

As the "cc" at the foot of the letter indicates, you will send a copy of your letter to the credit agency. Perhaps the possibility of an FTC investigation will make the agency cooperative; after all, the agency may have more shoddy dealings to hide from the FTC than just your isolated case. Then too, the FTC may actually apply some pressure to bring the agency into compliance with the Act.

Launching a super threat

If time keeps dragging on without results, you'll have to try something more potent to bring the credit agency to attention.

Soft spot. Recall the forty thousand dollars that James Millstone won and you'll recognize the soft spot here. A credit agency that gets sued for violating the FCRA can wind up paying stiff punitive damages and whopping attorney's fees. Just knowing that they may have to pay your attorney if you sue them is enough to make any agency uneasy.

"In the Matter of." Finish this phrase with "civil liability for Title 15 noncompliance." Actually, Title 15 (of the United States Code) contains a lot more stuff than just the

FCRA, but the phrase "Title 15 noncompliance" sounds so sweeping and ominous that it's hard to resist!

Heading. Give the name and address of the credit agency.

"Notice of Statutory Violation." Under this heading for the first paragraph, you will inform the agency of its violation of the civil-liability sections of the Fair Credit Reporting Act.

NOTICE OF STATUTORY VIOLATION

PLEASE TAKE NOTICE: Pursuant to Title 15, Sections 1681(n)–1681(o) of the United States Code, you are in violation of the Fair Credit Reporting Act.

"Statement of Complaint." Under this heading for the second paragraph, briefly recite the problem you are having with the agency. For example: "During my personal interview at your office on February 7, 1977, I disputed the accuracy of an item in your file on me. Your file erroneously indicated that a $1,500 lawsuit was pending against me. As I told you on February 7, and in several telephone conversations since then, that $1,500 lawsuit was dismissed on the merits eleven months ago. To date you have been unable or unwilling to confirm my allegation through your own reinvestigation, and the erroneous item remains in my file."

You may also want to tack on some highly generalized allegations concerning the distress and disruption which the credit agency's misconduct is causing you. (Rest assured that the credit-agency manager will recognize the makings of a hefty jury verdict in your tale of woe.) For example: "Your failure to correct my file has caused me loss of credit, great inconvenience, sleeplessness, anxiety, and distress."

(James Millstone won $2,500 just to compensate him for such suffering.)

"Demand for Action." Under this heading for the third paragraph, state exactly what you want the credit agency to do. Set a rather short deadline for compliance—say, fifteen days from the date of mailing. For example, if the agency has not renotified certain department stores about corrections in your credit file, you might write: "No later than March 15, 1977, you must notify (1) Daks Fifth Avenue, (2) Hillandale's Department Store, and (3) Betteroff-Goodman's, all situated in the City of New York, concerning the corrections made in my file on January 20, 1977."

"Ultimatum." Under this heading for the fourth paragraph, you will be dishing up some standard legalese to warn the credit agency about the prospect of an expensive lawsuit.

ULTIMATUM

If the above demand for action has not been satisfied in full by the date specified, I shall seek legal counsel to commence a civil proceeding against you for violation of Sections 616 and 617 of the Fair Credit Reporting Act. I shall be entitled to an award of my attorney's fees in any judgment against you under Sections 616(3) and 617(3) of said Act. In any proceeding against you, compensatory damages will be sought for the loss, inconvenience, and suffering to which you have subjected me. Punitive damages will also be sought according to the rulings in *Millstone v. O'Hanlon Reports, Inc.*, 383 F.Supp. 269 (E.D. Mo. 1974), aff'd, 528 F.2d 829 (8th Cir. 1976) (plaintiff awarded $2,500 compensatory damages, $25,000 punitive damages, and $12,500 attorney's fees); and *Nitti v. Credit Bureau of Rochester, Inc.*, 84 Misc.2d 277, 375

NYS2d 817 (Sup. Ct. 1975) (plaintiff awarded $10,000 punitive damages and $8,000 attorney's fees).

Truth in Lending

In June of 1972, Cheryl Meyers decided to buy a 1972 Dodge from Clearview Dodge Sales, Inc., on credit. Since Clearview did not finance credit purchases, it contacted Chrysler Credit Corporation, which agreed to finance Cheryl's purchase. A contract was drafted. The cash price of the Dodge in the contract included a charge of fifteen dollars for "tag, title and fees." However, these items were not itemized separately. Cheryl bought the car and then went to court, claiming that Clearview had violated the law by failing to itemize all charges separately. The court awarded Cheryl one thousand dollars in damages and attorney's fees of three thousand dollars.

What could Clearview have done that justified penalizing it four thousand dollars? Is failing to itemize a fifteen-dollar charge so dreadful a sin that only by giving a gift of one thousand dollars to Cheryl could there be absolution? The answer, surprisingly, is yes. As we shall see, buying on credit can be fraught with dangers, and the number of sellers who abuse the credit-sales procedure is matched only by the number of victims who have been bilked.

The concept of "buy now, pay later" is designed to increase the sale of goods and services. After all, it's easier to buy than to pay. What too few people realize is that it costs money to pay later. The cost, known as the finance charge, is often difficult to compute. Too many people buy now and worry about the finance charge later, usually when it's too late to do anything about it.

In addition, purchasing on credit can be confusing. The unscrupulous seller can define his terms any way he likes to make it appear that he is offering the buyer a great deal. Once the buyer has signed on the dotted line, he's hooked to a long-term commitment. If he then discovers that he's got a rotten deal, too bad.

In order to put the problem in context, consider the following example. Mario Smith decides he wants to buy a TV set on time. The set he wants costs $500. He has only $100. He goes to TV Heaven, Inc., and is told that with a $100 deposit the set will cost him only $12.80 a month for 40 months, plus one payment of $42.30. There is also a finance service charge of $13.25. The salesperson assures Mario that the interest rate he's being charged is 8.23 percent, the best deal in town.

Mario goes next door to TV Paradise, Inc., to price the same set. The salesperson says that credit purchasing raises the cost of the set a bit, to $542.30. However, Mario has to pay only $5.43 a week for three years, and there's no deposit required. There is, though, a "paperwork" charge of $47.80, standard in these cases. The salesperson assures Mario that he's paying something called a "deferred interest rate" of only 6.75 percent, a better deal than that offered by TV Heaven, Inc.

At this point, Mario has the choice of either enrolling in the Wharton School of Business for a few years in order to understand the credit terms or flipping a coin to decide where to buy. Most people in Mario's position simply buy wherever they find terms that they can afford. They rarely comparison-shop. They rarely take the time to figure it out on a calculator. They rarely look for hidden charges. They rarely worry about what an "interest rate" is or whether it's the same thing as a "deferred interest rate." In fact, most people (including us) don't even know if such a thing as a deferred interest rate exists. As a result, most uninformed people end up getting taken to the cleaners when they buy on credit.

If you have bought something on credit and think you've paid too much, the chances are very good that you're right. The only way to remedy the problem is to get the people who financed your purchase to give you back any overcharge. But how can you convince a seller who has your signed contract to admit that he bilked you and actually pay you the overcharge? The only way this can be done is by pointing out to the seller that he stands to lose much more money if he refuses to correct the deception he has perpetrated on you. After all, it is the desire to make money which motivates the unscrupulous credit seller, so the prospect of losing money, perhaps a great deal of money, is his soft spot.

The foundation we will use for our super threat will be the federal Truth in Lending Law. This law was passed in 1968 and is probably one of the best-kept secrets around. The purpose of the law is primarily to require sellers to clearly and conspicuously disclose their credit terms before a buyer signs anything. In this way, a buyer will know what he is getting in for, and he can shop around for the best credit terms. Furthermore, the law specifically defines the terminology which must be used to disclose credit terms. This makes shopping for credit even easier.

Unfortunately, the law can be confusing. As a result, very few buyers take the time to understand it. On the other hand, the same thing is true of many sellers; they don't understand the law either. So long as *you* don't know about the law, the seller has no problem. But if you're willing to put some effort into understanding the law, you might find a pot of gold waiting for you—about a thousand dollars' worth.

As we pointed out earlier, the Truth in Lending Law is designed to inform a buyer before he buys. If you are buying on a charge card or charge account, the credit terms will have been explained to you when you received the card or opened the account. However, when you are buying an item and establishing credit terms just for that purchase, the terms can vary from store to store. In this situation the law requires the seller to provide you with a great deal of information before you buy. Following is an explanation of all items that must be covered on a typical credit-cost disclosure statement.

1. *The cash price.* This is the price of the product if you were prepared to pay cash at the time of purchase without any other "extras" added on.

2. *The down payment or credit for a trade-in,* if any.

3. *The unpaid-balance-of-cash price.* This is the difference between the cash price and any down payment or credit for a trade-in.

4. *Any other charges.* These charges are those additional costs which you might want listed. These costs might include title costs, delivery costs, preparation charges, et cetera. Thus, these charges are not for the product itself but are being purchased by you *in connection* with the product. All these charges must be itemized separately.

5. *The unpaid balance.* This is the total of the cash price (the cost of the product) plus the cost of any other charges less any down payment or credit for a trade-in. This is the amount you still owe for the product or services you are buying. The other costs listed below relate to the financing of the purchase.

6. *Finance charge.* This is the amount you are paying for the privilege of paying on time. This amount may be composed of more than one charge. There will always be a "time price differential." This is the actual added charge for buying on credit. There may, however, be other charges which are required before you will receive credit. For example, if the seller requires that you have insurance before extending credit, then the insurance cost must be listed here,

since it is a charge you must pay in order to receive financing. These charges are different from the "other charges" listed in (4), in that those charges apply regardless of whether you are being financed or not. All the charges which must be listed here are those which are required in order to secure financing. These charges must be itemized.

7. *Deferred-payment price.* This is simply the total amount which is coming out of your pocket to make this purchase. It is computed by adding the cash price to the cost of "any other charges" and then adding on the total finance charge.

8. *Annual percentage rate.* This is the rate of interest that the seller is charging you for the privilege of borrowing his money to buy on time. The seller must compute this charge on an annual rate by comparing the "finance charge" to the total amount you are financing. In this way you can compare the rates being charged by different sellers. The higher the rate, the more the credit is costing you. The best deal will have the lowest rate.

Some unscrupulous companies may realize that if you shop around for credit you will choose the place with the lowest annual percentage rate. These businesses may try to artificially reduce the rate by playing a little game with you. Remember, the rate is computed by comparing the finance charge with the amount being financed. The less the finance charge, the lower the annual percentage rate (and the better the deal). So if a business can reduce the finance charge artificially, there will be an apparent lower rate. How can the business do this? Well, it can take charges which are required in order to secure financing (which should be listed under "finance charge") and tuck them in under "any other charges," or include them in the cash price. This will reduce the finance charge, and therefore the annual percentage rate. So make sure that all the charges required for financing are listed in "finance charge" and are therefore included in computing the annual percentage rate. For example, if you were told that you must have insurance in order to get financing, make sure the insurance cost is *not* listed under "any other charges." It doesn't belong there. It belongs under "finance charge," since it was required in order to get credit.

In addition, the following information must also be included on the credit-cost disclosure statement:

A. The date on which you must begin to pay the financing payments.

B. The number of payments you must make, how much each one is, and when it must be made by. If any single payment is twice as much (or more) as the other regularly scheduled payments, this payment must be identified as a "balloon payment." For example, if you are required to pay ten dollars a month for twenty months, but one of the payments is twenty dollars or more, that payment must be identified as a "balloon payment."

C. Any late-payment rules.

D. A description of any security interest held by the seller to secure payment of the credit extended to you. For example, if you buy a car on credit, the seller may retain a security interest in the car until you have made all your payments. This means that if you fail to pay, the seller can repossess your car.

E. An explanation of any penalty charges assessed against you in the event that you decide to pay any or all of the payments before they become due.

As you can see, the seller (or company financing a purchase) must provide you with a substantial amount of information. Having this information before you buy obviously can be very helpful. However, assuming you have gotten yourself in a bind already, how can you use the Truth in Lending Law?

The answer is that this law provides quite severe penalties in the event that the required information is not disclosed. As a general rule, the penalty is twice the finance charge (to a maximum of one thousand dollars) *plus attorney's fees*. There is a minimum penalty of one hundred dollars. You will remember that when Cheryl Meyers bought the Dodge from Clearview and received financing from Chrysler, the credit-cost disclosure statement did not separately itemize the cost of "tag, title and fees." You now realize that this cost should have been itemized and that the failure to do so was a violation of the Truth in Lending Law. Even though the violation was relatively minor, the court awarded damages of one thousand dollars plus attorney's fees of three thousand dollars.

The law also provides for class actions. Thus, if a business has systematically violated the law, all the people adversely affected may join together to sue. If this is done the business may be liable for one hundred thousand dollars in damages or 1 percent of the net worth of the business, whichever amount is less.

If you have entered into a credit purchase in which you were not provided with the required information, in writing, the seller (or financing company) probably violated the law. All you need do is check your copies of the documents you signed to see if the required information is present. If you have any doubts, you may want to consult with a Regional Office of the Federal Trade Commission (see Appendix F). Someone there will go over the contract with you and point out whether the seller (or finance company) has violated the law.

Opening volleys

Other than a polite complaint letter, there are no particular opening volleys recommended.

Launching a super threat

Soft spot. Clearly, the punitive damages of twice the finance charge opens up an ideal soft spot. However, we believe the credibility of the super threat derives from the possibility of collecting attorney's fees. Any business knows that if a court is directed by the law to order attorney's fees, a consumer will have no problem finding an attorney to follow through on the threat. In addition, attorney's fees can be high.

"In the Matter of." Insert a description of the transaction using, for example, the purchase-order number.

Heading. Insert the name of the owner of the business, the name of the business, and its address.

"Notice of ..." This language remains constant.

NOTICE OF VIOLATION OF 15 USC SEC. 1601 et seq.

PLEASE TAKE NOTICE: Pursuant to *Meyers* v. *Clearview Dodge Sales, Inc.,* 384 F. Supp. 722 (E.D. La. 1974), you are in violation of the Truth in Lending Law. You are now on NOTICE of this violation.

"Statement of Complaint." Indicate exactly why you believe the business has violated the law. Use the information you learned in the preceding discussion to describe exactly what the business is required by law to do. Then indicate what it did. For example, you were told that in order to purchase on time you must have insurance. You look at your purchase contract now and discover that the cost of insurance is not listed as part of the finance charge. You might then include the following in your statement of complaint: "Since the cost of insurance was required in order to secure financing, this cost should have been part of the finance charge. Failure to include this charge artificially reduced the annual percentage rate in violation of the law."

"Demand for Action." We will not advise you on what

to demand. You know what the law provides. Obviously, the more you demand, the less likelihood there is that the super threat will work. If you really feel you have an airtight case, you may want to go for double the finance charge. If you have some doubts, you may settle for better credit terms. Remember, though, that you are not entitled to attorney's fees if you lose in court.

"*Ultimatum.*" This is standard language.

ULTIMATUM

In the event you fail to perform the above demand within the time period specified, you will be deemed to have violated 15 United States Code Sec. 1601 et seq. You may be subjected to a penalty as provided by said law. Further, attorney's fees may be assessed against you pursuant to Regulation Z. (See Section 130, Truth in Lending Act.)

Correcting Billing Errors

The virtue of charge cards and charge accounts is that you don't have to carry cash with you. The drawback is that you get bills. While bills per se are not an overwhelming problem, whenever there are bills an erroneous bill can't be too far away. And as anyone who has ever tried to resolve a billing dispute with a hard-nosed billing department or a cold-nosed computer can tell you, few other problems can be quite as frustrating, aggravating, painful, or, in many cases, hopeless.

The types of billing disputes which commonly arise are numerous. Sometimes a department store charges for an item that you returned; a charge appears for something that you never bought; there's a computation error; a bill is sent to a wrong address; there's a late-payment charge when you paid on time; there's a failure to credit your payment at all; you're billed twice for the same item; you're billed for an item which is not identified on the bill; you buy something, pay for it, return it, and receive no credit. You name the problem and it can occur.

If you refuse to pay a bill, you may receive threats that your credit rating will be affected; that legal action will be instituted; and, in general, that you'd better pay or else! How, then, can you get "them" to listen?

The answer lies in the Fair Credit Billing Law. This recent federal law provides a billing-dispute resolution procedure, which must be followed by every business which uses credit or charge cards, or charge accounts for which a financing charge can be applied. Note that if you have any kind of card used to charge purchases, the law applies even if no finance charge is levied.

You may wonder whether this law has enough teeth in it to stop a computer in its tracks. We think it does, at least if you know how to use it. If you do, you will either get the dispute resolved or get enough money so you won't care about the dispute any more.

If you charge a purchase on a charge card, or on a charge account which uses no card but does charge interest (a finance charge) for payments, you are covered by the law. If you receive a bill which you believe is erroneous, you have sixty days in which to assert your rights under the law.

The law requires that within sixty days of receipt by you of the disputed bill the company which sent the bill must receive written notification from you contesting the bill. Note that your letter must be *received* within sixty days, so it's a good idea to send it out well before the sixty-day period expires. In addition, the letter must contain certain information:

1. Your name and account number (if any) and any other information necessary in order for the seller to determine which transaction you are contesting.

2. A statement to the effect that you believe a billing error has occurred and how much the error is for.

3. The reasons why you believe there is an error to the extent that you know.

In addition, you have the right to request copies of any documents which show your indebtedness. Here is a sample letter:

Certified Letter No. 12345678

February 14, 1977

Your name
Mailing address
City, state, zip code

Seller's name
Mailing address
City, state, zip code

Re: Your bill #34346 dated
February 11, 1977, for
$45.56 for the purchase of
One pair of slacks

Dear Sir:

This request is being made pursuant to Section 226.14 of Regulation Z under the Fair Credit Billing Law.

On January 25, 1977, I purchased a pair of slacks in your store for the sum of $45.56. Upon arriving home, I determined that the slacks were defective. I returned to your store the following day, January 26, and returned the slacks. I was assured that I would be credited for the purchase, since I had made the purchase on my charge card issued by you. Despite this assurance, on February 11, 1977, you sent me a bill which included a charge of $45.56 for the slacks that I returned.

I believe that a billing error has occurred in that I was improperly billed for $45.56. Please delete this charge from my account.

Sincerely,

/s/ Your name

In this case no request for documentary evidence was made, because no evidence would have been useful. However, if some evidence is useful to clarify the problem, be sure to request a copy of it. For example, if you are billed by a credit-card company for a charge which you believe is too high, be sure to request a copy of the credit slip you signed when making the purchase. An appropriate sentence to add might be: "Please send me copies of documentary evidence of my indebtedness."

Within thirty days of receipt of your notification, the company must mail or deliver a notice to you acknowledging receipt of your letter. Within ninety days of receipt of your letter, the company must inform you of how it intends to resolve your complaint. If it can notify you within thirty days of how it intends to resolve the dispute, the letter acknowledging receipt of your letter may be dispensed with.

The letter informing you as to how the company proposes to resolve your dispute cannot be arbitrary. The company must make a "reasonable investigation" before rejecting your claim. In two situations you are entitled to be told exactly how the investigation determined that your claim was not valid: When you complain that you are being billed for merchandise never received, and when you are contesting the amount of a credit-card purchase.

Thus, within ninety days of receipt of your letter you must have received a letter which either accepts your argument, in which case your account must be promptly corrected; partially accepts your argument, in which case your account will be adjusted and you will be provided with an explanation as to why your complaint was not fully accepted; or rejects your complaint entirely, in which case you must be provided with an explanation as to why you are wrong.

Clearly, the Fair Credit Billing Law places quite a burden on businesses which rely on charge cards or charge accounts. You might be quite skeptical that any business will actually follow the law. However, if you write the kind of complaint letter shown earlier, the business will realize that you know what you are doing and should resolve your complaint promptly. In the event that you don't receive the explanation required by the law, you may need a super threat to get results.

Some of you may now be thinking: "A super threat is a fine idea, but meanwhile I still have the bill with a due date on it. If I don't pay the disputed charge on time I may have to pay a finance charge. Also, my failure to pay on time may result in a report to a credit agency that I'm a deadbeat!" The law anticipated these thoughts. So long as you follow the proper procedures, you will be protected in the following ways:

Finance charge. During the period while you are contesting your bill, you cannot be charged a finance fee for that bill. (You must, however, pay any uncontested portion of the bill.) After the company has sent you the required explanation following an investigation of your complaint, if you still owe any money you must be given your normal period of time to pay up without a finance charge.

Credit rating. Adverse information cannot be given to a credit company because you are contesting your bill under the law. Only if you refuse to pay *after* the company has properly investigated your complaint and notified you that an amount is still owing may an adverse report be forwarded to a credit agency. And while you can't stop the company from reporting your *continuing* refusal to pay, you can limit the effect of the report. Remember, if the company determines that you do owe money on the disputed charge, you must be given your normal period of time to pay up and no credit report may be made. If instead of paying up you send a letter still refusing to pay because you contest the bill, then the company must do the following:

1. If the company reports your case to a credit agency, it must also report that you are contesting the bill.

2. Additionally, you must be provided with the name and address of every person and company who received the credit report.

Thus, if you carefully follow the required procedures your credit rating should remain intact.

Now let's get back to the super threat. What should you do if you follow the rules to contest a bill but the other side doesn't? The Fair Credit Billing Law provides some stiff penalties for the other side. First, if the company fails to follow the rules, it forfeits the right to collect the disputed charge (up to fifty dollars). In addition, the company may be liable for a penalty of up to one thousand dollars plus any attorney's fees which you might have to pay in order to enforce your rights. Finally, you are entitled to any actual damages which you might suffer as a result of the company's failure to follow the law. Obviously, with a remedy such as this you might want to retain an attorney to handle your case. However, if you want to try a super threat first, we suggest the following approach.

Opening volleys

Remember, under the law you must first notify the company that you dispute its bill. After sending such notification, sending a polite complaint letter will not be of much help. Therefore, you should move right to a super threat.

Launching a super threat

Soft spot. The statutory penalty of up to one thousand dollars plus your attorney's fees is a substantial sanction. Of particular significance is the provision for attorney's fees. If you have a good case, the company will know that you will have no problem finding an attorney to handle your case. You may not have much money to pay an attorney, but the business you sue does. Thus, your threat of bringing legal action is highly credible.

"In the Matter of." Insert a description of the transaction using, for example, the purchase-order number.

Heading. Insert the name of the owner of the business (if you know it), the name of the business, and its address.

"Notice of Violation of 15 USC Sec. 1601 et seq." This language remains the same for all such super threats.

NOTICE OF VIOLATION OF 15 USC Sec. 1601 et seq.

PLEASE TAKE NOTICE: Pursuant to 12 Code of Federal Regulations Section 226.14, you are in violation of the Fair Credit Billing Law.

"Statement of Complaint." Insert an explanation of exactly why you believe the business has violated the law. If you feel your preliminary complaint letter satisfactorily de-

scribes your complaint, you need only enclose a copy. In such a case, you would include a reference to the attached letter, which might read: "The basis of your violation is contained in my letter of [insert the date of the letter] to you, a copy of which is attached and incorporated herein by reference."

"*Demand for Action.*" Here you will insert your demand for resolution of your billing dispute. While the law provides for substantial damages in the event that a business fails to properly resolve a dispute, you would be ill advised to demand these damages in the super threat. Chances are great that the company will prefer to fight it out with you in court; after all, what has it got to lose? Rather, we suggest that you demand a resolution of your dispute. If the company still doesn't respond, then you can follow through on your super threat and retain an attorney.

"*Ultimatum.*" As pointed out in the preceding discussion, a company which fails to follow the billing-dispute resolution procedure is liable for up to one thousand dollars in damages, forfeiture of the amount in dispute (up to fifty dollars), and attorney's fees if you bring a legal action and win. While the damages can be high, the prospect of having to pay your attorney's fees hits an especially soft spot. Attorney's fees can be high. Most businesses correctly believe that a consumer will not pay three or four thousand dollars to an attorney just to recover a few hundred dollars in damages. However, under this law, if you win the case the business has to pay your attorney. This means that your threat to sue is highly credible.

ULTIMATUM

In the event you fail to perform the above demand within the time period specified, you may be deemed to have violated 15 USC Sec. 1601 et seq. You may be subjected to a penalty as provided by law. Further, attorney's fees may be assessed against you pursuant to Regulation Z (see Section 130, Truth in Lending Law).

Fighting Bill Collectors

Throughout this book we are examining different ways to exert your rights through the super threat. However, when you're up against a bill collector you are face to face with the master of the threat. Indeed, he makes his living threatening people: Pay up or else. The more people who pay up, the more money he makes. Is it any wonder that the bill collector frequently doesn't care whether you owe any money or not? After all, there's no money to be made by a bill collector if there's no bill to collect.

The outrageous techniques used by many bill collectors would be laughable if they were not so effective. For, unlike a super threat, the bill collector's letter need have no relationship to reality. Many will aim as low as necessary in order to get results. Consider these typical letters, actually sent out by the GC Service Corporation of Houston, Texas:

Does your child know that the books from Doubleday Book Club are not paid for? Is it fair for your child to be embarrassed at school when you are legally responsible for the bill? $9.20 is a small amount. Pay it now to avoid further contact. It will be humiliating for your child when our collector calls. You owe the $9.20 to Doubleday Book Club. Your child does not.

"You" ordered the merchandise from 69 Grolier Annual, Lawrence Bauer.
"You" ran up the bill, Lawrence Bauer.
"You" owe the money, Lawrence Bauer.
"You" are going to pay this bill, Lawrence Bauer.
"You" are going to send us full payment today.
"We" are going to see that you do.

Where is the money Pete Rodriquez? We want the $5.66 now! No more chances Pete Rodriquez, this is it. Your time is up. Either you pay now or our collector will get every last cent.

The approach being used by the GC Service Corporation could be described as the "street talk" collection letter. Surely, any letter which states that "Your time is up" or "Where is the money Pete Rodriquez?" belongs in a script for a grade-B crime movie. But, just as grade-B movies make money, so do these letters.

Another technique used by bill collectors might be called the "judge-jury-and-executioner" approach. Consider this actual letter sent out by a bill-collection company:

Final—72 hour—notice. We wish to put you on notice that your payment of this claim must be received by the creditor at once. You are further notified legal proceedings by the creditor following judgment may compel you to bring all financial records to court for examination. A writ of execution may be issued and may be satisfied by a levy on your automobile or other personal property, real estate, bank accounts, chattels, goods and accounts receivable. A public auction of the aforementioned property may be held after public advertisement of same and usual sales process is conducted by sheriff. Court costs, sheriff fees, judgments, and all other expenses relative to these proceedings may be assessed against the debtor. Litigation is expensive. Remit payment direct to creditor now to avoid these costs. . . .

If you received this kind of a letter, you might want to check outside to see if an auction of your property was already underway.

Still another type of debt-collection letter might be called the "oh-boy-are-you-in-trouble" letter. It's a combination of the other two types, a sort of street-talk-plus-judge-jury-and-executioner approach. Here's one that the Trans-American Collection Agency used:

IF YOU ARE SUED on a debt and the Court gives judgment against you, you are in SERIOUS TROUBLE. AN EXECUTION CAN BE ISSUED AGAINST YOU! Then an Officer of the Court may seize your goods, attach your wages, bank account or other property. He may also be instructed to bring YOU and YOUR FAMILY into Court and force you and them to tell UNDER OATH what property you own. This will be EXPENSIVE and EMBARRASSING to you. In addition, A JUDGMENT hanging over your head will cost you many times the amount of the debt, in loss of credit and respect in your community. IT'S IMPOSSIBLE TO ESCAPE A JUDGMENT.

Terms such as "execution" and claims such as "It's impossible to escape" and "A Judgment hanging over your head" imply that the last rites should be administered as soon as possible.

These letters are almost funny, but not quite. Some other techniques used by bill collectors are not funny at all; they are absolutely frightening. In one case a bill collector regularly called the mother of a debtor, stating, "You're a damn liar. I know damn good and well you know where [your son] is, and you are either going to get him to pay this debt to Zale Jewelry or I am going to make you pay for it."

Frequently debt collectors threaten debtors with criminal prosecution. In one Florida case the debt collector "visited [the alleged debtor's] residence and informed her that she was committing a crime by failing to return the automobile and that a police pick-up order had been issued for her and the automobile." In this case the debtor got so upset that she took an overdose of tranquilizers and was hospitalized.

What can you do about these tactics? Since not all bill collectors are irresponsible, you may be able to resolve any dispute with a clarifying letter explaining why you don't owe the debt. However, if this does not work you're going to have to go one better than the bill collector; you'll need a super threat.

There are two approaches which will slow a bill collector down. The first relies on the legal concept of *intentional infliction of mental distress*. Under this theory, a bill collector may be liable for damages if his tactics produce mental distress to the debtor. Whether or not a debt is actually owed is irrelevant. The second approach which a super threat can use relies on the Federal Trade Commission, which has decided that certain collection practices violate the law.

Let's take a closer look at the first super-threat approach. Remember the woman who, after being told that the police were going to pick her up along with her automobile if she did not do what the collector wanted, took an overdose of tranquilizers and was hospitalized? She went to court and accused the automobile dealer who was trying to repossess the car of intentional infliction of mental distress.

The court, in the case of *Abraham Used Car Company* v. *Silva*, decided that the automobile dealer had overstepped permissible bounds. A jury awarded compensatory damages of five thousand dollars and punitive damages (sting money) of thirty-five thousand dollars.

The debtor's mother who was bothered by offensive telephone calls went to court. In that case, *Lyons* v. *Zale Jewelry Company*, the court reviewed the applicable law: "The general rule is that a creditor has a right to urge payment of a just debt.... However, many courts have held that improper methods used to collect a debt may be the basis for the maintenance of an action for a mental or emotional disturbance produced thereby.... When the creditor's agents become vindictive and abusive in their collection efforts and resort to insulting and humiliating language, whether verbally or by letter, the courts have, in many instances, held that the creditor may be obliged to respond in damages for injuries caused to the debtor thereby." Thus, any bill collector who uses threatening language does so at his own risk.

What about the sample collection letters given at the beginning of this discussion? Are those letters, which threaten legal action, permissible? The answer is that there is nothing wrong with threatening legal action so long as you actually intend to sue if necessary. As a practical matter, few if any collection agencies bother to sue on small debts. Thus, claims that they will sue are simply false.

In the case of each of the examples of letters that collection agencies have sent out, the Federal Trade Commission decided that the letters constituted a deceptive trade practice. The FTC's reasons were twofold. First, the techniques used "cause embarrassment and harassment of alleged debtors [which] is contrary to the established public policies of the United States and is an unfair practice." Second, in most cases the statements made in the letter were false.

Let's take a look at one of these cases in a little more detail. Remember the letter which indicated that it was a "Final—72 hour—notice"? This letter promised that if you didn't pay right away a "writ of execution" would be issued, and the sheriff would sell everything you own. In fact, the company which sent out the letter did not, and could not, institute any legal action. It was only a mailing house which sent form letters and lent its name, Trans-American Collections, Inc., to the letterhead. Any statement to the effect that it intended to bring a legal action was a bald-faced lie.

Under recent amendments to the Federal Trade Commission Act, the Federal Trade Commission has sought to inform bill-collection companies of certain activities which constitute unfair or deceptive trade practices. A debt-collection company which has prior notice that certain activities are illegal and which nonetheless continues those activities may be liable for a fine of ten thousand dollars. This is the notice which the FTC has sent out:

>The Federal Trade Commission has determined that the following acts or practices used in the collection of debts are unfair or deceptive and are unlawful under Section 5(a)(1) of the Federal Trade Commission Act.
>   —It is an unfair or deceptive trade practice for a creditor to misrepresent his identity to the debtor or use a fictitious or misleading identity when he is seeking to collect a debt directly.
>   —It is an unfair or deceptive trade practice for a creditor to threaten to institute legal proceedings against a debtor when there is in fact no intent to actually initiate such proceedings.
>   —It is an unfair or deceptive trade practice for a creditor to represent that a debtor's credit rating will be adversely

affected, or that his name will be given to a credit-reporting agency, when such is not the case.

—It is an unfair or deceptive trade practice for a creditor to create a false impression that he has governmental or other legal authority to collect a debt.

—It is an unfair or deceptive trade practice to misrepresent the purpose of an inquiry directed at the debtor or at a third party in order to secure information concerning a debtor such as his whereabouts, assets or employment status.

Thus, any debt-collection company which uses the objectionable techniques we saw at the beginning of this section may be liable for a fine of up to ten thousand dollars for each violation. Under Section 205 of the Federal Trade Commission Improvement Act, the debt-collection company, in order to be held liable, must have had notice that its activities constitute a deceptive or unfair trade practice. We will use our super threat to provide that notice.

We have, therefore, two theories with which to draft a super threat: intentional infliction of mental distress and the damages recoverable for it in a court action; and liability of ten thousand dollars per violation to the FTC for committing an act after having received notice that the act constitutes a deceptive or unfair trade practice. Since debt-collection companies are masters of the threat, we will need the strongest super threat possible. We will, therefore, use both theories in our letter.

Opening volley

Some debt-collectors don't waste time trying to collect debts which are not actually owed. Therefore, a polite complaint letter informing the debt collector that you do not owe the debt is certainly in order. If that doesn't stop the threats, it's definitely time to launch your own super threat.

Launching a super threat

Many debt-collection agencies do little more than mail out form letters containing a series of escalating threats. In order to penetrate such a business, you should be sure to remember to send your super threat by certified mail.

Soft spot. Debt-collection agencies make money by spending a little bit of time and trouble trying to collect very many debts. The agencies keep only a small percentage of the actual amounts collected. They cannot afford to spend much time on any one debt. They also cannot afford to run the risk of losing a large sum of money in the attempt to get a small portion of one collectible debt. Consequently, their soft spot has two tender parts. The first is the prospect of spending a lot of time to collect one debt. The second is the possibility of losing a lot of money in order to make a little money. Our super threat utilizes both soft spots. The mere fact that you understand the law will show that you are potentially time-consuming trouble. In addition, the possibility of being assessed damages under Section 205 of the Federal Trade Commission Improvement Act or under a tort theory should convince the agency that you are more trouble than your debt is worth.

"In the Matter of." Insert sufficient information to identify the debt that they claim you owe. Debt collectors like to assign case numbers, because it looks official. If you have such a number, use it in your caption.

Heading. Insert the name and address of the debt-collection agency. If you happen to know the name of the person running the agency, put that name above the name of the business.

"Notice of..." We are using two notices. One informs the debt collector of his liability under the Federal Trade Commission Improvement Act. The other tells him that his conduct may expose him to liability under a tort theory.

NOTICE OF VIOLATION UNDER SECTION 205

AND

NOTICE OF TORTIOUS CONDUCT

PLEASE TAKE NOTICE: Pursuant to Section 205 of the Federal Trade Commission Improvement Act, you are committing an unfair and deceptive trade practice under Section 5(a)(1) of the Federal Trade Commission Act. Said practice is unlawful under *Wilson Chemical Co., Inc. et al.*, Docket 8474 (January 14, 1964), and subsequent cases. This letter constitutes formal notice under Section 205.

PLEASE TAKE FURTHER NOTICE: Your practices constitute tortious conduct through the intentional infliction of mental distress. Pursuant to *Wiggins v. Moskins Credit Clothing Store*, 137 F. Supp 764 (E.D. S.C. 1956), such conduct subjects you to damage liability. You are now on notice of such liability.

"*Statement of Complaint.*" Insert the facts of your case. Pay particular attention to describing what the bill collector is doing. For example, if you are receiving phone calls at night, put this in the statement. Remember, the gist of your complaint is the tactics being used by the bill collector. You are not disputing the bill. Disputes about the bill should be directed to the person who billed you in the first place.

"*Demand for Action.*" Insert your demands as precisely as you can. Do not say, "Don't bother me any more." Rather, demand that you not be called at night, not have letters sent to your employer, or whatever. Be as specific as possible. Also, indicate that this demand must be met "forthwith." For example, you might begin your demand with "Forthwith discontinue the activities described above."

"*Ultimatum.*" This language will remain constant for all such super threats.

ULTIMATUM

In the event that you fail to accept the above demands, a petition will be filed with the Regional Office of the Federal Trade Commission seeking the maximum penalty of $10,000 for violation of Section 205. Further, a class-action investigation may be authorized to determine whether your practices have subjected others to similar damages. A class action may then be instituted.

Further, legal counsel may be retained to commence an action for your tortious conduct. Such action may result in substantial damages. See *Abraham Used Car Co. v. Silva*, 208 So.2d 500 (1968) ($35,000 award); see also "Torts—Emotional Disturbance," 64 A.L.R.2d 100, 119.

If your super threat does not get action, you may send a polite complaint letter to your Federal Trade Commission Regional Office (see Appendix F).

13

Up Against the Internal Revenue Service

"April is the cruellest month," wrote the poet T. S. Eliot, and every American taxpayer would certainly agree. Each April you sharpen your pencils and fence with the year's most inscrutable crossword puzzle: the Form 1040 Income Tax Return. As if this workout were not aggravating enough, you may also wind up as one of two million or so taxpayers whose returns are audited by the IRS. If you receive a letter from the IRS that begins, "We are examining your federal income tax return and find that we need additional information to verify your correct tax," you'll know that you're one of the unlucky two million. Brace yourself: The IRS wants more money.

How can you fight the Tax Man when he claims that you owe more income tax than you've paid? There are basically two paths to take, and you can pursue either or both, depending largely on your stamina and the amount of time you can devote to the battle. The first path leads through IRS-land, with several stops along the way. The second path takes you out of enemy territory and onto neutral ground.

Choosing this second path affords you the opportunity for—believe it or not—a super threat against the IRS.

The first path is the auditing process, conducted by IRS personnel, usually at various IRS offices. There may be as many as four stops along this path. Ordinarily, the first one occurs at an IRS office in the IRS district where you filed your return. (You can request that this initial meeting be transferred to another, more convenient location if, for example, your residence has changed or your books and records are kept in a different IRS district.)

An IRS auditor will examine your tax return with you to determine whether any adjustment (a euphemism for "increase") should be made in your tax liability. You will have been notified in advance regarding any records that you should bring with you in order to substantiate or clarify any disputed items on your return. If you wish, you can be accompanied by an attorney, a certified public accountant, the person who prepared your return, or any other individual entitled to practice before the IRS. In fact, you can authorize any one of these persons to appear on your behalf if you prefer not to attend the examination yourself.

At the end of the examination the auditor will explain to you (or your representative) any change he may propose to adjust your tax liability. Don't let yourself be railroaded into signing an agreement with the auditor. If you disagree with his proposals and believe that the tax you originally computed (or some other in-between figure) is justified, psych yourself up for stop number two in IRS-land. Ask to see the auditor's supervisor, and restate your position to the supervisor. Maybe the supervisor will prove more receptive to your argument.

If no agreement is reached at your meeting with the supervisor, the IRS will be sending you a so-called thirty-day letter. It will contain a copy of the IRS examination report, explaining proposed adjustments to your tax liability, and instructions regarding your further appeal rights, which must be exercised within thirty days.

Should you choose to take full advantage of your appeal rights, you'll wind up making stops three and four in IRS-land. Stop three is the district conference, which will be held at the office of the IRS District Director. There, you or your representative can dispute the findings in the IRS examination report. If no satisfactory agreement can be hammered out at the district conference, you can opt for the last stop in IRS-land: the appellate-division conference. It will be conducted at the office of the IRS Regional Commissioner.

Suppose you don't receive what you consider to be a sympathetic hearing at any of the four stops in IRS-land— not an entirely unlikely prospect, since you are, after all, bearding the lion in its den. Or suppose the very idea of making all four stops strikes you as more trouble than it's worth. At any point along the route, you can take a detour out of IRS-land into neutral territory.

This second path will lead you into the United States Tax Court, where you will sue the Internal Revenue Service. That's right: You versus the IRS. Don't panic. The whole process is much simpler than you might suspect, and it can yield surprisingly favorable results.

To begin with, the United States Tax Court is not connected in any way with the IRS. It's a wholly independent judicial tribunal, which decides whether tax deficiencies claimed by the IRS are correct. The court has a special *small-tax-case procedure* for taxpayers who are disputing relatively small tax claims made by the IRS. To be precise, you can bring a small-tax case against the IRS whenever the sum of taxes demanded from you is *$1,500 or less for any one tax year*. If the IRS demands more than $1,500 for any one tax year, you can still resort to the small-tax procedure so long as the part of the IRS demand that you're contesting is $1,500 or less. (The overwhelming majority of taxpayers audited by the IRS are eligible to invoke the small-tax case procedure, because usually no more than $1,500 is in dispute.)

Four aspects of the small-tax-case procedure make it particularly appealing. First, the United States Tax Court is an impartial forum, with no ax to grind. Second, it will cost you only a ten-dollar filing fee to have your day in court with the Tax Man. Third, you don't have to travel to Washington, D.C., to have your case heard. Small-tax cases can be tried in any one of over a hundred cities across the country. (A list of these cities appears in Appendix G.) As you will learn shortly, you can select the place for your trial when you file your case.

Finally, small-tax proceedings are conducted in an informal "people's court"–type atmosphere. *You do not need a lawyer to represent you.* Most taxpayers represent themselves. There are no tricky rules of evidence to foul you up. Any evidence you offer will be admitted by the judge if he believes that it will help to prove your side of the case. For example, if you have various receipts or canceled checks or other documents which support the amount of tax you reported, rather than the amount claimed by the IRS, bring these papers to court with you. (If the originals have been lost, bring whatever copies you may have.)

The tax-court judge will even assist you in presenting the facts through your own testimony and that of other witnesses. After you and any other witnesses have testified, you can argue your case orally, in writing, or both. (Any written argument you wish to make should be filed soon after the trial, so as not to delay the judge's decision.)

You should be aware that the judge's decision in your case is *final*—it cannot be appealed. Thus, if the judge decides that the tax deficiency claimed by the IRS is correct— in whole or in part—you will have no recourse to a higher court. On the other hand, if the decision goes in your favor—

that is, the IRS is not entitled to the tax it had claimed—the IRS can't appeal. You will have defeated the United States Government.

To be candid, your chances of total victory are slim. Of all the small-tax cases tried and decided in fiscal years 1975 and 1976, the IRS won over 60 percent. Only about 11 percent were won each year by taxpayers. The remainder—about 27 percent per year—resulted in split decisions, partly in favor of the taxpayer and partly in favor of the IRS.

Don't be discouraged by the odds against you, because they fail to reflect one of the most important byproducts of the small-tax-case procedure: namely, *out-of-court settlements*. The chances are better than fifty–fifty that your case will never actually get to trial, because the IRS will offer you an out-of-court settlement that you'll find acceptable. In fiscal year 1976, 2,310 out of 3,422 small-tax cases were settled this way, with the IRS accepting about 57 cents on every dollar originally claimed in tax deficiencies. During the preceding fiscal year, 1,970 cases out of 3,203 were settled, with the IRS collecting only 54 cents on the dollar.

So you can see how invoking the small-tax-case procedure may yield unexpected benefits. Let's run through the steps that will position you for launching a super threat against the IRS.

Preliminary skirmishes

These will be fought along the path through IRS-land at any one or more of the four stops that we've already visited.

Opening volleys

Whenever you want to bypass any of the stops in IRS-land and go directly to tax court, simply ask the IRS to issue you a ninety-day letter, known in legalese as a *statutory notice of deficiency*. Issuance of a ninety-day letter is a necessary prerequisite for suing the IRS in tax court. The ninety-day letter will indicate the tax year in question and the amount of the tax deficiency for that year which the Commissioner of Internal Revenue has determined that you owe. The letter will tell you that the deficiency will be assessed against you after ninety days from the date of mailing the letter, unless within that period you file a petition with the United States Tax Court—which is exactly what you're going to do. That petition is your super threat.

Launching a super threat

As you can no doubt guess, the super threat differs from the others we've seen so far. It is not a "notice," which threatens to take some action unless an ultimatum is met. It is, instead, an official legal petition, which actually initiates a judicial proceeding.

Soft spot. If you're fully tuned in to the strategy behind a super threat, you may well be puzzled at this point. Once a taxpayer actually goes ahead and initiates a small-tax case, what leverage does he have against the IRS? It's not as if potential legal action were being threatened, in which case the IRS might still have something it wished to avoid. Here, the action has already been taken; the damage has been done, so to speak. In what way, therefore, is the IRS threatened? Where's the soft spot?

Time is the soft spot. With no offense intended, let us assure you that your small-tax case represents a royal waste of time to the IRS. A $1,500 (or less) dispute may be a big deal to you, but it's small potatoes to the IRS. The Feds would prefer to maximize their returns by concentrating their efforts on fat cats. They don't want to waste a staff attorney's valuable time in matching wits with you in a small-tax trial. That is precisely the sort of unwanted drain on legal talent which your petition poses. And it is only because you have actually filed a petition, rather than merely threatening possible legal action, that the IRS will know it must either waste time with you in court or settle with you out of court.

Filing the petition. Here's where you get a chance not only to sound like a lawyer but to act like one. Don't panic. The United States Tax Court has a straightforward fill-in-the-blanks petition for taxpayers who are suing the IRS. Simply write to:

>Clerk of the Court
>United States Tax Court
>400 Second Street, N.W.
>Washington, D.C. 20217

Ask for the forms and instructions necessary to file a petition with the United States Tax Court in a small-tax case. The instructions that the clerk will include with your petition will tell you exactly how to fill it out. (A copy of the current form petition appears on the next page.)

Once you have filled out the petition, you "file" it simply by mailing it back to the tax court at the address given above. *You must file the petition no later than ninety days after the IRS's ninety-day letter was mailed to you.* (The date shown on the ninety-day letter itself is the date on which the letter was mailed to you.) In order for your petition to be filed before the deadline, the petition must actually be received by the tax court within the ninety-day period or in an envelope properly addressed to the court and bearing a United States postmark showing a legible date that falls within the ninety-day period. *If your petition is even one day late, the tax court will dismiss your case for late filing.* So plan ahead and mail early.

When you mail in your petition, be sure to enclose three other items: a copy of your ninety-day letter; a check or money order in the amount of ten dollars, made payable

UNITED STATES TAX COURT

_____)
                      Petitioner(s))
        v.   )   Docket No.
)
COMMISSIONER OF INTERNAL REVENUE)
                    Respondent)

PETITION

1. Petitioner(s) request(s) the Court to redetermine the tax deficiency(ies) for the year(s) _____, as set forth in the notice of deficiency dated _____, A COPY OF WHICH IS ATTACHED. The notice was issued by the Office of the Internal Revenue Service at

_____
(CITY AND STATE)

2. Petitioner(s) taxpayer identification (e.g. social security) number(s) is (are) _____.

3. Petitioner(s) make(s) the following claims as to his tax liability:

Year	Amount of Deficiency Disputed	Amount of Addition to Tax, if any, Disputed	Amount of Overpayment Claimed
_____	_____	_____	_____
_____	_____	_____	_____
_____	_____	_____	_____

4. Set forth those adjustments, i.e. changes, in the notice of deficiency with which you disagree and why you disagree.

_____
_____
_____
_____
_____
_____
_____
_____

Petitioner(s) request(s) that the proceedings in this case be conducted as a "small tax case" under section 7463 of the Internal Revenue Code of 1954, as amended, and Rule 172 of the Rules of Practice of the United States Tax Court. *(See page 8 of the enclosed booklet.) A decision in a "small tax case" is final and cannot be appealed by either party.

_____	_____
SIGNATURE OF PETITIONER (HUSBAND)	PRESENT ADDRESS
_____	_____
SIGNATURE OF PETITIONER (WIFE)	PRESENT ADDRESS

_____
SIGNATURE AND ADDRESS OF COUNSEL, IF RETAINED BY PETITIONER(S)

*If you do not want to make this request, you should place an "X" in the following box. ☐

to "Clerk, United States Court"; and a "Request for Place of Trial." The last item is a simple request form, which the clerk will have sent to you along with your petition and instructions. Consult Appendix G and select the city nearest to you where you would like your trial held, then record this city on the request form. Be sure to make copies of all papers that you send to the tax court and keep them for your records.

The tax court will send a copy of your petition to an IRS lawyer, who will file an answer with the court. A copy of that answer will be sent to you. Then a trial date will be set; you will be notified about it by the court at least sixty days in advance of the trial.

As we already stated, the trial may never take place. At almost any time after your petition has been forwarded to the IRS, you may be offered a settlement. That offer may not come until the last minute—for example, outside the courtroom itself on the day of your trial. If no offer, or only an unacceptable one, is forthcoming, then you will proceed with the trial and hope for total or at least partial victory. One thing's for certain: Win, lose, or draw, you're bound to feel vindicated, simply because you stood up to the Tax Man and had your day in court. That sense of gratification alone is worth the ten-dollar filing fee.

14

Collecting on an Insurance Policy

For most prudent Americans, especially those with family responsibilities, insurance is a necessity for daily living. We insure our cars, our houses, our health, our lives. Through insurance we hope to secure ourselves against loss and assure our peace of mind in time of catastrophe. Indeed, the regular payment of premiums, as painful as it can be, offers some consolation as an investment in a safer, more stable future. Everything goes smoothly until the risk insured against occurs: Your apartment is burglarized; your home burns down; your spouse dies; you're disabled in an accident. Then you're transformed from a premium-paying policyholder into a claimant demanding benefits. You will rapidly discover how good or bad your insurance really is.

Probably the only thing tougher than reading an insurance policy is trying to collect on one. Insurance companies are in business primarily to take in premiums, not to pay out on claims. The former activity is pursued with computerlike determination, backed up by the persuasive sanction that your policy may be canceled, or, its coverage limited, if your premiums are not paid on time and in full. When it comes to honoring the terms of a policy, however, many insurance companies play ping-pong, batting you back and forth between the home office and the local claims office, while you're required to complete and file extensive questionnaires and proof-of-loss forms. Delay, skepticism, and outright resistance will often characterize your insurer's reaction to your claim. Don't forget—insurers never do—that your claim represents a potential drain on company profits.

Hard-nosed business tactics and harassment on the part of insurance companies are held in dim view by the courts. Legally speaking, insurers stand in a special relationship with persons whom they insure. The insurance business affects the public interest and offers services of a quasi-public nature. Therefore, in the eyes of the law policyholders and claimants are entitled to fair and aboveboard treatment —let alone treatment that is neither oppressive nor outrageous. "To some extent," one California judge has written, "the special relationship and duties of the insurer exist in recognition of the fact that the insured does not contract '... to obtain a commercial advantage but to protect [himself] against the risks of accidental losses. Among the considerations in purchasing ... insurance, as insurers are well aware, is the peace of mind and security it will provide in the event of an accidental loss. . . .' "

When insurers intentionally or recklessly disrupt a claimant's peace of mind, they open themselves up to extremely costly lawsuits. Thanks to a recent trend in court cases, there is a potent source for a super threat, should one become necessary while you're wrangling with an insurer over a claim. In a number of lawsuits against insurers, claimants have won substantial jury verdicts for punitive damages. (Shortly, you'll see how one claimant was awarded $180,000 in punitive damages.)

When an insurance company is the defendant, it may be found guilty of intentionally or wantonly disregarding the rights of a claimant. Such misconduct can take many forms. For example, the insurer "stonewalls"—that is, flatly denies any liability on its policy with you, even though that policy has, by its own terms, become incontestable or beyond dispute. Instead of completely denying liability, the insurer may make you a chintzy take-it-or-leave-it offer, one that bears no reasonable relationship to the facts presented in your claim. Another form of insurance-company misconduct consists of the persistent use of highhanded pressure tactics to make you settle for less than you deserve. (The claimant who won $180,000 had been subjected to just this sort of foul play.)

An insurance company that plays dirty may be sued for *tortious breach of contract* and the *intentional infliction of emotional distress*. Translating this legalese into plain English: You have performed your part of the bargain with the insurer, by paying premiums. The insurer, however, has breached the terms of your policy, by refusing to honor a just claim. Taking advantage of its superior bargaining position, the insurer has willfully or recklessly imposed upon you at a particularly vulnerable time and as a result caused you not only economic deprivation but also emotional distress. It is for this oppressive conduct that the law allows the recovery of punitive damages. The operation of these general principles can be illustrated by a few recent court victories, which claimants won over their stubborn insurers.

In a 1970 Ohio case, *Kirk* v. *Safeco Insurance Company*, the Kirks had a "homeowner's policy" with Safeco. After their home was burglarized one night, the Kirks filed a claim for various stolen household effects and articles of clothing. The Kirks had done an unusually thorough job in ascertain-

COLLECTING ON AN INSURANCE POLICY   223

ing the amount of their losses and even determining replacement prices. They calculated liability on the policy at several thousand dollars. After supposedly negotiating with the Kirks through a local claims office, Safeco sent them a nasty letter offering a thousand dollars. This so-called offer had no reasonable basis whatsoever.

The Kirks sued Safeco for malicious breach of the insurance policy. Judge Williams found the value of the items stolen from the Kirks to be $4,450. He also ruled that Safeco's conduct indicated a lack of any intention to honor the Kirks' claims. Safeco's breach of the Kirks' insurance contract was willful, wanton, and malicious, so Judge Williams tacked on punitive damages ($1,550), together with attorney's fees ($2,000), for a total award to the Kirks of $8,000.

A life-insurance policy was contested in the 1975 Indiana case of *Rex Insurance Company* v. *Baldwin*. Rufus Baldwin had purchased a policy on his life from Rex Insurance, naming his wife, Myrtle, as beneficiary. The policy was purchased on July 20, 1970, and two years later it became incontestable—that is, according to the terms of the policy, Rex could not deny liability except for failure by the insured to pay premiums. On November 25, 1972, Rufus Baldwin died. At that time the policy was in full force and effect, all premiums had been paid, and the policy had been incontestable for over four months.

However, when the widow, Myrtle Baldwin, submitted proof of her husband's death to Rex and demanded payment of $1,000 (the full amount of the policy), Rex made no move to pay off. Even after Myrtle complained to the Indiana Insurance Commissioner, Rex persisted in denying any liability under the policy. Despite the fact that the policy had become incontestable, Rex claimed that it didn't have to pay, because Mr. Baldwin had allegedly not reported an existing illness on his application for life insurance. The premiums paid on the policy ($332.80) were returned by Rex to Myrtle Baldwin, and she was told to sue if she wanted to collect on the $1,000 value of the policy.

She did. The court awarded her the full amount of the policy, $1,000, plus punitive damages of $2,500. Given the fact that the policy had become incontestable, Rex's refusal to pay off, and its insistence that Myrtle sue, evidenced a heedless disregard for Myrtle's rights and her well-being.

One of the largest recoveries against an outrageously uncooperative insurance company came in the 1970 California case of *Fletcher* v. *Western National Life Insurance Company*. U. L. Fletcher was a married man and the father of eight children, seven of whom were in school. Fletcher worked as a scrap operator for a rubber company, performing heavy manual labor. In order to protect his family, Fletcher purchased a disability-insurance policy from Western National Life. This policy provided for monthly payments of $150 should Fletcher become totally disabled because of sickness or injury. In the event of disability caused by sickness, these payments were limited to a maximum period of two years, while thirty years was the maximum period in case of a disability due to injury.

In January, 1965, Fletcher had an accident at work while lifting a 361-pound bale of rubber. He injured his lower back and legs. The doctor's diagnosis was a herniated intervertebral disc with probable irritation of spinal nerves. Fletcher's physician placed him on disability, and Fletcher was fired by the rubber company.

Shortly after the accident, Fletcher filed proof of loss with Western National. The company began paying him $150 per month, but this was done under the sickness provision of the policy, rather than the injury provision, because the company knew that its liability would continue for only two years under the sickness provision, instead of thirty years under the injury provision. This difference in liability periods could have saved Western National as much as $50,000.

Apparently not satisfied with this cost-cutting maneuver, Western National wrote to Fletcher on August 25, 1966, accusing him of concealing the fact of a congenital back defect on his application for insurance: "We have just completed making an intensive investigation of your disability claim. We are quite surprised to find you had a congenital back ailment which was not disclosed in your application. ... We consider such information material, and quite frankly, would not have issued you an Accident and Sickness Policy had we been aware of your true medical condition. Consequently, we feel there is definite misrepresentation on your part in not informing us of this condition." This letter was written to Fletcher despite the complete absence of any investigation by Western into a possible congenital back defect, the complete absence of any facts indicating that Fletcher knew of any such condition, and in the face of Fletcher's own denial of any such congenital condition. Western's letter went on to demand that Fletcher *return* the $150 monthly benefits that he had already received (a total of $2,250), less the amount of the premiums he had paid on the policy. Payment of any further monthly benefits was terminated.

While poor Fletcher was still reeling from Western's inexplicable campaign against him, he received another letter from the company, on October 4, 1966. Western admitted having received Fletcher's denial of any knowledge of a preexisting back ailment, but nevertheless reasserted the accusation that Fletcher had made a material misrepresentation on his insurance application. In a magnanimous gesture, however, Western indicated a willingness "to make a compromise agreement" for the purpose of avoiding "further cost of litigation." Western proposed that Fletcher be allowed to retain the benefits already paid to him ($2,250), in return for the cancellation of his policy and the execution of a full release by him. "It is only fair to tell you," Western warned Fletcher, "that if we have to, we are willing to take whatever action necessary to have this policy cancelled. The action, however, is expensive to both parties and it is only for this reason we wish to effect a compromise settlement at this time."

Fletcher wisely consulted an attorney, who filed suit against Western National. The court found that Western's refusal to pay Fletcher's claim was malicious. The company had deliberately pressured Fletcher to either surrender his policy or enter into a disadvantageous "settlement" of a trumped-up dispute. Western never had any probable cause to believe that Fletcher had made misrepresentations on his application or that his injury was due to anything other than the January, 1965, accident.

Fletcher testified that he had been upset when Western accused him of misrepresentation. After his monthly benefits were discontinued, Fletcher and his family suffered economic hardship. The court ruled that Fletcher had been subjected to the kind of distress for which punitive damages can be awarded. "It is true," observed Judge Kaufman, "that plaintiff's testimony did not indicate that he suffered any traumatic emotional distress of the character of shock, horror, or nausea, but the requisite emotional distress may consist of any highly unpleasant mental reaction such as fright, grief, shame, humiliation, embarrassment, anger, chagrin, disappointment or worry." Fletcher won a judgment of $60,000 in compensatory damages, plus $180,000 in punitive damages. (Actually, the jury returned a verdict of $640,000 in punitive damages, but this was reduced by the trial judge to $180,000.)

The reasoning contained in *Fletcher* and the other cases we have discussed applies to any situation in which an insurer fails to properly pay a legitimate claim. The likelihood of substantial damage awards is increased, though, if the insurance coverage is for health-related problems. A sick or injured person is especially susceptible to emotional distress. So if a health-insurance company such as Blue Cross is giving you the runaround, the possibility of a large damage award is especially likely.

We will rely on the precedent set in the *Fletcher* case when we compose a super threat for recalcitrant insurers. But before resorting to extreme measures, let's review the escalating steps that lead to the super-threat launch pad.

Preliminary skirmishes

Regardless of whether your policy covers valuables, home, health, or life, psych yourself up for a fight as soon as you file a claim with your insurer. If the claim is settled promptly and to your satisfaction, consider yourself fortunate. But if your claim is disputed, or the size of it is questioned, or payment is stalled off for an unreasonable length of time, call or visit the agent who sold you the policy. Explain to the agent why the insurer's treatment of your claim is unjustified, and ask the agent to intervene on your behalf. The agent is licensed by the state; he or she should be aware that the State Commissioner of Insurance can investigate an agent who fails or refuses to assist customers with their grievances.

Opening volleys

If you are not satisfied with the agent's response, there are two polite complaint letters that you can write. The first will go to the company that issued your policy, and the second, if necessary, will go to the State Commissioner of Insurance in your state.

Address the first letter to the claims department at the home office or headquarters of your insurer. In general, this letter should follow the formula for any polite complaint letter. Considering the special nature of an insurance complaint, however, the letter should cover six basic points:

1. Give the number of your policy and any other appropriate identification, such as the type of policy.

2. Give the date on which you purchased the policy and the agent from whom you purchased it.

3. State your understanding that the policy was sold to you as one which covered the kind of loss on which your pending claim is based.

4. Explain briefly the unsatisfactory treatment of your claim that has given rise to your current complaint.

5. Request that your claim be paid by a specific date. (Pick a date within, say, the next ten to thirty days.)

6. Close by warning the company that if your claim has not been paid by the deadline, you intend to file a formal complaint with the State Commissioner of Insurance, alleging that the company engages in unfair practices and should not be authorized to do business in the state.

A polite-complaint form letter, which you can adapt to suit your particular purposes, follows:

Certified Letter No. 12345678

[Date of mailing here]

Name of insured
Mailing address
City, state, zip code

Claims Department
Name of insurance company
Home office address
City, state, zip code

Re: [Insert type or name of policy and policy number]

Dear Sirs:

I purchased the above-mentioned insurance policy from you on [insert date] through [insert name of agent or agency].

Based upon the representation made to me in connection with the purchase of this policy, it was my understanding and expectation that the policy would pay for [insert the particular accident, loss, or other occurrence for which you have filed a claim].

Unfortunately, I have been disappointed by your treatment of the claim that I filed under this policy on [insert date]. [Briefly describe the unsatisfactory treatment.] It is my understanding that insurance companies have a legal obligation to deal fairly with the public whom they serve. So far, you have not lived up to that trust.

I hereby request that my claim be paid in full by [insert specific date].

If my claim has not been paid in full by the date specified, I shall be compelled to plead my case before the State Commissioner of Insurance. I do not believe that insurance companies which persist in treating members of the public as unfairly as you have treated me should be authorized to continue doing business in this state.

Sincerely,
[your signature]
/s/ Name of insured

Make extra copies of this letter, because you may need them for future correspondence, as you will see.

The Commissioner of Insurance in each of the fifty states has jurisdiction over all agents and brokers licensed to sell insurance in the state, as well as insurance companies doing business in the state. A polite complaint letter to the commissioner with jurisdiction over your insurer may precipitate the kind of official intervention that you need to settle your claim. Your polite complaint letter should be addressed directly to the commissioner (a list of state commissioners appears in Appendix H). This letter will actually be a brief cover letter, referring to your prior polite complaint letter to the insurer, a copy of which you will enclose. Tell the commissioner in the briefest possible terms about the grievance you have against your insurer. Refer the commissioner to your enclosed copy for a fuller description. Explain what response, if any, you have received to your enclosed letter. State your belief that the insurer is not justified in treating your claim as unfairly and unreasonably as it has, and that the commissioner ought to investigate the insurer's operations within the state to determine how many other citizens have been similarly mistreated. Indicate at the bottom of the letter (with an appropriate "cc" notation) that a copy of the letter is being sent to the insurer, and send that copy to the insurer's home office.

Launching a super threat

A super threat can expedite the processing and payment of your insurance claim. A company that is stalling or jerking you around will be sobered by the possible consequences of its misconduct. (See Appendix A for a sample super threat that follows the instructions given below.)

If your insurance company has been particlarly stubborn, malicious, and dishonest, you may prefer to see a lawyer directly, rather than sending a super threat. You are not going to be able to demand in any super threat the punitive damages that you might actually be awarded in court. All you can do in the super threat is raise the *prospect* of punitive damages as leverage to make the insurer budge.

Soft spot. Here it's money—combined with uncertainty over just how much money. Insurance companies are painfully aware of how free juries can be when it comes to doling out insurance money. Jurors can become utterly prodigal when allowed to punish a big mean insurance company for browbeating some poor, premium-paying little guy.

"*In the Matter of.*" Here you will insert "the tortious breach of" and then supply the name, if any, and number of your insurance policy. For example, "IN THE MATTER OF the tortious breach of Major Medical Policy No. MBE-120914."

Heading. Give the name and address of the president and home office of your insurer, where you will be sending your super threat.

"*Notice of Tortious Breach.*" Under this heading for the first paragraph, you will be notifying the insurer of its tortious breach of your insurance contract and citing, by way of authority, *Fletcher* v. *Western National Life Insurance.* (You can rest assured that the enormous jury verdict awarded in *Fletcher* is known and feared by insurance companies from coast to coast.)

NOTICE OF TORTIOUS BREACH

PLEASE TAKE NOTICE: Pursuant to *Fletcher* v. *Western National Life Insurance Co.,* 10 Cal. App. 3d 376, 89 Cal. Rptr. 78 (Ct. App. 1970), you have committed a tortious breach of contract.

"*Statement of Complaint.*" Under this heading for the second paragraph, you will briefly recite the nature of your grievance and refer to your prior letters (such as to the insurer and the insurance commissioner), copies of which you will enclose. You should add on some highly generalized allegations about the distress that the insurer's misconduct is causing you. For example, if an insurer has stubbornly stalled off paying you the value of a life-insurance policy, you might write, "Since January 5, 1977, the date on which I first filed a claim on the above-mentioned life-insurance policy, your company has delayed paying me the proceeds on grounds that are wholly arbitrary and unjustified. This misconduct on your part was more fully described in my letter to you of March 25, 1977, as well as my letter of April 15, 1977, to the State Insurance Commissioner, copies of which are enclosed. Your persistent disregard for and resistance to the just merits of my claim have caused me, and continue to cause me, constant distress, anxiety, worry, and needless hardship." Or, if an insurer has arbitrarily discontinued payments under a health-insurance policy, your "Statement of Complaint" might begin with a sentence such as "On February 10, 1977, your company incorrectly and unjustifiably discontinued payment of sick benefits to me under the above-mentioned policy."

"Demand for Action." Under this heading for the third paragraph, you will state precisely what you want the insurer to do, and you will set a specific date for compliance. Don't allow the insurer much more than ten days for compliance, and emphasize the importance of prompt compliance. For example, "At the earliest possible opportunity, and in no event later than April 1, 1977, the Square Deal Insurance Company must render payment to me in full for the amount claimed by me in my claim filed on January 10, 1977."

The language of the "Demand for Action" may have to be adjusted somewhat to suit your particular problem. For example, if you want the insurer to resume discontinued payments under a health or disability policy, you might write, "At the earliest possible opportunity, and in no event later than April 10, 1977, the Square Deal Insurance Company must render payment to me in full for the amount of sick benefits owing to me and must resume regular payment of future sick benefits as they become due under the above-mentioned policy."

"*Ultimatum.*" Under this heading for the fourth paragraph, you will be warning the insurer of your intention to seek counsel for the legal recovery of both compensatory and punitive damages.

ULTIMATUM

If the above demand for action has not been satisfied in full by the date specified, then I shall seek legal counsel with the intention of commencing a civil action against you for tortious breach of contract and the intentional infliction of emotional distress. In any such litigation, the jury verdict sought shall include compensatory damages as well as punitive damages based upon your willful, wanton, and reckless misconduct.

15

Travel and Moving

Getting away from it all is a billion-dollar business. There are innumerable hotels, airlines, cruise ships, and travel agents all ready to sing you "Yellow Bird" and fly you on the "wings of man" to a land where problems don't exist. For a large percentage of travelers this promise is fulfilled. However, the odds will probably catch up with you. You will then join the ranks of frustrated vacationers who paid good money to have a rotten time.

While there are many ways in which a vacation can be ruined, we will look at two of the most common mishaps: the travel agent blew it, or the charter airline blew it.

Travel Agents

In order to understand the problem with travel agents, consider the following fact and question. The fact: In most states the only requirement to become a travel agent is that you be able to spell "travel agent." The question: Who is a travel agent the agent for? The answer to the question is: Nobody really knows. Maybe he's your agent. Maybe he's the airline's or hotel's agent. The point is that travel agents do make mistakes, and the law is not quite sure if they are liable for them. Most travel agents feel they only book reservations and wish you good luck; if you get into trouble, sue the hotel or the airline or the car-rental company. The problem for you is that most of these businesses are located in the place you went to on vacation. To sue them you'll have to return there, and that will mean another airline, another hotel, another car rental, et cetera. (Of course, your travel agent will be happy to make the booking.)

The trick is to make the travel agent liable for the bookings that he makes. Not only is this logical, but it is also convenient. After all, you probably chose the travel agent because he was located nearby. If he is convenient to visit, he is convenient to sue.

Consider the 1974 New York case of *Bucholtz* v. *Sirotkin Travel Ltd.* Helen Bucholtz and her husband planned a trip to Las Vegas. They asked Sirotkin Travel Ltd., a travel agency, to make the necessary arrangements. Sirotkin told the Bucholtzes that bookings had been made at the Alladdin Hotel in Las Vegas. After a change in departure dates, the Bucholtzes took off. After they landed, they found that no reservations had been made at the Alladdin Hotel, and they were required to find other accommodations at a motel half a mile out of town.

On their return home, Mrs. Bucholtz planned another trip: to court. She claimed that Sirotkin had breached its contract to provide accommodations at the Alladdin Hotel, and she asked the court for damages. The court agreed with her: "In this case nothing was done by the travel agency to verify or confirm either the plane reservation or the hotel reservation. If this duty is the responsibility of the travel agency, then the travel agency is liable in negligence for its failure to exercise reasonable care in making the reservations."

The magic word is "negligence." A person or business can be liable for substantial damages if its negligence causes damage. And the danger of having to pay a substantial money judgment can be a very soft spot for anybody. In the case of the Bucholtzes, the court awarded damages equivalent to one third the cost of their trip. But, as we will see in the next case, the damages can be even higher.

The Paterson and Majewski families planned a joint Christmas holiday in the Canary Islands. They went to Astral Travel Service to make the arrangements. Astral suggested a package tour called "Xmas Jet Set Sun Fun/Canary Isle." The package included a stay at the "deluxe Semiramis Hotel," which was described as a "Five-Star" hotel. The two families bought the package from Astral and took off on December 26. They landed in the Canary Islands some thirty hours later. That was their first mistake. They should never have landed.

After waiting two hours in the Canary Island airport, they and the other tour members were bused to the Semiramis Hotel. On their arrival, they were handed a letter from the hotel informing them that there were no reservations. The tour operator put our exhausted tourists back in a bus and delivered them to the Porto Playa Hotel.

The Porto Playa Hotel was only a four-star hotel. But after almost forty hours of travel, who cared? The problem was not the number of stars the hotel had but the fact that the hotel was not yet completely built. Instead of a balcony, the Paterson and Majewski families had scaffolding. Electrical connections were not complete, and the recreational facilities were still in the planning stage. The two families tried to plan how they could get back home as quickly as possible, but all flights were booked, and they were stuck at the almost-hotel Porto Playa until their scheduled departure on January 1.

When they got back home, the two families joined together to sue the Astral Travel Service. Astral in turn sued Odysseys Unlimited, the people who put the tour package together and sold it to Astral (which in turn sold it to the Paterson and Majewski families). The result was the 1974 lawsuit *Odysseys Unlimited, Inc. v. Astral Travel Service*.

The two families claimed that Astral had breached its contract and had been negligent. They asked for return of the cost of the trip and ten thousand dollars in damages. Astral responded, in effect, "Who, me? It was Odysseys' fault." Odysseys responded, in effect: "Sorry." The court responded by holding Astral liable to the two families. After all, the court reasoned, the two families had no relationship with Odysseys. In fact, they had no idea who Odysseys was, until they met the tour operator on their own ill-fated odyssey. Their dealings were with the Astral Travel Service, and Astral was negligent.

The question of how much the damages should be was dealt with by the court in the following language: "Because the contract was violated and the accommodations contracted for not furnished, a more realistic view of awarding damages to Majewski and Paterson would include not only the difference in the cost of the accommodations but also compensation for their inconvenience, discomfort, humiliation and annoyance." In this case the court awarded the defendants about $2,500 in damages. However, the important point is not the actual damages awarded but the recognition by the court that a travel agent is liable for "inconvenience, discomfort, humiliation and annoyance" suffered by a client. Who is to predict how much a jury might award?

In this case, at least 246 other tourists encountered the problems that the two families were forced to endure.

The possibility of a class action, therefore, existed. The prospect of a class action makes for a potent super threat indeed. The 1973 case of *Siegel* v. *Council of Long Island Educators* is a good example.

In the *Siegel* case, a number of individuals signed up for a package tour to Israel. The accommodations got fouled up, and the tourists were deprived of three days of touring. Apparently, the travel agent failed to make the necessary arrangements. Ten people who went on the trip got together and sued the travel agent. The court awarded each of them $218.68 in damages.

If you have been subjected to a vacation which turned into a nightmare because of an incompetent travel agent, there's not much you can do while still on the trip. You might want to call the agent to inform him of the problem and warn him that unless he uses his good offices to solve it he may be in for a surprise when you get home. However, you will most likely have to try to make the best of your vacation and wait until you return home before you seek compensation for your lost week or two.

Opening volleys

On returning home, you should obviously notify your travel agent if you haven't done so already. Most agents are members of an association of travel agents. If you do not get a prompt response to your complaint, you might inform the agent that you will seek the assistance of the association. While associations do not license travel agents, they do exert some degree of pressure to resolve complaints. Be sure to find out from your agent which associations he belongs to. The addresses of the associations are:

Consumer Affairs Office
American Society of Travel Agents
711 Fifth Avenue
New York, N.Y. 10022

(primarily for complaints involving air fares)
Compliance Office
International Air Transport Association
500 Fifth Avenue
New York, N.Y. 10036

Launching a super threat

Soft spot. A travel agency may be liable to you for its negligence if it makes a careless error in planning your trip. Damages may include actual losses as well as compensation for aggravation.

"In the Matter of." Provide sufficient information to identify the trip. Provide the departure and return dates and any special name your trip might have had (for example, a "Sun/Fun Guided Tour of Malawi").

Heading. Insert the name of the president of the travel agency. If the agency is franchised or part of a chain, be sure to send a copy of the super threat to the head of the chain or the franchisor.

"Notice of Tortious Breach." This paragraph contains standard language which remains constant.

NOTICE OF TORTIOUS BREACH

PLEASE TAKE NOTICE: Pursuant to *Bucholtz* v. *Sirotkin Travel Ltd.,* 80 Misc.2d 333, 363 NYS2d 415 (App. Term 1973), you have committed a tortious breach of contract.

"Statement of Complaint." Here you will explain exactly what happened on the trip. There will certainly be a temptation to describe all the gory details. Try to avoid this. Lay out the facts chronologically, indicating what you expected and what you received.

"*Demand for Action.*" Deciding what you want from the travel agent may be a problem. After all, the only compensation you can receive is cash. How do you translate frustration into dollars and cents? There is no formula. However, a reasonable method of computing your actual damages might be the following. If you were forced to find alternative accommodations or services because of a mistake by the agent, the added costs which resulted would properly be considered as damages. Further, if you lost time which should have been spent enjoying yourself, you might prorate out the cost of the lost time. For example, if a ten-day trip cost you one thousand dollars and you lost two days, it would be logical to assume that you suffered two hundred dollars in damages.

From the cases we have discussed, you might be tempted to make a large claim for the aggravation that you suffered. Bear in mind, however, that the travel agency is much less likely to give in to your demand if you include money damages for aggravation. Indeed, the possibility of the agency's having to pay a large amount as punitive damages is our soft spot. If you demand this money as part of the super threat, the travel agency has nothing to lose by going to court with you. Thus, if you are adamant about being compensated for aggravation, don't expect the super threat to be 100 percent successful. However, if you are content to get back your actual losses, then a super threat may get results.

"*Ultimatum.*" This paragraph contains standard language. In the event that the problems you encountered were shared with other travelers, you should add a class-action possibility to the ultimatum: "Furthermore, since other individuals share my cause of action, I may seek a class action to avoid a multiplicity of law suits. See *Siegel* v. *Council of Long Island Educators,* 75 Misc.2d 750 (1973)."

ULTIMATUM

In the event you fail to respond as requested, I shall seek legal counsel to commence a civil action against you for negligence and tortious breach of contract. I shall seek actual damages as well as compensation for mental distress. I shall also seek punitive damages. See *Odysseys Unlimited, Inc. v. Astral Travel Service*, 354 NYS2d 88 77 Misc.2d 502 (1974). [Add class-action sentence, if appropriate.]

Charter Flights

Charter flights can be a bargain or a bust. And charter-flight organizers can make a good income. Indeed, their income can be very high if they collect money for a charter flight and then never charter an airplane. You might assume that such a procedure would, at a minimum, annoy many people, and you would be right. But the practitioner of this type of fraud doesn't worry too much. He knows there are very few regulations governing charter-flight operators. He also knows that a large proportion of his defrauded clients will not bother to sue him. And as the last resort he can always declare his corporation bankrupt and start all over again. Meanwhile, he pays himself a fat salary. So what has he got to lose?

In order for a super threat to work against a fraudulent charter-flight operator, it has to cut through one of his defenses. You could use a class-action approach to overcome his confidence that not all defrauded clients will sue. However, he could still use the bankruptcy route and make collection of any refund impossible. The best solution, therefore, would be to eliminate the shield of bankruptcy. And that is exactly what we will try to do. The case we will use is *Civil Aeronautics Board* v. *Scottish-American Association, Inc.*, decided in 1976.

This case involves a charter organizer, Scottish-American, which sold seats on charter flights bound for Scotland. The tickets were in large part sold through a travel agency, Travel-A-Go-Go. Both the travel agency and the charter organizer were operated by the same person, Francis John Folan.

As is the general practice, purchasers of charter-flight tickets sold by Folan's corporation were required to put a deposit down and then pay the balance within a specified time period before the flight was scheduled to depart. However, in the case of at least one charter group the money deposited for a flight was used instead to cover the costs for a different flight. As a result, when it came time to leave one charter group found itself without a plane to fly on.

A complaint was filed with the Civil Aeronautics Board (CAB). The CAB ordered Scottish-American and Travel A-Go-Go to return all monies to the customers whose charter flight had been canceled. This should have been good news for the otherwise disappointed would-be travelers. However, it turned out that neither Scottish-American nor Travel-A-Go-Go had enough money to make the necessary restitution. As we noted earlier, this is not unusual. However, in this case the CAB went one step further—into court. They asked that Folan be held *personally liable* to make restitution. Folan claimed that only the corporation was liable, and if it didn't have enough money, too bad.

The federal district court decided that Folan was not entitled to hide behind the corporate shield. In the law, this sort of judicial decision is rather eloquently known as "piercing the corporate veil." Folan had to pay back the defrauded consumers *out of his own pocket.* The reasoning of the court was simple: "The avoidance of personal liability is a privilege of doing business in the corporate form. Such a privilege may be lost, and the so-called corporate veil pierced 'to prevent fraud and to achieve equity.' "

Preliminary skirmishes

If you show up for a charter flight and find no airplane, you may want to explain the danger of personal liability to the charter-tour operator (if you can find him). This may give you leverage to secure a scheduled flight from him at the charter cost.

Opening volleys

You can try a polite complaint letter to the charter organizer. If you don't get satisfaction you can write to the Civil Aeronautics Board, Consumer Advocate's Office, Washington, D.C. 20428. It's possible that the CAB will exert some pressure on your behalf. (Of course, if you bought the flight through a travel agent you should consider a super threat directed at the agent. This is discussed on page 239.) However, many charter organizers are in business for a quick buck, and politeness may not work. Then it's time to launch a super threat.

Launching a super threat

Soft spot. The soft spot is the personal liability of the charter organizer and the possibility of a class action.

"In the Matter of." Give your name and the flight number, and the date and time when the flight had been scheduled to depart.

Heading. Insert the name of the charter organizer. Follow his name with this language: "individually and as an officer of." Then insert the name of the company operating the charter. Also include the address of the organizer.

"Notice of Personal Liability." This will be the heading of your first paragraph.

NOTICE OF PERSONAL LIABILITY

PLEASE TAKE NOTICE: Pursuant to *Civil Aeronautics Board* v. *Scottish-American Association, Inc.,* 14 Avi. 17,327, 411 F. Supp. 883 (E.D.N.Y., 1976), you may be personally liable in a single action or a class action.

"*Statement of Complaint.*" Insert the facts of your case. There is not much you will have to write other than that you bought a ticket and there was no plane. However, you should provide enough details to make it clear which flight you were conned out of. You might also include a description of any particular problems that the flight cancellation caused. For example, if you missed an important conference you should mention this fact.

"*Demand for Action.*" Insert the amount owed to you as a result of the canceled flight. This amount will be what you actually paid for your ticket.

DEMAND FOR ACTION

On or before [insert date] you must forward to me the amount paid to you for the above-mentioned flight.

"*Ultimatum.*" This is standard language. We are including a threat of a class action. Though there is no case directly on this point, there is no reason why you can't be the person to bring the first one. It certainly can't hurt to raise the idea of a class action anyway.

ULTIMATUM

Your failure to timely respond to this demand may result in personal liability in the event of insufficient funds available from the business organization. This personal liability may also include any and all other participants in the above-mentioned flight who have a similar cause of action.

Moving Companies

Webster's offers three definitions for the verb "to move": "(1) to change the place of or position of in any manner; (2) to arouse the feelings or passion; and (3) of the bowels, to have an evacuation." Anyone who has had a problem moving from one house to another would probably agree with all three definitions.

Interstate moving companies are regulated by the Interstate Commerce Commission (ICC). This Commission has issued a number of regulations designed to protect the consumer. One of these regulations requires the moving company to give you a booklet before you move, entitled "Summary of Information for Shipper of Household Goods." This booklet outlines all the rights that you have.

It is especially important when moving to take preventive steps to avoid problems, since many of the difficulties you will face will pit your word against theirs. For example, if your dinner glasses arrive broken, the moving company might argue that they were broken when they were originally packed. Resolving this kind of problem, even with a super threat, can be very difficult. It's better to take the steps outlined in the ICC booklet and avoid the problem in the first place.

However, this advice will be of little comfort to those of you who have managed to get yourselves into a fix despite the best intentions of the Interstate Commerce Commission. For you, a super threat may be necessary.

We will examine two common problems which arise frequently in interstate moves. The first occurs when your moving company violates one of the ICC regulations, which usually means there is an overcharge. The second problem occurs when the moving company fails to deliver your household goods on time.

If you believe you have been overcharged, you probably have been billed substantially more than the amount estimated. (It's also possible that you received no written estimate, which is a violation of the law.) Under the ICC regulations, estimates must be made based on a personal inspection of your belongings by a representative of your moving company. Charges are based upon the weight of your goods. A general rule of seven pounds per cubic foot of goods must be used. Thus, a violation of the regulations occurs if you received no written estimate, or the estimate was not based on a personal inspection, or the estimate given bears no reasonable relationship to the rule of seven pounds per cubic foot of goods.

The ICC regulations also protect you by giving you various rights to insure that you are billed only for the actual weight of your goods. You have the right to be present at the weighing of your goods. You also have the right to receive official copies of the weight receipts issued by the official weighmaster both before and after the moving truck is loaded with your belongings. Various other rights are spelled out in the booklet "Summary of Information for Shippers of Household Goods." If a moving company violates any of these regulations, the violation may result in an overcharge.

Thus, assuming you feel you have been overcharged,

it's quite likely your moving company has violated an ICC regulation.

Opening volleys

Other than the normal polite complaint letter, no special procedures are recommended prior to a super threat.

Launching a super threat

In order to show that you mean business your super threat will incorporate a petition to the Interstate Commerce Commission requesting a license suspension. While the Commission does not routinely act on every petition, there still is a distinct possibility of such action. In the event that the super threat does not produce satisfactory results, you may want to send off the petition to your regional office of the Interstate Commerce Commission. The addresses of the regional offices are given in Appendix I.

Soft spot. Interstate moving companies are licensed by the Interstate Commerce Commission. A violation of ICC rules or regulations can be grounds for license suspension. Even a short suspension can be a severe blow to any moving company.

"In the Matter of." Provide sufficient information for the moving company to identify which move you are writing about. Giving your name, the date of the move, the pickup and drop-off locations, and the bill-of-lading number should suffice (the bill of lading is the document given to you when the movers come to pick up your goods). A typical caption might read: "IN THE MATTER OF move of Joe Wander from New York, New York, to San Diego, California, on March 3, 1977, under Bill of Lading Number 123456."

Heading. Insert the name and address of the moving company.

"Notice of Violation of ICC Regulations." This is standard boilerplate and should remain in all such super threats.

NOTICE OF VIOLATION OF ICC REGULATIONS

PLEASE TAKE NOTICE: You are in violation of Part 1056 of Title 49 of the Code of Federal Regulations known as the "Household Goods Regulations."

"*Statement of Complaint.*" Insert here the facts of your case. Be sure to include the dollar amount of any estimate as well as the final bill price. You may consult the ICC booklet to determine which of your rights were violated. Be sure to give enough facts to show the violation. For example, if you requested copies of the weighmaster's receipts for your shipment and did not receive them, be sure to state this fact.

"*Demand for Action.*" Here you will specify exactly what it is you want the moving company to do for you. Either the company will owe you money, due to an overpayment, or you will be contesting a bill. Be sure to provide a time limit for your demand. For example, a typical demand might be: "On or before March 2, 1977, provide me with a revised bill showing a total cost of $1,845.00, the amount originally estimated by you."

"*Ultimatum.*" This is standard boilerplate. In order to understand this boilerplate, you should know that the term "proviso (2)" refers to a class of goods which moving companies transport. The ICC frequently suspends a company's license to haul "proviso (2)" goods as punishment for violating rules or regulations. We use the term here to impress the company with your familiarity with ICC sanctions. We also cite a typical case to back up the ultimatum, namely, the *Aero Mayflower* case, in which the ICC imposed its "proviso (2)" sanction.

ULTIMATUM

If you do not comply with my demand for action, the enclosed petition will be filed with the regional office of the Interstate Commerce Commission. Action on the petition may result in suspension of license to haul "proviso (2)" commodities pursuant to *Aero Mayflower Transit Company, Inc., Allied Van Lines, Inc.* v. *Interstate Commerce Commission and United States of America* (United States Court of Appeals, Seventh Circuit, May 7, 1976).

[Your signature]
―――――――――
Your name

Mailing address
City, state, zip code

Petition. On a separate piece of paper type out the petition, using the form which follows. Underneath "Interstate Commerce Commission" at the top of the petition insert the address of the regional office nearest you (from Appendix I). As always, under "Date of mailing" be sure to put in the same date used in your demand for action—the date by which you are demanding satisfaction. Attach a copy of the petition to your super-threat letter.

PETITION

Interstate Commerce Commission
[insert address of regional office]
          and
[insert name of moving company]

Date of mailing:
[insert date here]

PETITIONER requests action be instituted pursuant to Section 212(a) of the Interstate Commerce Act for violation of 49 Code of Federal Regulations 1056 et seq.

PETITIONER avers that the statements made on the attached NOTICE are true and were served upon the above-captioned company by mail.

PETITIONER respectfully requests that action be instituted pursuant to the Law to suspend the license of the above-captioned company for breach of the "Household Goods" regulations.

Respectfully submitted

[Your signature]
Your name

Mailing address
City, state, zip code

Delayed Delivery. The second problem which can be dealt with by a super threat involves the delay in delivery of goods being moved. This is a particularly aggravating problem. You can live with overcharges or damaged household goods, but you can't live if you've received no goods at all.

A solution to this problem lies in the recent case *Hubbard* v. *Allied Van Lines*. The Hubbards were moving from New Haven, Connecticut, to Columbia, South Carolina. Allied Van Lines agreed to deliver the goods on or about July 18. Instead, about 80 percent of the shipment arrived on August 8, and the rest on October 10.

The Hubbards felt that Allied could have delivered on time except that Allied had used its equipment to haul some other more important shipment. And the Hubbards were angry. Mr. Hubbard was starting a new career as a law professor, and Mrs. Hubbard was pregnant. They argued in court that the delay had caused them mental distress. They sought punitive damages. In total, they asked the court to award twenty-five thousand dollars in damages. Allied Van Lines tried to defend itself by arguing that the Carmack Amendment to the Interstate Commerce Act limits a moving company's liability and therefore the Hubbards were not entitled to any damages except for damaged goods.

The court agreed with the Hubbards. The Carmack Amendment did not limit liability of a moving company in the event of a delayed delivery. Even more important, though, was the court's conclusion that damages, including punitive damages, could be awarded: "We hold that a private right of action exists under 49 U.S.C. § 316(d) and that in a proper case punitive damages and damages for mental distress may be recovered."

The importance of this decision is that it tells moving companies that they may be held liable if they discriminate against you by making you a low-priority customer. They are not free to delay your shipment simply because they need to use their trucks for some other move. Even more important, the *Hubbard* decision makes a moving company liable for damages for your mental distress and for punitive damages. These damages can be extraordinarily high, since they are usually determined by unpredictable juries. And moving companies know it.

Opening volleys

If you're caught waiting overtime for delivery of your goods there is not much time for any preliminaries. A phone call certainly is in order. If you are the patient type you'll probably be willing to put up with the moving company's first excuse. However, if you get fed up with excuses you should fire off a super threat as soon as possible.

Launching a super threat

Soft spot. Here the soft spot is potential damages, both punitive and actual. The amount of any judgment is highly unpredictable. There are only a few, quite recent cases in this area. No moving company wants to find out just how high a judgment might be.

"In the Matter of." Provide sufficient information for the moving company to identify which move you are writing about. Give your name, the date your goods were picked up, and where or when they were scheduled for delivery. Include your bill-of-lading number, which should appear on the papers given to you by the moving company when your goods were picked up.

"Notice of Violation of 49 U.S.C. §316(d)." This paragraph is standard boilerplate.

NOTICE OF VIOLATION OF 49 U.S.C. §316(d)

PLEASE TAKE NOTICE: You are in violation of Section 316(d) of Title 49 of the United States Code, *Hanke v. Global Van Lines Inc.,* 533 F.2d 396 (8th Cir. 1976).

"Statement of Complaint." Insert here the facts of your case. Indicate the delivery date which you were promised. Also indicate any facts which might prove that delay in delivery of your goods will cause you a hardship. For example, if there is a pregnant woman in your family, note this fact. If anyone in your family is suffering particular distress at not being able to move in properly, note this also. If any portion of your belongings which are caught en route are needed for a particular purpose, be sure to point this out. In

general give any facts which might be the basis for a claim of damages which resulted from the delay.

"*Demand for Action.*" Insert the demands you want to make. Since your goods are already overdue, you will want to choose a delivery date in the very near future.

"*Ultimatum.*" This is standard language.

ULTIMATUM

If you do not comply with my demand for delivery you may be liable for damages, both actual and punitive, including liability for infliction of mental distress pursuant to *Hubbard* v. *Allied Van Lines,* 1976 ICC 57, 177 (Court of Appeals, Fourth Circuit, August 5, 1976). Liability for this violation may be substantial in light of the facts in this case.

Appendix A
Sample Super Threats

Here are four sample super threats based on hypothetical fact patterns. Each super threat relies on the rules enunciated in one of the preceding chapters. In order to understand the super threat, therefore, you must read the relevant chapter. All the fact patterns are fictitious and are not intended to depict actual persons or businesses.

Sample Super Threat for Dangerous Animals (Chapter 4)

Jack Eisenberg lived with his wife and two young children on a quiet street outside of Westwood, California. His neighbors, the Wechslers, had been robbed twice. Harry Wechsler told Jack that he was going to get some protection. Jack thought he was going to buy a gun. Instead, Harry brought home a German shepherd, named "Tiger," which clearly had been trained not to be friendly.

The Wechslers kept Tiger tied up in front of the house, to scare off intruders. Tiger would leap, snarling at anyone who walked by the house, including Jack's children.

Jack called up Harry to ask him to keep Tiger indoors. He told him he was scared that the dog might get loose and hurt someone. He also told him that the snarling dog scared his children and that someone might get hurt by being frightened. Harry did nothing.

Jack wrote a polite letter to Harry, figuring that might do the trick. It didn't. Jack then decided to call the police, since Tiger was clearly a menace. The police thought Tiger was cute. Fed up, Jack decided to take action. He felt the danger was not extreme enough to hire a lawyer and immediately bring legal action. He thought a super threat might work.

Jack decided to demand that Tiger be kept indoors. He felt that would eliminate the danger while allowing the Wechslers to have the protection they wanted. He also decided to give the Wechslers one week to comply with his demand.

Since Tiger was a dog, Jack used the super threat for *domitae naturae*. He was sure to insert in his "Statement of Complaint" enough facts to show that Tiger was dangerous. He sent his super threat by certified mail and included the receipt number at the end of his letter.

NOTICE

IN THE MATTER OF Harry Wechsler
Harry Wechsler
21212 Flotsam Lane
Westwood, California 90099

Date of mailing:
July 2, 1977

NOTICE OF LIABILITY FOR POSSESSION OF DANGEROUS ANIMAL

PLEASE TAKE NOTICE: Your possession of a *domitae naturae* constitutes a condition which is dangerous and may cause serious injury or death. Pursuant to *Maxwell v. Fraze*, 344 S.W.2d 262 (Mo. App. 1961), this letter constitutes notice of the dangerous propensity of your animal.

STATEMENT OF COMPLAINT

Your dog has viciously lunged at people passing in front of your house. Our children, who must pass in front of your house on the way to school, have been repeatedly frightened. Further, if the rope which restrains the dog breaks, serious injury is likely. Even if the rope holds, the fright caused may result in injury.

DEMAND FOR ACTION

On or before July 10, 1977, cease tying up your dog in front of your house.

ULTIMATUM

You are now on NOTICE of the dangerous characteristics of your animal. Your failure to accept the reasonable demands contained herein will expose you to liability in the event your animal causes any injury. See *Groner* v. *Hedrick,* 403 Pa. 148, 169 A.2d 302 (1961) ($17,000 award). This liability may be substantial in the event your animal causes serious injury or death.

[Signature]
Jack Eisenberg

21214 Flotsam Lane
Westwood, California 90099

Certified Mail No. 12345678

Sample Super Threat for Deceptive Trade Practices
(*Chapter 9*)

Jane Crane, who lived in Georgia, was having trouble with her RCO television set. On March 23, 1977, she called the Static Repair Shop, and Sid Sly, the manager, visited her home. Jane told Sid that although the set needed servicing, it was ten years old, and therefore she was not willing to pay for any extensive repairs. Sid assured Jane that he would notify her of the estimated cost before doing any work. Pleased with this arrangement, Jane let Sid take the set back to the shop with him.

Contrary to his word, Sid went ahead and repaired the set without first giving Jane a cost estimate. On March 30, Sid called Jane to tell her that the charge for his work would be $125. Outraged by Sid's dishonesty and the exorbitant service charge, Jane refused to pay. Sid refused to return the set.

On April 1, Jane wrote Sid a polite complaint letter. She pointed out how Sid had misrepresented the characteristics of his repair service when he promised a cost estimate in advance of any actual work. Jane insisted that Sid return the set to her no later than April 15. In an attempt to be accommodating, and perhaps settle the dispute more quickly, Jane even offered to pay Sid $40 for his work. But Sid remained adamant. As of April 15, he still refused to return Jane's set unless she first paid him the full $125.

Jane immediately wrote a super threat for Sid. In it she renewed her offer of $40 in return for Sid's compliance with her demands. Forty dollars was about as much as Jane was willing to pay in order to have the set back in good working condition. Considering the severity of her ultimatum, Jane figured the $40 offer would leave Sid a reasonable escape hatch.

NOTICE

IN THE MATTER OF violation of Georgia Fair Business Practices Act of 1975

Sid Sly
Static Repair Shop
100 Main Street
Winston, Georgia 97431

Date of mailing:
April 15, 1977

NOTICE OF DECEPTIVE TRADE PRACTICE

PLEASE TAKE NOTICE: Pursuant to Ga. Code Ann. secs. 106-1201–106-1217 (G.C.A. Adv. Codif. Serv.), you have committed an unlawful deceptive trade practice.

STATEMENT OF COMPLAINT

On March 23, 1977, you removed my RCO television set (serial no. 34567) from my home and took it to your shop. You told me that you would give me a price estimate before doing any actual repair work. Instead, you performed the work without notifying me of the cost in advance. The deceptive trade practice in which you are engaged was more fully described to you in my letter of April 1, 1977, a copy of which is enclosed.

DEMAND FOR ACTION

No later than April 30, 1977, you must deliver the RCO television set to me in good working order, in return for which I will pay you the sum of $40, which shall be deemed just, reasonable, and full compensation for your work.

ULTIMATUM

If the above demand for action has not been satisfied in full by the date specified, then I shall seek legal counsel with the intention of commencing a civil action against you for the willful and wanton commission of an unlawful deceptive trade practice. Under the Georgia Fair Business Practices Act of 1975, you may be subjected to liability for the actual amount of my loss, plus punitive damages in the amount of three times my actual loss, as well as the amount of my attorney's fees and court costs.

[Signature]
Jane Crane

7 Lake Road
Winston, Georgia 97433

Certified Mail No. 12345678

Sample Super Threat for Mail Fraud (Chapter 11)

Judy Kurtis was always looking for a bargain. When the mail brought an offer from the Beauty Unlimited Co. promising eighty dollars' worth of cosmetics for only two dollars, she could not refuse. After all, the printed offer showed a picture of ten large bottles of cosmetics which Judy knew cost at least eighty dollars at the store. Judy sent off her two dollars, figuring she had made a real killing.

Three weeks later a small package arrived containing ten small plastic containers. Each container held a small amount of a cosmetic. This was hardly what Judy had bargained for. She reread the offer to see if she had made a mistake. While the offer never promised ten large bottles of cosmetics, any reasonable person would have assumed that was what she would receive.

Judy was angry. She felt she had been ripped off. She considered writing a polite complaint letter, but dismissed the idea. The Beauty Unlimited Co. knew exactly what it was doing. There was no mistake a polite letter could clear up. So Judy decided to launch a super threat.

She tried to find out who the owner of Beauty Unlimited Co. was, but she couldn't. Therefore, she decided to use the name "John Doe" in her heading.

Since she was sending out her letter on June 20, 1977, she decided to demand her money back by July 15, 1977. A couple of weeks should be enough time for them to respond.

Judy remembered to send her super threat by certified mail. She also decided to send a copy of the letter to her local consumer-affairs office. While she didn't expect the office to help her out, she did feel that if enough people contacted the office with a complaint against Beauty Unlimited Co., they might take some action.

NOTICE

IN THE MATTER OF order of May 16, 1977 for ten cosmetics.

"John Doe"
individually and as an
officer of
Beauty Unlimited Co.
1421 West 18th Street
New York, N.Y. 10087

Date of mailing:
June 20, 1977

NOTICE OF VIOLATION

PLEASE TAKE NOTICE: You are in violation of Title 39, Section 3005 of the United States Code (see *United States* v. *Outpost Development Corp.*, 369 F. Supp. 399 [C.D. Cir.], aff'd, 414 US 1105 [1973]), and Title 18, Section 1341 of the United States Code (see *United States* v. *Uhrig*, 443 F.2d 239 [7th Cir..], cert. denied, 404 S 832 [1971]).

STATEMENT OF COMPLAINT

On or about May 16, 1977, I received an offer from you through the mails. This offer indicated that you would send me $80 worth of cosmetics for $2. This offer contained a picture of full bottles of cosmetics. Instead, I received ten small plastic containers of the cosmetics.

DEMAND FOR ACTION

On or before July 15, 1977, return to me the sum of $2.00. This amount reflects the payment made to you as a result of your false representations. Include instructions for return of any goods I have received from you, said return to be at your expense.

ULTIMATUM

In the event you fail to respond to my demand in a timely manner, I shall file a formal petition with the Postal Service, Inspection Division, pursuant to Title 39, Section 3005 of the United States Code. This may result in a stop-order being issued against your receipt of any mail. Further, a "Request for Investigation" may be filed with the United States Attorney, which may result in criminal penalties, *United States v. Uhrig, supra.*

[Signature]
Judy Kurtis

112 Oak Street
Fair Lawn, New Jersey 11004

Certified Mail No. 12345678

Sample Super Threat for Collecting on an Insurance Policy (Chapter 14)

The James Wilson family owned a tastefully furnished seven-room summer house on the Massachusetts shore. To secure himself against losses due to theft or destruction, James Wilson maintained a homeowner's insurance policy on the house. In January, 1976, the house was vandalized, and many valuable furnishings were stolen.

On February 9, 1976, James filed a claim for $7,300 with his insurer, the Square Deal Insurance Company. He submitted all necessary proof-of-loss forms and told the agent that he was anxious to receive payment soon so that the house could be refurbished for the summer season.

Not until late March, however, did an adjuster from Square Deal inspect the badly damaged home. At every turn, the adjuster discounted the severity of the vandalism, as well as the value of the items that had been stolen. On April 5, 1976, Square Deal offered to pay Wilson $1,800, which he rejected as totally unrealistic. Negotiations dragged on into May, despite Wilson's protestations that his family's vacation plans were being completely disrupted by Square Deal's intransigence.

On May 5, 1976, James wrote a polite complaint letter to Square Deal. He objected to the company's arbitrary disregard for his proof of the amount of his losses. He demanded full payment of his claim within ten days. Square Deal still wouldn't budge from its $1,800 offer, and on May 15 James wrote a polite complaint letter to the State Insurance Commissioner.

By June 15, 1976, the weather was getting hot, and with it James's temper at being deprived of the full enjoyment of his summer home. With no prospect of quick action from the insurance commissioner, and Square Deal still stalling, James wrote the following super threat.

NOTICE

IN THE MATTER OF the
tortious breach of
Homeowner's Policy No. SSC-3201

W. Harmon Jones, President
Square Deal Insurance Company
10 City Plaza
Clifton, Massachusetts 27546

Date of mailing:
June 15, 1976

NOTICE OF TORTIOUS BREACH

PLEASE TAKE NOTICE: Pursuant to *Fletcher* v. *Western National life Insurance Co.*, 10 Cal. App. 3d 376, 89 Cal. Rptr. 78 (Ct. App. 1970), you have committed a tortious breach of contract.

STATEMENT OF COMPLAINT

Since February 9, 1976, the date on which I first filed a claim on the above-mentioned homeowner's policy, your company has delayed paying me the full proven amount of my claim and has, instead, persisted in offering an amount that is wholly arbitrary and unjustified. This misconduct on your part was more fully described in my letter to you of May 5, 1976, as well as my letter of May 15, 1976, to the State Insurance Commissioner, copies of which are enclosed. Your persistent disregard for and resistance to the just merits of my claim have caused, and continue to cause, both me and my family constant distress, anxiety, worry, and needless disruption of our lives.

DEMAND FOR ACTION

At the earliest possible opportunity, and in no event later than June 25, 1976, the Square Deal Insurance Company must render payment to me in full for the amount claimed by me in my claim filed on February 9, 1976.

ULTIMATUM

If the above demand for action has not been satisfied in full by the dates specified, then I shall seek legal counsel with the intention of commencing a civil action against you for tortious breach of contract and the intentional infliction of emotional distress. In any such litigation, the jury verdict sought shall include compensatory damages as well as punitive damages based upon your willful, wanton, and reckless misconduct.

[Signature]
James Wilson

666 Cyprus Drive
Mayflower, Massachusetts 27549

Certified Mail No. 12345678

Appendix B
Repair-and-Deduct
Statutes and Cases

Alaska

Statute: Alaska Statutes, Secs. 34.03.100, 34.03.180 (1975 Supp).
Provisions: After notifying the landlord in writing of the repairs and services needed, the tenant may immediately procure these repairs and services and deduct their actual and reasonable cost from his rent.

Arizona

Statute: Arizona Revised Statutes Annotated, Secs. 33-1324, 33-1363 (1974).
Provisions: Landlord must make the necessary repair or supply the necessary service within twenty days after being notified by the tenant. In the case of an emergency, the work must be done as promptly as conditions require. If the landlord fails to do his duty, the tenant can hire a licensed contractor to do the work. After submitting an itemized bill to the landlord, the tenant can deduct from his rent the actual and reasonable cost of the work—not exceeding $150 or one half the monthly rent, whichever is greater.

California

Statute: California Civil Code, Secs. 1941, 1942 (1954).
Provisions: Landlord must make the necessary repairs within pairs within a "reasonable time" after being notified by the tenant. (After a maximum of thirty days, a "reasonable time" is presumed to have passed.) If the landlord fails to do his

duty, the tenant can have the repairs made and deduct the expense—not exceeding one month's rent—from his rent. The statute does not allow this remedy to be used by the tenant more than once in any twelve-month period.

Colorado

Case: *Shanahan v. Collins*, 539 P.2d 1261 (Colo. 1975).

Delaware

Statute: Delaware Code Annotated, Title 25, Secs. 5306, 5307 (1974).
Provisions: Landlord must make necessary repairs within thirty days after being notified by the tenant. If the landlord fails to do his duty, the tenant can then further notify the landlord of his intention to make the repairs at the landlord's expense. A tenant who does so cannot deduct more than fifty dollars from his rent for the repair work.

Georgia

Case: *Dougherty v. Taylor & Norton Co.*, 5 Ga. App. 773, 63 S.E. 928 (1909).

Hawaii

Statute: Hawaii Revised Statutes, Secs. 521-42(a), 521-64 (1975 Supp).
Provisions: Landlord must make necessary repairs within twelve business days after being notified by the tenant. (Only five business days are allowed in the case of a health hazard.) If the landlord fails to do his duty, the tenant can then further notify the landlord in writing of his intention to make the repairs at the landlord's expense. A tenant who does so cannot deduct more than two hundred dollars from his rent for the actual expenses. The statute states that total

deductions within each six-month period shall not exceed three months' rent.

Illinois

Case: *Jack Spring, Inc.* v. *Little,* 50 Ill.2d 351, 280 N.E.2d 208 (1972).

Kentucky

Statute: Kentucky Revised Statutes, Secs. 383.595, 383.635 (1976 Cumm. Supp.).
Provisions: Landlord must make the necessary repairs within fourteen days—or a shorter time in an emergency—after being notified by the tenant. (The tenant's notification should recite the repairs needed and that the tenant intends to have the work done at the landlord's expense if the landlord does not comply.) If the landlord willfully fails to do his duty, the tenant can have the work done. After submitting an itemized bill for actual expenses to the landlord, the tenant can deduct that amount from his rent.

Louisiana

Statute: Louisiana Code Annotated, Arts. 2692–2694 (1972).
Provisions: The statute does not say how much time a landlord has to do his duty after being notified by the tenant, so the tenant ought to allow a reasonable amount of time under the circumstances. If the landlord fails to do his duty, the tenant can then repair and deduct on his own if (1) the repairs are "indispensable" and (2) their cost is "just and reasonable."

Massachusetts

Statute: Massachusetts General Laws Annotated, Ch. 111, Sec. 127L (1976–77 Supp.).

Provisions: Landlord is required to begin the repairs within five days after being notified by the tenant, and the work must be substantially completed within fourteen days after the same notification date. (These times may be shortened in cases of emergency.) If the landlord fails to do his duty, the tenant can have the repair work performed and deduct its "reasonable" cost from his rent. The statute does not allow a tenant to use this remedy to deduct more than four months' rent in any twelve-month period.

Michigan

Statute: Michigan Compiled Laws Annotated, Sec. 125.534 (1976–77 Supp.).
Provisions: Before the tenant can invoke this law, there must be a housing-code violation recorded against his apartment building by the local housing agency. Then the tenant can bring an enforcement proceeding in court. The judge can authorize the tenant to correct the violation and deduct the cost from his rent "upon such terms as the court determines to be just."

Montana

Statute: Montana Code Annotated, Secs. 42-201, 42-202 (1974).
Provisions: Landlord must make the necessary repairs within a "reasonable time" after being notified by the tenant. If the landlord fails to do his duty, the tenant can make the repairs and deduct their cost—not to exceed one month's rent—from his rent.

Nebraska

Statute: Nebraska Revised Statutes, Secs. 76-1419, 76-1427 (1974 Cumm. Supp.).

Provisions: The statute does not say how much time a landlord has to provide essential services to the tenant after being notified of their lack by the tenant, so the tenant ought to allow a reasonable amount of time under the circumstances. If the landlord fails to do his duty, the tenant can procure essential services on his own and deduct their actual and reasonable cost from his rent.

New Jersey

Case: *Marini v. Ireland*, 56 N.J. 130, 265 A.2d 526 (1970).

New York

Case: *Jackson v. Rivera*, 65 Misc.2d 468, 318 N.Y.S.2d 7 (Civ. Ct. N.Y. Co. 1971).

North Dakota

Statute: North Dakota Century Code, Secs. 47-16-12, 47-16-13 (1960).
Provisions: Landlord must make the necessary repairs within a "reasonable time" after being notified by the tenant. If the landlord fails to do his duty, the tenant can make his own repairs and deduct their cost from his rent.

Ohio

Statute: Ohio Revised Code, Secs. 5321.04, 5321.07 (1975 Supp.).
Provisions: Landlord must remedy the condition complained about by the tenant "within a reasonable time considering the severity of the condition and the time necessary to remedy such condition, or within thirty days, whichever is sooner." If the landlord fails to do his duty, then the tenant can seek a court order allowing him to deposit his rent money into court and use it for repair work.

Oklahoma

Statute: Oklahoma Statutes Annotated, Title 41, Secs. 31, 32 (1951).
Provisions: Landlord must make the necessary repairs within a "reasonable time" after being notified by the tenant. If the landlord fails to do his duty, the tenant can make the repairs and deduct their cost from his rent.

Oregon

Statute: Oregon Revised Statutes, Secs. 91.770, 91.805 (1975).
Provisions: The statute does not say how much time the landlord has to make repairs after being notified by the tenant, so the tenant ought to allow a reasonable amount of time under the circumstances. If the landlord fails to do his duty, the tenant can make the repairs. After submitting receipts or an itemized bill to the landlord, the tenant can deduct the actual and reasonable costs—not exceeding two hundred dollars—from his rent.

South Dakota

Statute: South Dakota Compiled Laws Annotated, Secs. 43-32-8, 43-32-9 (1967).
Provisions: Landlord must make the necessary repairs within a "reasonable time" after being notified by the tenant. If the landlord fails to do his duty, the tenant can make the repairs and deduct their cost from his rent. There is a special provision for repairs that cost more than one month's rent: Tenant can notify landlord of the specific reason that the rent will be withheld from the landlord. Then the tenant can deposit that rent in a bank account and maintain it there until either (1) the landlord makes the repairs, or (2)

enough rent money has been withheld for the tenant to make the repairs from money deposited in the bank account.

Washington

Statute: Washington Revised Code Annotated, Secs. 59.18.-060, 59.18.070, 59.18.090, 59.18.100 (1975 Supp.).

Provisions: Landlord must commence the necessary repairs within a reasonable time after being notified by the tenant. Generally, a reasonable time shall not exceed seven days, although it can be as little as twenty-four hours in case of emergency. The repairs must be completed with reasonable promptness. The tenant can make the repairs himself if (1) the landlord fails to do his duty; (2) the cost of the repairs does not exceed *half a month's rent;* and (3) the repairs need not be performed by licensed or registered contractors. After the landlord has had an opportunity to inspect the tenant's work, the tenant may deduct the cost of the repairs from his rent. The statute does not allow the tenant to use this remedy to deduct more than half a month's rent or seventy-five dollars, whichever is less, in any twelve-month period.

By way of an alternative method of repair-and-deduct, the statute also allows the tenant to submit bids for the repair work to the landlord. The tenant may submit at least two bids at the time he notifies the landlord of the defect to be repaired. These bids should be from licensed contractors, or if no such licensing requirement applies to the work in question, then the bids may simply be from responsible persons capable of doing the work. If the landlord does not commence repair of the defective condition within a reasonable time after being notified by the tenant, the tenant can contract with the lowest bidder to have the work performed. After completion of the work and an opportunity for the landlord to inspect it, the tenant can deduct the cost from his rent—not exceeding *one month's rent*. The statute does not allow the tenant to use this alternative remedy to deduct more than one month's rent in any twelve-month period.

Virginia

Statute: Code of Virginia, Sec. 32-64 (1973).
Provisions: Virginians, alas, your statute is of little use to you, unless your apartment building is without toilets. If the landlord has not supplied the necessary toilet facilities, you can install them in accordance with prevailing health standards and deduct the cost from your rent.

Appendix C
Warranty-of-Habitability Statutes and Cases

Alaska

Statute: Alaska Statutes, Secs. 34.03.100, 34.03.160, 34.03.180 (1975 Supp.).

Arizona

Statute: Arizona Revised Statutes Annotated, Secs. 33-1324, 33-1361 (1974).

California

Statute: California Civil Code, Sec. 1941 (1954).

Connecticut

Statute: Connecticut General Statutes Annotated, Sec. 47-24 (1960).
Case: *Todd* v. *May,* 6 Conn. Supp. 731, 316 A.2d 793 (Cir. Ct. 1973).

Delaware

Statute: Delaware Code Annotated, Title 25, Sec. 5303 (1974).

District of Columbia

Case: *Javins* v. *First National Realty Corp.,* 428 F.2d 1071 (D.C. Cir.), cert. denied, 400 U.S. 925 (1970).

Florida

Statute: Florida Statutes Annotated, Secs. 83.51, 83.56 (1973).

Hawaii

Statute: Hawaii Revised Statutes, Sec. 521-42 (1975 Supp.).

Illinois

Case: *Jack Spring, Inc.* v. *Little,* 50 Ill.2d 351, 280 N.E.2d 208 (1972).

Iowa

Case: *Mease* v. *Fox,* 200 N.W.2d 791 (Iowa 1972).

Kansas

Case: *Steele* v. *Latimer,* 214 Kan. 329, 521 P.2d 304 (1974).

Kentucky

Statute: Kentucky Revised Statutes Annotated, Secs. 383.595, 383.625 (1976 Cumm. Supp.).

Maine

Statute: Maine Revised Statutes Annotated, Title 14, Sec. 6021 (1975 Supp.).

Maryland

Statute: Maryland Real Property Code Annotated, Sec. 8-211 (1975 Supp.).

Massachusetts

Case: *Boston Housing Authority* v. *Hemmingway,* 363 Mass. 184, 293 N.E.2d 831 (1973).

APPENDIX C WARRANTY-OF-HABITABILITY STATUTES AND CASES 275

Michigan

Statute: Michigan Compiled Laws Annotated, Sec. 554.139 (1976–77 Supp.).

Case: *Rome* v. *Walker*, 38 Mich. App. 458, 196 N.W.2d 850 (1972).

Minnesota

Statute: Minnesota Statutes, Sec. 504.18 (1974).

Missouri

Case: *King* v. *Moorehead*, 495 S.W.2d 65 (Mo. Ct. App. 1973).

Nebraska

Statute: Nebraska Revised Statutes, Sec. 76-1419 (1974 Cumm. Supp.).

New Hampshire

Case: *Kline* v. *Burns*, 111 N.H. 87, 276 A.2d 248 (1971).

New Jersey

Case: *Marini* v. *Ireland*, 56 N.J. 130, 265 A.2d 526 (1970).

New York

Statute: New York Real Property Law, Sec. 235-b (1976 Supp.).

Ohio

Statute: Ohio Revised Code, Secs. 5321.04, 5321.07 (1975 Supp.).

Oregon

Statute: Oregon Revised Statutes, Sec. 91.770 (1975).

Pennsylvania

Case: *Commonwealth* v. *Monumental Properties, Inc.*, 459 Pa. 450, 329 A.2d 812 (1974).

Virginia

Statute: Code of Virginia, Secs. 55-248.13, 55-248.25 (1975 Cumm. Supp.).

Washington

Statute: Washington Revised Code Annotated, Sec. 59.18.060 (1975 Supp.).
Case: *Foisy* v. *Wyman*, 83 Wash.2d 22, 515 P.2d 160 (1973).

Wisconsin

Case: *Pines* v. *Perssion*, 14 Wis.2d 590, 111 N.W.2d 409 (1961).

Appendix D
Uniform Commercial Code State Citations

State	Statutory Citation
Alabama	Code of Ala. Tit. 7A, SS 1-101 to 10-104
Alaska	A.S. SS 45.05.002 to 45.05.794
Arizona	A.R.S. SS 44-2201 to 44-3202
Arkansas	Ark.Stats. SS 85-1-101 to 85-9-507
California	West's Ann.Com.Code SS 1101 to 10104
Colorado	C.R.S. '73, SS 4-1-101 to 4-11-102
Connecticut	C.G.S.A. SS 42a-1-101 to 42a-10-104
Delaware	6 Del.C SS 1-101 to 10-104
District of Columbia	D.C.C.E. SS 28:1-101 to 28:10-104
Florida	West's F.S.A. SS 671.1-101 to 680.10-105
Georgia	Code SS 109A-10101 to 109A-10-106
Hawaii	HRS 490:1-101 to 490:10-104
Idaho	I.C. S 28-1-101 et seq.
Illinois	S.H.A. ch. 26, SS 1-101 to 11-108
Indiana	I.C.1971, 26-1-1-101 to 26-1-9-507
Iowa	I.C.A. SS 554.1101 to 554.11109
Kansas	K.S.A. SS 84-1-101 to 84-10-102
Kentucky	KRS 355.1-101 to 355.10-102
Maine	11 M.R.S.A. SS 1-101 to 9-507
Maryland	Code, Commercial Law, SS 1-101 to 10-104
Massachusetts	M.G.L.A. c.106, SS 1-101 to 9-507
Michigan	M.C.L.A. SS 440.1101 to 440.9994
Minnesota	M.S.A. SS 336.1-101 to 336.10-105

Mississippi	Code 1972, SS 75-1-101 to 75-10-104
Missouri	V.A.M.S. SS 400.1-107 to 400.10-102
Montana	R.C.M.1947, SS 87A-1-101 to 87A-10-103
Nebraska	Neb.U.C.C. SS 1-101 to 10-104
Nevada	N.R.S. 104.1101 to 104.9507
New Hampshire	RSA 382-A:1-101 to 382-A:9-507
New Jersey	N.J.S.A. 12A:1-101 to 12A:10-106
New Mexico	1953 Comp. SS 50A-1-101 to 50A-9-507
New York	McKinney's Uniform Commercial Code, SS 1-101 to 10-105
North Carolina	G.S. SS 25-1-101 to 25-10-107
North Dakota	NDCC 41-01-02 to 41-09-53
Ohio	R.C. SS 1301.01 to 1309.50
Oklahoma	12A Okl.St.Ann. SS 1-101 to 10-104
Oregon	ORS 71.1010 to 79.5070
Pennsylvania	12A P.S. SS 1-101 to 10-104
Rhode Island	Gen.Laws 1956, SS 6A-1-101 to 6A-9-507
South Carolina	Code 1962, SS 10.1-101 to 10.10-103
South Dakota	SDCL SS 57-1-1 to 57-40-2
Tennessee	T.C.A. SS 47-1-101 to 47-9-507
Texas	V.T.C.A., Bus. & C. SS 1.101 to 11.108
Utah	U.C.A.1953, 70A-1-101 to 70A-10-104
Vermont	9A V.S.A. SS 1-101 to 9-507
Virgin Islands	T. 11A V.I.C. SS 1-101 to 9-507
Virginia	Code 1950, SS 8.1-101 to 8.11-108
Washington	RCWA 62A.1-101 to 62A.10-104
West Virginia	Code, 46-10101 to 46-11-108
Wisconsin	W.S.A. 401.101 to 409.507
Wyoming	W.S.1957, SS 34:1-101 to 34:10-105

Appendix E
Deceptive-Trade-Practices Statutes

Alaska

Statute: Alaska Unfair Trade Practices and Consumer Protection Act.
Citation: Alaska Stat. Secs. 45.50.471–45.50.561 (1973 Cumm. Supp.).
Damages: Consumer can be awarded either the actual amount of his loss or two hundred dollars, whichever is greater. Treble damages may be awarded in the case of a willful violation of the Act.
Attorney's fees: Reasonable attorney's fees and court costs may also be awarded to the consumer.

Arizona

Statute: Arizona Consumer Fraud Act.
Citation: Ariz. Rev. Stat. Ann. Secs. 44-1521–44-1534 (1967).
Leading court case: *Sellinger* v. *Freeway Mobile Home Sales, Inc.*, 110 Ariz. 573, 521 P.2d 1119 (1974). (In any super threat relying on the Arizona statute, cite the *Sellinger* case as well as the statute.)
Damages: Consumer can be awarded the actual amount of his loss. Punitive damages may also be awarded in the case of a willful violation of the Act.
Attorney's fees: Not presently recoverable under the Act.

California

Statute: California Consumers Legal Remedies Act.
Citation: Calif. Ann. Civ. Code Secs. 1770–1784 (1973).

Damages: Consumer can be awarded the actual amount of his loss as well as punitive damages.
Attorney's fees: May also be awarded to the consumer.

Colorado

Statute: Colorado Consumer Protection Act.
Citation: Colo. Rev. Stat. Secs. 6-1-101–6-1-114 (1973).
Damages: Consumer can be awarded the actual amount of his loss.
Attorney's fees: Consumer may also be awarded attorney's fees plus court costs.

Connecticut

Statute: Connecticut Unfair Trade Practices Act.
Citation: Conn. Gen. Stat. Ann. Secs. 42-110a–42-110l (1976 Supp.).
Damages: Consumer can be awarded both the actual amount of his loss and punitive damages.
Attorney's fees: Consumer may also be awarded reasonable attorney's fees plus court costs.

Delaware

Statute: Delaware Uniform Deceptive Trade Practices Act.
Citation: Del. Code Ann. Secs. 2531–2536 (Rev. 1974).
Damages: Consumer is entitled to recover treble damages (three times amount of his actual losses).
Attorney's fees: May also be awarded to the consumer provided there has been a willful violation of the Act.

District of Columbia

Statute: District of Columbia Consumer Protection Procedures Act.
Citation: D.C. Law 1-76, Secs. 2–6 (July 22, 1976).

Damages: Consumer is entitled to recover treble damages (three times the amount of his actual losses) plus punitive damages.
Attorney's fees: Reasonable attorney's fees can also be recovered.

Florida

Statute: Florida Deceptive and Unfair Trade Practices Act.
Citation: Fla. Stat. Ann. Secs. 501.201–501.213 (1976–77 Cumm. Supp.).
Damages: Consumer can be awarded the actual amount of his loss.
Attorney's fees: Reasonable attorney's fees can be awarded to the consumer.

Georgia

Statute: Georgia Fair Business Practices Act of 1975.
Citation: Ga. Code Ann. Secs. 106-1201–106-1217 (G.C.A. Adv. Codif. Serv.).
Damages: Consumer can be awarded the actual amount of his loss. In the case of a willful violation of the Act, punitive damages can be awarded in the amount of three times the actual loss.
Attorney's fees: Reasonable attorney's fees plus court costs can be awarded to the consumer.

Hawaii

Statute: Hawaii Deceptive Practices Statute.
Citation: Haw. Rev. Stat. Secs. 480-2, 480-3, 480-13 (1975 Supp.).
Damages: When a consumer wins his case under Hawaii's statute, he is awarded either one thousand dollars or three times his actual damages—whichever amount is greater.
Attorney's fees: Consumer can also be awarded reasonable

attorney's fees plus court costs.

Idaho

Statute: Idaho Consumer Protection Act.
Citation: Idaho Code Secs. 48-601–48-619 (1975 Cumm. Supp.).
Damages: Consumer can be awarded either the actual amount of his loss or five hundred dollars—whichever sum is greater. Punitive damages may also be awarded, at the court's discretion.
Attorney's fees: Reasonable attorney's fees plus court costs may be awarded to the consumer.

Illinois

Statute: Illinois Consumer Fraud and Deceptive Business Practices Act.
Citation: Ill. Ann. Stat., Chp. 121½, secs. 261–272 (1976–77 Cumm. Supp.).
Damages: Consumer may recover the actual amount of his loss.
Attorney's fees: Reasonable attorney's fees and court costs may also be awarded.

Indiana

Statute: Indiana Deceptive Consumer Sales Act.
Citation: Ind. Stat. Ann. Secs. 24-5-0.5-1–24-5-0.5-6.
Damages: Consumer can be awarded the actual amount of his loss.
Attorney's fees: Consumer can be awarded reasonable attorney's fees plus court costs.

Kansas

Statute: Kansas Consumer Protection Act.
Citation: Kans. Stat. Ann. Secs. 50-623–50-643 (1975 Cumm. Supp.).
Damages: Consumer can be awarded either the actual amount of his loss or a civil penalty (two thousand dollars for each violation of the Act)—whichever sum is larger.
Attorney's fees: Reasonable attorney's fees can also be awarded to the consumer.

Kentucky

Statute: Kentucky Consumer Protection Act.
Citation: Kent. Rev. Stat. Secs. 367.110–367.300 (1976 Cumm. Supp.).
Damages: Consumer can be awarded the actual amount of his loss plus punitive damages "where appropriate."
Attorney's fees: Consumer can also recover reasonable attorney's fees plus court costs.

Louisiana

Statute: Louisiana Unfair Trade Practices and Consumer Protection Law.
Citation: La. Stat. Ann. Secs. 51-1401–51-1418 (1976 Cumm. Supp.).
Damages: Consumer can be awarded the actual amount of his loss. Three times the amount of the loss may be awarded under certain circumstances.
Attorney's fees: Consumer can also recover reasonable attorney's fees plus court costs.

Maine

Statute: Maine Unfair Trade Practices Act.
Citation: Me. Rev. Stat. Ann., Title 5, Secs. 206–214 (1973 Supp. Pamphlet).

Damages: Consumer can be awarded the actual amount of his loss.
Attorney's fees: Reasonable attorney's fees plus court costs can also be awarded to the consumer.

Maryland

Statute: Maryland Consumer Protection Act.
Citation: Md. Ann. Code Secs. 13-101–13-501 (1975).
Damages: Consumer can recover the actual amount of his loss.
Attorney's fees: Not presently recoverable under the Act.

Massachusetts

Statute: Massachusetts Consumer Protection Act.
Citation: Mass. Gen. Laws Ann., Chp. 93A, Secs. 1–11.
Damages: Consumer can recover the actual amount of his loss. In the case of a willful violation of the Act, the consumer can be awarded punitive damages of up to three times, but not less than two times, the actual amount of the loss.
Attorney's fees: Consumer can also be awarded attorney's fees and costs.

Minnesota

Statute: Minnesota Prevention of Consumer Fraud Act.
Citation: Minn. Stat. Ann. Secs. 325.79–325.80, 325.907 (1976 Cumm. Supp.).
Damages: Consumer can recover the actual amount of his loss.
Attorney's fees: Consumer can also recover reasonable attorney's fees and court costs.

Mississippi

Statute: Mississippi Consumer Protection Act.
Citation: Miss. Code Ann. Secs. 75-24-1–75-24-23 (1976 Cumm. Supp.).
Damages: Consumer can be awarded the actual amount of his loss.
Attorney's fees: Reasonable attorney's fees may also be recovered.

Missouri

Statute: Missouri Merchandising Practices Act.
Citation: Mo. Stat. Ann. Secs. 407.010–407.130 (1976 Cumm. Supp.).
Damages: Consumer can recover both the actual amount of his loss and punitive damages, at the court's discretion.
Attorney's fees: May be recovered by consumer on the basis of the actual hours put in by his attorney.

Montana

Statute: Montana Unfair Trade Practices and Consumer Protection Act of 1973.
Citation: Mont. Rev. Code Ann. Secs. 85-401–85-418 (1975 Cumm. Supp.).
Damages: Consumer can be awarded either the actual amount of his loss or two hundred dollars, whichever sum is larger. Consumer may also be awarded three times the actual amount of his loss at the discretion of the court.
Attorney's fees: Reasonable attorney's fees may also be awarded.

Nebraska

Statute: Nebraska Consumer Protection Act.
Citation: Neb. Rev. Stat. Secs. 59-1601–59-1623 (1976 Cumm. Supp.).

Damages: Consumer can be awarded the actual amount of his loss. (N.B. If the damages cannot be accurately measured, then the award may be increased to a reasonable amount, not to exceed one thousand dollars.)
Attorney's fees: Consumer may also be awarded reasonable attorney's fees plus court costs.

New Hampshire

Statute: New Hampshire Consumer Protection Act.
Citation: N.H. Rev. Stat. Ann. Secs. 358-A:1–358-A:13 (1975 Cumm. Supp.).
Damages: Consumer can recover the actual amount of his loss as well as punitive damages of up to one hundred dollars.
Attorney's fees: Consumer may also be awarded reasonable attorney's fees plus court costs.

New Jersey

Statute: New Jersey Consumer Fraud Act.
Citation: N.J. Stat. Ann. Secs. 56:8-1–56:8-20 (1976–77 Cumm. Supp.).
Damages: The victorious consumer will be awarded three times the amount of his actual loss.
Attorney's fees: Consumer will also be awarded reasonable attorney's fees and costs.

New Mexico

Statute: New Mexico Unfair Practices Act.
Citation: N.M. Stat. Ann. Secs. 49-15-1–49-15-14 (1975 Supp.).
Damages: The consumer can be granted injunctive relief against someone who is violating the Act; money damages will not be awarded, however.
Attorney's fees: If there is a willful violation of the Act, the consumer can recover his attorney's fees.

North Carolina

Statute: North Carolina Consumer Protection Act.
Citation: N.C. Gen. Stat. Ann. Secs. 75-1–75-29 (1975).
Damages: Consumer will be awarded three times the actual amount of his loss.
Attorney's fees: Reasonable attorney's fees may also be awarded if there has been a willful violation of the act.

Rhode Island

Statute: Rhode Island Deceptive Trade Practices Act.
Citation: R.I. Gen. Laws Ann. Secs. 6-13.1-1–6-13.1-7 (1975 Supp.).
Damages: Consumer can be awarded either the actual amount of his loss or two hundred dollars, whichever sum is larger. The court may also award punitive damages to the consumer.
Attorney's fees: Reasonable attorney's fees plus court costs can also be awarded.

Oregon

Statute: Oregon Unlawful Trade Practices Act.
Citation: Ore. Rev. Stat. Secs. 646.605–646.656.
Damages: Consumer can be awarded either the actual amount of his loss or two hundred dollars, whichever sum is larger. The court may also award punitive damages to the consumer.
Attorney's fees: Reasonable attorney's fees plus court costs can also be awarded.

Ohio

Statute: Ohio Consumer Sales Practices Act.
Citation: Ohio Rev. Code Secs. 1345.01–1345.13 (1975 Cumm. Supp.).

Damages: Consumer can be awarded the actual amount of his loss. (N.B. In addition, punitive damages have been awarded by Ohio courts and should be sought by consumers.)
Attorney's fees: Not presently recoverable under the Act.

South Carolina

Statute: South Carolina Unfair Trade Practices Act.
Citation: S.C. Code Ann. Secs. 66-71–66-71.15 (1975 Cumm. Supp.).
Damages: Consumer can recover the actual amount of his loss. If the violation of the Act was willful, then the consumer will be awarded three times the amount of his loss.
Attorney's fees: Reasonable attorney's fees plus court costs can also be recovered by the consumer.

South Dakota

Statute: South Dakota Deceptive Trade Practices Act.
Citation: S.D. Comp. Laws Ann. Secs. 37-24-1–37-24-35 (1972 Rev.).
Damages: Consumer can recover the actual amount of his loss.
Attorney's fees: Not presently recoverable under the Act.

Texas

Statute: Texas Deceptive Trade Practices Consumer Protection Act.
Citation: Tex. Bus. & Comm. Code Ann. Secs. 17.41–17.63 (1976–77 Cumm. Supp.).
Damages: The victorious consumer will be awarded three times the actual amount of his loss.
Attorney's fees: Consumer may also recover reasonable attorney's fees plus court costs.

Utah

Statute: Utah Consumer Sales Practices Act.
Citation: Utah Code Ann. Secs. 13-11-1–13-11-23 (1975 Cumm. Supp.).
Damages: Consumer can recover either the actual amount of his loss or one hundred dollars, whichever sum is greater.
Attorney's fees: Reasonable attorney's fees can also be recovered.

Vermont

Statute: Vermont Consumer Fraud Act.
Citation: Vt. Stat. Ann., Title 9, Secs. 2451–2462 (1976 Cumm. Supp.).
Damages: Consumer can be awarded the actual amount of his loss. Three times this amount may also be awarded by way of punitive damages.
Attorney's fees: Reasonable attorney's fees are recoverable.

Virginia

Statute: Virginia Deceptive Trade Practices Laws.
Citation: Va. Code Ann. Secs. 59.1-68.3, 59.1-68.5 (1975 Cumm. Supp.).
Damages: Consumer can recover either the actual amount of his loss or one hundred dollars, whichever sum is greater.
Attorney's fees: Reasonable attorney's fees are also recoverable.

Washington

Statute: Washington Consumer Protection Act.
Citation: Wash. Rev. Code Ann. Secs. 19.86.010–19.86.920 (1976 Cumm. Supp.).
Damages: Consumer can be awarded the actual amount of his loss. Three times this amount (not to exceed one thou-

sand dollars) can also be awarded by way of punitive damages.
Attorney's fees: Reasonable attorney's fees and court costs are recoverable too.

West Virginia

Statute: West Virginia General Consumer Protection Act.
Citation: W. Va. Code Ann. Secs. 46A-6-101–46A-6-108 (1976 vol.).
Damages: Consumer can be awarded either the actual amount of his loss or two hundred dollars, whichever sum is greater.
Attorney's fees: Not presently recoverable under the Act.

Wisconsin

Statute: Wisconsin Unfair Trade Practices Statute.
Citation: Wisc. Stat. Ann. Sec. 100.20 (1973).
Damages: The victorious consumer will be awarded two times the actual amount of his loss.
Attorney's fees: Consumer will also be awarded reasonable attorney's fees and court costs.

Wyoming

Statute: Wyoming Consumer Protection Act.
Citation: Wyom. Stat. Ann. Secs. 40-102–40-113 (1975 Cumm. Supp.).
Damages: Consumer can recover the actual amount of his loss.
Attorney's fees: No provision for recovery of attorney's fees under the Act.

Appendix F
Federal Trade Commission Regional Office

Atlanta: Alabama, Florida, Georgia, North Carolina, South Carolina, Tennessee
730 Peachtree Street N.E., Atlanta, Ga. 30308
S. Edward Combs, Regional Director
Boston: Connecticut, Maine, Massachusetts, New Hampshire, Rhode Island, Vermont
150 Causeway Street, Boston, Mass. 02114
William M. Gibson, Regional Director
Chicago: Illinois, Indiana, Minnesota, Wisconsin
55 East Monroe Street, Chicago, Ill. 60603
Stephanie W. Kanwit, Regional Director
Cleveland: Kentucky, Michigan, Ohio, West Virginia
1240 East 9th Street, Cleveland, Ohio 44199
Paul R. Peterson, Regional Director
Dallas: Arkansas, Oklahoma, Texas
500 South Ervay Street, Dallas, Tex. 75201
Carl L. Swanson, Jr., Regional Director
Kansas City: Colorado, Iowa, Kansas, Missouri, Nebraska, North Dakota, South Dakota, Wyoming
911 Walnut Street, Kansas City, Mo. 64106
Newman T. Guthrie, Regional Director
Los Angeles: Arizona, Southern California, New Mexico
1100 Wilshire Boulevard, Los Angeles, Ca. 90024
Carol G. Emerling, Regional Director
New Orleans: Louisiana, Mississippi
333 St. Charles Street, New Orleans, La. 70130
Donald M. Van Wart, Assistant Director
New York: New York, New Jersey
26 Federal Plaza, New York, N.Y. 10007

Richard A. Givens, Regional Director
San Francisco: Northern California, Hawaii, Nevada, Utah
450 Golden Gate Avenue, San Francisco, Ca. 94102
William A. Arbitman, Regional Director
Seattle: Alaska, Idaho, Montana, Oregon, Washington
915 Second Avenue, Seattle, Wash. 98174
William C. Erxleben, Regional Director
Washington, D.C.: Delaware, District of Columbia, Maryland, Pennsylvania, Virginia
2120 L St. N.W., Washington, D.C. 20037
Michael J. Vitale, Regional Director

Appendix G
Trial Locations for Small-Tax Cases

When you sue the Internal Revenue Service in United States Tax Court, you may select one of the cities listed below as the place for your trial. Record that city on the "Request for Place of Trial," which you file with the clerk of the court.

Alabama: Birmingham, Mobile, Montgomery
Alaska: Anchorage
Arizona: Phoenix, Tucson
Arkansas: Fort Smith, Little Rock
California: Fresno, Los Angeles, San Diego, San Francisco
Colorado: Denver
Connecticut: New Haven
Delaware: Wilmington
District of Columbia: Washington
Florida: Jacksonville, Miami, Tallahassee, Tampa
Georgia: Atlanta, Macon, Savannah
Hawaii: Honolulu
Idaho: Boise, Pocatello
Illinois: Chicago, Danville, Peoria, Springfield
Indiana: Evansville, Fort Wayne, Indianapolis
Iowa: Cedar Rapids, Des Moines
Kansas: Wichita
Kentucky: Louisville
Louisiana: New Orleans, Shreveport
Maine: Portland
Maryland: Baltimore
Massachusetts: Boston, Springfield
Michigan: Detroit, Grand Rapids
Minnesota: Duluth, Minneapolis, St. Paul

Mississippi: Greenville, Jackson, Biloxi
Missouri: Kansas City, St. Louis
Montana: Billings, Helena
Nebraska: Omaha
Nevada: Las Vegas, Reno
New Hampshire: Concord
New Jersey: Atlantic City, Newark
New Mexico: Albuquerque
New York: Albany, Buffalo, New York City, Syracuse
North Carolina: Asheville, Greensboro, Raleigh
North Dakota: Bismarck
Ohio: Cincinnati, Cleveland, Columbus, Toledo
Oklahoma: Oklahoma City, Tulsa
Oregon: Portland
Pennsylvania: Harrisburg, Philadelphia, Pittsburgh, Scranton
Rhode Island: Providence
South Carolina: Charleston, Columbia
South Dakota: Aberdeen
Tennessee: Knoxville, Memphis, Nashville
Texas: Dallas, El Paso, Houston, Lubbock, San Antonio
Utah: Salt Lake City
Vermont: Burlington
Virginia: Norfolk, Richmond, Roanoke
Washington: Seattle, Spokane
West Virginia: Charleston, Clarksburg, Huntington
Wisconsin: Eau Claire, Green Bay, Milwaukee
Wyoming: Cheyenne

Appendix H
State Insurance Commissioners

Any of the commissioners named below may have been replaced at the expiration of his term by a new commissioner, so you might want to check for the name of the current commissioner before you address correspondence directly to him.

Alabama:
    Charles Payne
    Commissioner of Insurance
    Administrative Building
    Montgomery 36104
    (205) 832-6140

Alaska:
    Richard L. Block
    Director of Insurance
    State Office Building
    Juneau 99811
    (907) 465-2515

Arizona:
    John N. Trimble
    Director of Insurance
    1601 West Jefferson
    Phoenix 85007
    (602) 271-4862

Arkansas:
    William H. L. Woodyard III
    Insurance Commissioner

12th & University Avenue
Little Rock 72204
(501) 371-1325

California:
Wesley J. Kinder
Insurance Commissioner
600 South Commonwealth
Los Angeles 90005
(213) 620-2580

Colorado:
J. Richard Barnes
Commissioner of Insurance
106 State Office Building
Denver 80203
(303) 892-3201

Connecticut:
T. F. Gilroy Daly
Insurance Commissioner
Rm. 425 State Office Building
Hartford 06115
(203) 566-5275

Delaware:
J. Francis Richardson
Insurance Commissioner
21 The Green
Dover 19901
(302) 678-4251

District of Columbia:
Maximilian Wallach
Superintendent of Insurance

614 H Street N.W., Suite 512
Washington 20001
(202) 629-4514

Florida:
Bill Gunter
Insurance Commissioner
State Capitol
Tallahassee 32304
(904) 488-7056

Georgia:
Johnny L. Caldwell
Insurance Commissioner
238 State Capitol
Atlanta 30334
(404) 656-2056

Guam:
Manuel A. Chaco
Insurance Commissioner
P.O. Box 2796
Agana 96910

Hawaii:
Wayne Minami
Insurance Commissioner
P.O. Box 3614
Honolulu 96811
(808) 548-7505

Idaho:
Monroe C. Gollaher
Director of Insurance
206 State House

Boise 83720
(208) 384-2250

Illinois:
Michael P. Duncan
Director of Insurance
160 N. LaSalle Street, Room 1600
Chicago 60601
(312) 793-2420

Indiana:
H. Pete Hudson
Commissioner of Insurance
509 State Office Building
Indianapolis 46204
(317) 633-4892

Iowa:
Herbert W. Anderson
Commissioner of Insurance
State Office Building
Des Moines 50319
(515) 281-5705

Kansas:
Fletcher Bell
Commissioner of Insurance
State Office Building
Topeka 66612
(913) 196-3071

Kentucky:
Harold B. McGuffey
Insurance Commissioner
Capitol Plaza Tower

Frankfort 40601
(502) 564-3630

Louisiana:
>Sherman Bernard
Insurance Commissioner
P.O. Box 44214, Capitol Station
Baton Rouge 70804
(504) 389-5671

Maryland:
>Edward J. Birrane, Jr.
Insurance Commissioner
One South Calvert Bldg.
Baltimore 21202
(301) 383-5690

Massachusetts:
>James M. Stone
Commissioner of Insurance
100 Cambridge Street
Boston 02202
(617) 727-3357

Michigan:
>Thomas C. Jones
Commissioner of Insurance
111 North Hosmer Street
Lansing 48913
(517) 373-0220

Minnesota:
>Berton W. Heaton
Commissioner of Insurance
Metro Square Building

St. Paul 55101
(612) 296-6907

Mississippi:
George Dale
Commissioner of Insurance
P.O. Box 79
Jackson 39205
(601) 354-7711

Missouri:
Henry W. Edmiston
Director of Insurance
P.O. Box 690
Jefferson City 65101
(314) 751-2451

Montana:
Elmer V. Omholt
Commissioner of Insurance
Capitol Building
Helena 59601
(406) 449-2040

Nebraska:
E. Benjamin Nelson
Director of Insurance
1335 L Street
Lincoln 68508
(402) 471-2201 Ex. 20

Nevada:
Dick L. Rottman
Insurance Commissioner
Nye Building

APPENDIX H STATE INSURANCE COMMISSIONERS 301

    Carson City 89710
    (702) 885-4270

New Hampshire:
    Frank E. Whaland
    Insurance Commissioner
    169 Manchester
    Concord 03301
    (603) 271-2261

New Jersey:
    James J. Sheeran
    Commissioner of Insurance
    201 East State Street
    Trenton 08625
    (609) 292-5363

New Mexico:
    Kenneth C. Moore
    Superintendent of Insurance
    P.O. Drawer 1269
    Santa Fe 87501
    (505) 827-2451

New York:
    Thomas A. Harnett
    Superintendent of Insurance
    Two World Trade Center
    New York 10047
    (212) 488-4124

North Carolina:
    John R. Ingram
    Commissioner of Insurance
    P.O. Box 26387

Raleigh 27611
(919) 829-7343

North Dakota:
J. O. Wigen
Commissioner of Insurance
Capitol Building, Fifth Floor
Bismarck 58501
(701) 224-2244

Ohio:
Harry V. Jump
Director of Insurance
447 E. Broad Street
Columbus 43215
(614) 466-3584

Oklahoma:
Gerald Grimes
Insurance Commissioner
408 Will Rogers Memorial Bldg.
Oklahoma City 73105
(405) 521-4246

Oregon:
Lester L. Rawls
Insurance Commissioner
158 12th Street, N.E.
Salem 97310
(503) 378-4271

Pennsylvania:
William J. Sheppard
Insurance Commissioner
108 Finance Building

Harrisburg 17120
(717) 787-5173

Puerto Rico:
    Manuel Juarbe
    Commissioner of Insurance
    P.O. Box 3508
    San Juan 00904
    (809) 722-0141

Rhode Island:
    Peter F. Mullaney
    Insurance Commissioner
    100 North Main Street
    Providence 02903
    (401) 277-2223

South Carolina:
    John W. Lindsay
    Insurance Commissioner
    2711 Middleburg Drive
    Columbia 29204
    (803) 758-2185

South Dakota:
    Lowell L. Knutson
    Director of Insurance
    Insurance Building
    Pierre 57501
    (605) 224-3563

Tennessee:
    Millard Oakley
    Commissioner of Insurance
    114 State Office Building

Nashville 37219
(615) 741-2241

Texas:
Joe D. Hawkins
Commissioner of Insurance
1110 San Jacinto Boulevard
Austin 78786
(512) 475-2273

Utah:
Clifton N. Ottosen
Commissioner of Insurance
275 E. Second South Street
Salt Lake City 84111
(801) 533-5611

Vermont:
Commissioner of Insurance
State Office Building
Montpelier 05602
(802) 828-3301

Virginia:
John G. Day
Commissioner of Insurance
700 Blanton Building
Richmond 23209
(804) 786-3741

Virgin Islands:
Juan Luis
Commissioner of Insurance
P.O. Box 450
Charlotte Amalie

St. Thomas 00801
(809) 774-2991

Washington:
Karl V. Herrmann
Insurance Commissioner
Insurance Building
Olympia 98504
(206) 753-7301

West Virginia:
Donald W. Brown
Insurance Commissioner
1800 Washington Street, E.
Charleston 25305
(304) 348-3386

Wisconsin:
Harold R. Wilde, Jr.
Commissioner of Insurance
123 West Washington
Madison 53702
(608) 266-3583

Wyoming:
John T. Langdon
Insurance Commissioner
500 Randall Boulevard
Cheyenne 82001
(397) 777-7401

Appendix I
Interstate Commerce Commission Field Offices

Alabama:
    2121 Building Suite 1616
    2121 Eighth Avenue North
    Birmingham 35203

    700 Commerce Building
    P.O. Box 2112
    Mobile 36602

Alaska:
    G-31 Federal Building
    P.O. Box 1532
    Anchorage 99510

Arizona:
    3427 Federal Building
    230 North First Avenue
    Phoenix 85025

Arkansas:
    3108 Federal Building
    Little Rock 72201

California:
    1321 Federal Building
    300 North Los Angeles Street
    Los Angeles 90012

13001 Federal Building
450 Golden Gate Avenue
P.O. Box 36004
San Francisco 94102

Colorado:
Room 492, U.S. Customs House
721 19th Street
Denver 80202

Connecticut:
324 U.S. Post Office
135 High Street
Hartford 06101

District of Columbia:
ICC Building Bureau of Operations
317 Labor Building
12th & Constitution, N.W.
Washington 20423

Florida:
288 Federal Building
Building Box 35008
400 West Bay Street
Jacksonville 32202

Monterey Building, Suite 101
8410 N.W. 53rd Terrace
Miami 33166

Georgia:
Room 300
1252 West Peachtree Street N.W.
Atlanta 30309

Idaho:
>550 West Fort Street
>Box 07
>Boise 83724

Illinois:
>Everett McKinley Dirksen Building
>Room 1386
>219 South Dearborn Street
>Chicago 60604
>
>414 Leland Office Building
>527 East Capitol Avenue
>Mailing address: P.O. Box 2418
>Springfield 62705

Indiana:
>345 West Wayne Street
>Room 204
>Fort Wayne 46802
>
>429 Federal Building and U.S. Court House
>46 East Ohio Street
>Indianapolis 46204

Iowa:
>518 Federal Building
>210 Walnut Street
>Des Moines 50309

Kansas:
>234 Federal Building
>Topeka 66603
>
>501 Petroleum Building
>221 South Broadway
>Wichita 67202

Kentucky:
    216 Bakhaus Building
    1500 West Main Street
    Lexington 40505

    426 U.S. Post Office
    601 West Broadway
    Louisville 40202

Louisiana:
    T-9038 Federal Building and U.S. Post Office
    701 Loyola Avenue
    New Orleans 70113

Maine:
    305 U.S. Post Office and Courthouse
    76 Pearl Street
    Portland 04112

Maryland:
    814-B Federal Building
    Charles Center
    31 Hopkins Plaza
    Baltimore 21201

Massachusetts:
    150 Causeway Street, Room 501
    Boston 02114

    338–342 Federal Building
    436 Dwight Street
    Springfield 01103

Michigan:
    1110 David Broderick Tower Building
    10 Witherell Street
    Detroit 48226

225 Federal Building
325 West Allegan Street
Lansing 48933

Minnesota:
414 Federal Building and U.S. Courthouse
110 South Fourth Street
Minneapolis 55401

Mississippi:
145 East Armite Building
Room 212
Jackson 39201

Missouri:
600 Federal Building
911 Walnut Street
Kansas City 64106

210 North 12th Street
Room 1465
St. Louis 63101

Montana:
2702 1st Avenue, North
Billings 59101

Nebraska:
285 Federal Building and U.S. Courthouse
100 Centennial Mall North
Lincoln 68508

Suite 620 Union Pacific Plaza
110 North 14th Street
Omaha 68102

Nevada:
203 Federal Building
705 North Plaza Street
Carson City 89701

New Hampshire:
313 Federal Building
55 Pleasant Building
Concord 03301

New Mexico:
1106 Federal Office Building
517 Gold Avenue S.W.
Albuquerque 87101

New Jersey:
9 Clinton Street, Room 618
Newark 07102

204 Carroll Building
428 East State Street
Trenton 08608

New York:
518 New Federal Building
Maiden Lane & Broadway
Albany 12201

910 Federal Building
111 West Huron Street
Buffalo 14202

26 Federal Plaza
Room 1807
New York 10007

104 O'Donnell Building
301 Erie Boulevard, West
Syracuse 13202

North Carolina:
Room CC-516 Mart Office Building
800 Briar Creek Road
Charlotte 28205

624 Federal Building
310 New Bern Avenue
P.O. Box 26896
Raleigh 27611

North Dakota:
P.O. Box 2340, Federal Building and U.S. Post Office
657 Second Avenue North
Fargo 58102

Ohio:
5514-B Federal Building
550 Main Street
Cincinnati 45202

181 Federal Building
1240 East Ninth Street
Cleveland 44199

220 Federal Building and U.S. Courthouse
85 Marconi Boulevard
Columbus 43215

313 Federal Building
234 Summit Street
Toledo 43604

Oklahoma:
>240 Old Post Office and Courthouse
215 Northwest Third Street
Oklahoma City 73102

Oregon:
>114 Pioneer Courthouse
555 S.W. Yamhill Street
Portland 97204

Pennsylvania:
>278 Federal Building
228 Walnut Street
P.O. Box 869
Harrisburg 17108

>William J. Green, Jr., Federal Building
600 Arch Street, Room 3238
Philadelphia 19106

>2111 Federal Building
1000 Liberty Avenue
Pittsburgh 15222

>314 U.S. Post Office
North Washington Avenue and Linden Street
Scranton 18503

Rhode Island:
>187 Westminster Street
Room 401
Providence 02903

South Carolina:
>RM 302, 1400 Building
1400 Pickens Street
Columbia 29201

South Dakota:
    369 Federal Building
    Pierre 57501

Tennessee:
    435 Federal Building
    167 North Main Street
    Memphis 38103

    Federal Building, 801 Broadway A422
    Nashville 37203

Texas:
    1012 Herring Plaza
    317 East Third Street
    Amarillo 79101

    Room 13C12
    1100 Commerce Street
    Dallas 75242

    9A27 Fritz Garland Lanham Federal Building
    819 Taylor Street
    Fort Worth 76102

    8610 Federal Building and U.S. Courthouse
    515 Rusk Avenue
    Houston 77002
    Mailing address: P.O. Box 61212
    Houston 77061

    Room B-400 Federal Building
    727 E. Durango
    San Antonio 78206

Utah:
>5301 Federal Building
>125 South State Street
>Salt Lake City 84138

Vermont:
>87 State Street, Room 303
>Mailing Address: P.O. Box 548
>Montpelier 05602

Virginia:
>10-502 Federal Building
>400 North Eighth Street
>Richmond 23240
>
>Mailing address: P.O. Box 210
>722 Richard H. Poff Federal Building
>210 Franklin Road, S.W.
>Roanoke 24011

Washington:
>858 Federal Building
>915 Second Avenue
>Seattle 98174

West Virginia:
>3108 Federal Building
>500 Quarrier Street
>Charleston 25301
>
>416 Old Post Office Building
>12th and Chapline Streets
>Wheeling 26003

Wisconsin:
>139 West Wilson Street
>Room 202
>Madison 53703

>135 West Wells Street
>Room 807
>Milwaukee 53203

Wyoming:
>1006 Federal Building and Post Office
>100 East B. Street
>Casper 82601

Index

Abernathy (company), 119–20
Abraham Used Car Company v. Silva, 205, 210
Acosta, Yvette, 87–8
Adams v. *Hamilton Carhartt Overall Co.*, 58
advertisements, 95, 118, 130, 155, 166–7
Aero Mayflower case, 248–9
Ahmed v. *Collins*, 148, 152
Alaska, 78, 93, 129
Allied Van Lines, 250–1, 253
Allied Van Lines, Inc. v. *Interstate Commerce Commission and United States of America*, 249
American Society of Travel Agents, 238
animal problems; dangerous, 59–64; noisy, 55–9; and personal liability, 59–64, 256; soft spots of, 33, 57, 62; super threats for, 44, 57–9, 61–4, 254–6
Arizona, 78–9, 93, 129
Arthur Murray Dance Studios, 142, 145–7

Astral Travel Service, 236–7

Baldwin, Myrtle, 223–4
Baldwin, Rufus, 223
bankruptcy; as shield for charter flight operators, 241
Best Gift Shop, 115–16

Boe Huchman Marine (company), 116–17
Book-of-the-Month Club, 160, 161
Boston Housing Authority v. *Hemmingway*, 274
Bowen, Mr. and Mrs., 149
Bowen v. *Johnson*, 149
Braddock, Mary, 48–9
Braddock v. *Barbecue Cottage*, 48–9, 51
Braitman, Nathan and Olga, 102–3
Braitman v. *Overlook Terrace*, 102–3
Brown, Mr., 121
Bucholtz, Helen, 235–6
Bucholtz v. *Sirotkin Travel Ltd.*, 235–6, 239
business: as a nuisance to neighbors, 47–51; soft spots of, 50; super threats for, 50–1. *See also* individual types

California, 78–9, 93, 129
Canfield v. *Howard*, 90–1
Carey, Mr., 145–6
Catania, Michael, 121
charter flight operators: and bankruptcy shield, 241; and fraud, 241–3; personal liability of, 242–5; soft spot of, 243; super threat for, 243–5
Chrysler Credit Corporation, 185, 191

317

Civil Aeronautics Board (CAB), 242–3
Civil Aeronautics Board v. *Scottish-American Association, Inc.*, 242–4
Civil Rights Act of 1871 (Section 1983 of U.S. Code): and civil rights movement, 69–70; and public utilities, 69–74
civil servants: personal liability of, 70–2
Clearview Dodge Sales, Inc., 185, 191–2
Code of Federal Regulations: and billing disputes, 199–201; and mail-order industry, 155–9, 161–5 and moving companies, 248–50
Collins, Constance, 148
Collins v. *Schoonfield*, 74
Colorado, 78, 129
Columbia Stereo Tape Club, 160–2
Commonwealth v. *Monumental Properties, Inc.*, 276
Connecticut, 93, 129
Constitution, the, 70–4
consumer affairs offices: and fraud, 150, 170; and SOS letters, 15, 18
consumers: credit problems of, 176–85; private right of action of, 129–30, 135, 137, 251. *See also* deceptive trade practices; fraud; warranties
Copley v. *Mills*, 63
Cova v. *Harley Davidson Motor Co.*, 126
crank letters: in tenant-landlord disputes, 7–11; weakness of, 9–12, 26
Credit Bureau of Rochester, Inc., 179–80, 185–4
credit problems: bill collection companies, 201–10; billing disputes, 193–201; credit-cost disclosure statements, 187–91; Fair Credit Billing Law, 194–201; and Federal Trade Commission, 191, 204, 205–7, 210; finance charges, 185–93, 197–8; penalties in, 190–3, 198–201, 204, 205, 206–7, 210; soft spots in, 187, 191–2, 199, 208; super threats for, 191–3, 197, 198–201, 204, 207–10; and Truth in Lending Law, 187–93; unscrupulous sellers, 186–7, 189
credit-reporting agencies, 173; civil liability of, 178–85; and contested bills, 197–8, 207; errors by, 174–80; and Fair Credit Reporting Act, 176–84; and Federal Trade Commission, 40, 176, 177, 180–2; renotification responsibility of, 176, 178, 180; and rights of consumers, 176–85; soft spot of, 182; super threat for, 182–5; and U.S. Code, 182–3

damages: compensatory, 33, 71, 102–3, 128, 141–2, 144, 146, 148, 149, 153, 179, 184, 198, 205, 226, 233, 236–41, 264; punitive, 21–2, 34, 48, 49, 51, 52–4, 58, 60, 63, 67, 71, 86, 88, 110, 128, 130, 141–2, 144–53, 179–80, 182, 184–5, 190–3, 198–201, 204, 205, 221–2, 223, 224, 226, 230–3, 241, 251–3, 259, 264
Davidson, Edward, 60–1
Davoust, Richard and Danny, 55–6, 57
Davoust v. *Mitchell*, 55, 59
deceptive trade practices: badmouthing of competitors, 133–4; of bill-collection companies,

205–7, 209; and characteristics of goods, 133; and leasing goods, 130; and misrepresentation of goods, 127–40, 142, 143; and price cuts, 132; and quality, 133; and services, 127, 130, 131, 148–9; soft spot in, 138; and sponsorship or affiliation, 132–3; statutes against, 129–30, 132, 134–40; super threats for, 137–40, 256–9; and used goods, 132, 142. *See also* fraud; individual states
Delaware, 78, 93
Denecke, Justice, 128
Detroit, Michigan, 103–4
Dietz, James and Mary, 94–7
Direct Mail Advertising Association, 156
District of Columbia, 93, 129
Doubleday and Company, 162
Dougherty v. *Taylor & Norton Co.*, 266

Eliot, T. S., 211
Eugene Surplus Sales Store, 127–9, 134

Fair Credit Billing Law, 194–201
Fair Credit Reporting Act, 176–84
Federal Trade Commission: and credit problems, 40, 176, 177, 180–2, 191, 204, 205–7, 210; and mail-order industry, 154–5, 157–9, 161, 163–5
Federal Trade Commission Improvement Act, 124, 157–9, 163–5, 206–10
Fletcher, U. L., 224–6
Fletcher v. *Western National Life Insurance Company*, 224–7, 231, 263
Florida, 93, 129
Foisy v. *Wyman*, 276

Foland, Francis John, 242
fraud: and automobiles, 148–50; and charter flights, 241–3; common-law, 129, 141; criminal liability in, 167–72; damages awarded in, 141–2, 144–53; defined, 141; elements in, 142–5; and gullible people, 144, 147; mail, 165–72; personal liability in, 151, 153, 243; soft spot in, 151; super threats for, 142, 151–3. *See also* deceptive trade practices

GAF Corporation, 115
Garcia, José, 80
Gates, Dr. Paul, 119–20
Gates v. *Abernathy*, 119–20
GC Service Corporation, 201–2
General Electric Credit Corporation, 115–16
General Electric Credit Corporation v. *Hoey*, 115–16
Georgia, 78, 90, 104, 129
Gilbert v. *Duke Power Company*, 74
Goldberg, Mr., 118–19
Gorman family, 52
Gorman v. *Sabo*, 52, 53
Groner, Bertha, 60
Groner v. *Hedrick*, 60, 64, 256

Hanke v. *Global Van Lines, Inc.*, 252
Hannigan, William, 169–70
Hawaii, 78, 93, 129
Hawkins Pontiac, 117–18
Hewlett House of Tires, 48
Hoey, Benjamin, 115–16
Holland Furnace Company v. *Robson*, 142–3
housing agencies, 81–3, 97
housing codes, 94
Hubbard family, 250–1

320 SUPER THREATS

Hubbard v. *Allied Van Lines,* 250–1, 253

Idaho, 129
Illinois, 78, 93, 129
income tax problems: appealing audited returns, 211–13; out-of-court settlements for, 215, 217, 219; soft spot in, 216; super threat for, 212, 216–19; and United States Tax Court, 213–19
Indiana, 129
insurance companies: claims on, 220–1; misconduct of, 33, 221–33; soft spot of, 34, 230; special relationship with clients of, 34, 221; super threats for, 221, 230–3, 262–4
Internal Revenue Service: and audited returns, 211–13; issuing statutory notice of deficiency, 215–16; soft spot of, 216; and United States Tax Court, 213–19. *See also* income tax problems
International Air Transport Association, 239
Interstate Commerce Act, 250; Carmack Amendment of, 251
Interstate Commerce Commission (ICC); and moving companies, 245–50
Iowa, 93
Ireland, Alice, 79–80

Jackson, Mr., 150
Jackson v. Rivera, 269
Jack Spring, Inc. v. Little, 83, 267, 274
Javins v. First National Realty Corp., 273
Johnson Dodge, 149
Johnston, Reese, 103–4
Johnston v. Harris, 103–4

J. Truett Payne Company, Inc. v. Jackson, 150
juries: and award of punitive damages, 86, 144, 146–53, 183, 226, 230–1, 251; in child-injury cases, 67, 68; in fraud cases, 143, 144, 146–53, 169; in insurance cases, 34, 221, 226, 230–1, 233, 264; in moving company cases, 251; in tenant-landlord disputes, 21, 22, 28, 76, 86, 110

Kansas, 93, 129
Kaufman, Judge, 226
Kentucky, 78, 93, 129
King v. Moorehead, 275
Kinley v. Atlantic Cement Co., 51
Kirk, Mr. and Mrs., 222–3
Kirk v. Safeco Insurance Company, 222–3
Kline, Sarah, 105–6
Kline v. Burns, 275
Kline v. 1500 Massachusetts Avenue Apartment Corporation, 20, 23, 105–6, 108

landlords: and common-law negligence, 20–8, 76–7, 86–92, 101–10; crank letter to, 7–11; and implied warranty of security, 20, 23, 106–10; maintenance and repair services required of, 75–101; personal liability of, 20–8, 76–7, 86–92, 101–10; polite complaint letters to, 12–14, 19, 78, 81, 84, 90–1, 97, 99, 107, 108–9; and repair-and-deduct laws, 76–86; soft spots of, 22, 76, 83, 90, 98, 108; SOS letters to, 15–18; super threats to, 6–7, 19–28, 76, 77, 80, 83–92, 97–101, 102, 106–10; and tenant security, 6–28 *passim,* 75–6, 77,

94, 101–10; and warranty-of-habitability laws, 76–7, 92–101
laws, ix–x; demystification of, x; and institutionalization of conduct standards, 32–3
lawsuits: class action, 151, 153, 191, 210, 238, 240, 241, 243–5; private right of action, 129–30, 135, 137, 251. See also damages; juries; liability, personal
lawyers: civil rights, 69–70; conservative character of, 28–9; and detecting soft spots, 32; fees of, ix–x, 27–8, 121, 124–5; fees of, paid by adversary, 31, 122–4, 128–9, 130, 138, 179–80, 182, 184–5, 191–3, 198–201, 223, 259; in insurance company disputes, 226, 230; letters of, 21–2, 23, 25, 28; in neighborhood disputes, 52, 53; and super threats, 27–9; in tenant-landlord disputes, 27–8, 85, 101
leasing goods, 130
legalese, 106, 129, 215, 222; in super threats, 25–6, 30, 42, 44, 91–2, 98, 100, 109, 184
legal rights, ix–x; legal remedies to obtain, 5, 31–4
letters: confirming, after telephone call, 36–7; lawyers', 21–2, 23, 25, 28. See also crank letters; polite complaint letters; SOS letters
liability, personal: and attractive nuisances, 66–8; of charter flight operators, 242–5; of civil servants, 70–2; and fraud, 151, 153, 243; of landlords, 20–8, 76–7, 86–92, 101–10; in neighborhood disputes, 54; of pet owners, 59–64, 256; of travel agents, 235–41; of utility companies, 73–4
Lobell, Mr., 89
Louisiana, 78, 114, 129
Lyons v. Zale Jewelry Company, 205

Machacado, Nilda, 60–1
Machacado v. City of New York, 60–1
Magnuson-Moss Warranty Act, 113–14, 117, 121–4
mail-order industry: and Code of Federal Regulations, 155–9, 161–5; complaints against, 154–5; criminal liability in, 167–72; fraud in, 165–72; and mail stop-orders, 22–3, 166–7, 170–2; negative-option plans, 159–65; soft spots of, 22–3, 157, 163, 166, 170–1; super threats for, 156–9, 163–5, 166, 167, 170–2, 259–61; and U.S. Code, 166–8, 171–2, 260–1
Maine, 93, 129
Majewski family, 236–7
Mandell, Mr. and Mrs., 48
Mandell v. Pasquaretto, 48, 50
manufacturers. See warranties
Marini v. Ireland, 79, 269, 275
Maryland, 93, 129
Massachusetts, 78, 93, 129
Maxwell v. Fraze, 62, 255
Mease v. Fox, 274
Melby, Ward, 117–18
Melby v. Hawkins Pontiac, 117–18
Mendelsohn, Mr., 89
Meyers, Cheryl, 185, 191
Meyers v. Clearview Dodge Sales, Inc., 185, 191–2
Michigan, 78, 93, 103–4
Millstone, James, 174–5, 179, 182, 184

Millstone v. *O'Hanlon Reports, Inc.*, 179, 184
Mindell, Mr., 115
Mindell v. *Raleigh Rug Company*, 115
Minnesota, 93, 129
Mississippi, 129
Missouri, 93, 129
Mitchell family, 55–6, 59
Mitchell v. *Akers*, 68
Montana, 78, 129
Morbeth Realty Corporation v. *Rosenshine*, 97
moving companies: delayed deliveries of, 250–3; and Interstate Commerce Commission, 245–50; liability of, 251–3; overcharges of, 246–50; soft spots of, 247, 252; super threats for, 246, 247–50, 251–3

Nebraska, 78, 93, 129
negligence: in tenant-landlord disputes, 20–8, 76–7, 86–92, 101–10; by travel agents, 236–41. *See also* liability, personal
neighborhood problems: business nuisance, 47–51; hazards, 43, 65–8; malicious neighbors, 51–4; soft spots of, 50, 53, 67; super threats for, 43, 50–4, 65, 67–8. *See also* animal problems
New Hampshire, 90, 93, 129
New Jersey, 78–9, 93, 94–7, 102–3, 129
New Mexico, 129
New York, 78, 80, 93–4, 97
New York City, 80, 87–9, 102, 104
Nitti, Louis, 179–80
Nitti v. *Credit Bureau of Rochester, Inc.*, 179–80, 184–5
North Carolina, 129
North Dakota, 78

nuisances: animal, 33, 55–9; attractive, 65–8; and environment, 48; neighborhood, 47–54
Nunez, Emilio, 88

Odysseys Unlimited, Inc., 237, 241
Odysseys Unlimited, Inc. v. *Astral Travel Service*, 237
O'Hanlon Reports, Inc., 174–5, 179, 184
Ohio, 78–9, 93, 129
Oklahoma, 78
Oregon, 78, 93
Oregon Unlawful Trade Practices Act, 128–9
Ortho Comfort Stores, 148
Outpost Development Corporation, 165–7, 171

Paterson family, 236–7
Pennsylvania, 93
Pines v. *Perssion*, 276
police: in neighborhood problems, 50, 52, 53, 57; personal liability of, 70–1
polite complaint letters: for credit problems, 180–1, 191, 194–7, 199–200, 207; for deceptive trade practices, 134–7, 139; drawbacks of, 24, 26; guidelines for, 13–14, 37–40, 42; to insurance companies, 227–30, 231–2; to outside sources, 19, 40, 81–3, 97, 170, 172, 181–2, 210, 238, 243; as preliminary to super threat, 12, 14, 34, 37, 81–3, 90, 97, 107, 135–7, 156, 163, 191; in tenant-landlord disputes, 7, 12–14, 19, 78, 81–3, 84, 90–1, 97, 99, 107, 108–9
politicians: appeals to, 17, 50
Postal Service: and mail fraud, 22–3, 166–7, 172, 261

Prosser: *Law of Torts*, 151–2
Public Service Commission, 72–3

Raleigh Rug Company, 115
repairpersons: misrepresentations of, 127, 130, 131, 148–9. *See also* warranties
Rex Insurance Company, 223–4
Rex Insurance Company v. Baldwin, 223–4
Rhode Island, 129
Robson, Mary Jane, 142–3
Rome v. Walker, 99, 275
Rudolf, Gabriel, 116–17

Sabo family, 52, 53
Sackheim, Max, 159–60
Safeco Insurance Company, 222–3
salespersons: and implied warranty, 115, 118–21; misrepresentations of, 127–40, 142, 143
Sargent v. Ross, 90–1
Sawyer, Raymond, 160–1
Scherman, Harry, 159–60
Scott, Floyd G., 127–9, 134
Scott v. Western International Sales, Inc., 127–9
Scottish-American Association, Inc., 242–3, 244
Sellinger v. Freeway Mobile Home Sales, Inc., 279
Shanahan v. Collins, 85, 266
Siegel v. Council of Long Island Educators, 238, 240
Simmons, Mr., 165–7
Sirotkin Travel Ltd., 235–6, 239
Small Claims Court, 80, 124–6
Snell, Justice, 146–7
soft spots: and super threats, 22, 30. *See also* individual situations
SOS letters, 7, 15–19, 26
South Carolina, 129
South Dakota, 78, 129

state attorney general: and fraud, 150, 170
State Commissioner of Insurance, 40, 223, 227–30, 232
Steele v. Latimer, 274
super threats: by certified mail, 44–5, 208; deadlines in, 24, 44, 84, 91, 100; escape hatch in, 24, 29, 44, 58, 84, 100; fallibility of, 30–1; format of, 40–6; to gain an edge over adversary, 26–9; guidelines for, 21–9; intimidation function of, 23; legal authorities in, 23–4, 28–9, 42, 45, 85; preliminaries to, 12, 14–15, 30, 34, 80–3, 89–90, 97–8, 107, 134–7, 156, 163, 191, 227–30, 251; presentation of facts in, 42–4; reasonable demands in, 25, 44, 50–1, 58, 84, 99–100; and self-interest, 5, 25; and soft spots, 22, 30; strategy behind, 5–6; trade-off function of, 31–2; uncertainty in, 22; use of legalese in, 25–6, 30, 42, 44, 91–2, 98, 100, 109, 184. *See also* individual situations
Syester, Agnes, 145–7
Syester v. Banta, 145–7

telephone calls: and confirming letter, 36–7; guidelines for, 35–7; as preliminary to super threat, 34, 80–1, 97, 251
tenant organizations, 17, 97–8, 107
tenants: and common-law negligence, 20–8, 76–7, 86–92, 101–10; crank letters of, 7–11; and implied warranty of security, 20, 23, 106–10; maintenance and repair services for, 75–101; polite complaint letters of, 12–14, 19, 78, 81–3, 84, 90–1, 97,

tenants: (cont.)
99, 107, 108–9; rent reductions for, 76, 96–101; rent withheld by, 76, 96–101; repair-and-deduct laws for, 76–86; security for, 6–28 *passim*, 75–6, 77, 94, 101–10; SOS letters of, 15–18; super threats of, 6–7, 19–28, 76, 77, 80, 83–92, 97–101, 102, 106–10; warranty-of-habitability laws for, 76–7, 92–101

Texas, 129

threats, 3–5, 11, 14. *See also* super threats

Timber Ridge Town House v. Dietz, 94–7, 100

Todd v. May, 273

Trans-American Collection Agency, 203, 206

travel agents: liability of, 235–41; problems with, 234–8; soft spot of, 236, 239; super threat for, 239–41, 243

Travel-A-Go-Go, 242

travel problems. *See* charter flight operators; travel agents

Truth in Lending Law, 187–93, 201

TV consumer-help reporters, 17–18, 98

Uhrig, Joseph, 168–9, 171–2

Uniform Commercial Code: and implied warranty, 114–16, 118–26

United States Code: and credit problems, 182–3, 193; and mail-order industry, 166–8, 171–2, 260–1; Title 42, Section 1983 of, 70–4

United States Tax Court, 213–19

United States v. Hannigan, 169–70

United States v. Outpost Development Corp., 166–7, 171, 260

United States v. Uhrig, 168–9, 171–2, 260–1

Utah, 129

utility companies: contesting bills of, 69–74; and due process clause, 72–4; public dislike of, 69; service termination procedures of, 72–4; soft spot of, 73; super threats for, 70, 72–4; and U.S. Code, 69–74

Vermont, 129

Virginia, 78, 93, 129

warranties: and advertisements, 118; express (written), 111–14, 122–4; implied, 111–26; implied, of security, 20, 23, 106–10; and repairing defective products, 117–18; and salespersons, 115, 118–21; soft spots of, 123–4, 125; state and federal laws on, 112–26; super threats to enforce, 122–6; and Uniform Commercial Code, 114–15, 116; warranty-of-habitability laws, 76–7, 92–101

Washington, 78–9, 93, 129

Washington, D.C.: tenant security in, 104–6

Western National Life Insurance Company, 224–6, 231

West Virginia, 129

Whitman, Codie, 104–5

Wiggins v. Moskins Credit Clothing Store, 209

Williams, Judge, 223

Wilson Chemical Co., Inc. et al., 209

Wisconsin, 93, 129

World Executive, Inc., 168–9

Wright, J. Skelly, 75

Wyoming, 129

Zale Jewelry Company, 204, 205

Ziskin, Edis, 118–19